THE FIRST WORL

Financing the
First World War

FINANCING
THE FIRST
WORLD WAR

HEW STRACHAN

OXFORD
UNIVERSITY PRESS

OXFORD
UNIVERSITY PRESS

Great Clarendon Street, Oxford OX2 6DP

Oxford University Press is a department of the University of Oxford.
It furthers the University's objective of excellence in research, scholarship,
and education by publishing worldwide in

Oxford New York

Auckland Bangkok Buenos Aires Cape Town Chennai
Dar es Salaam Delhi Hong Kong Istanbul Karachi Kolkata
Kuala Lumpur Madrid Melbourne Mexico City Mumbai Nairobi
São Paulo Shanghai Taipei Tokyo Toronto

Oxford is a registered trade mark of Oxford University Press
in the UK and in certain other countries

Published in the United States
by Oxford University Press Inc., New York

British Library Cataloguing in Publication Data

Data available

Library of Congress Cataloging in Publication Data

Data available

ISBN 0-19-925727-2

1 3 5 7 9 10 8 6 4 2

Typeset by Kolam Information Services Pvt. Ltd, Pondicherry, India
Printed in Great Britain on acid-free paper by
Biddles Ltd., King's Lynn, Norfolk

PREFACE

No general history of the First World War has given proper attention to its financing. Niall Ferguson's *The Pity of War* is an honourable exception to that remark, but then again it does not aspire to be a general history of the war. The neglect may be a reflection on the limitations of military historians. Economists, like generals, have technical vocabularies of their own, and these can create barriers to comprehension by those not trained in their use. However, that is not an observation applicable to those writing and acting during the war itself. The impact of John Maynard Keynes's attack on the Versailles settlement of 1919, *The economic consequences of the peace*, was so great, both immediately and subsequently, precisely because it was fluent and comprehensible. Exactly the same point can be made about his wartime memoranda, composed when he was working for the British Treasury. Keynes and those like him were political economists, not mathematicians, and it was policy that they aspired to shape.

The conventional wisdom about financiers and their role in the war might run something like this. International finance was not in the least belligerent before the war. Its links crossed national frontiers, and credit depended on stability and trade. Moreover, many commentators could not see how the world's stock markets could adapt to long-term hostilities, or how states could finance major war through conventional means. In the event—or so the standard wisdom might run—they were proven wrong on two counts. First, states proved the expectations of the pre-war economists spectacularly wrong. They found ways to fund the war over a period of four and half years, and even then they did not stop fighting because of financial collapse. This book does not dissent from that proposition.

The second count is one with which this book is less happy. It would aver that finance was not even a major aspect of the economic policy of the belligerent states. What mattered was the ability of industry to produce armaments. The monetary implications of the war were therefore postponed until after its conclusion. It was the post-war generation that confronted the costs and paid for them through inflation and then recession. The key debate for financial historians, therefore, has not been about the war itself but about its consequences. Ultimately it asks whether the crash of 1929 was a consequence of the First World War.

The total number of military deaths in the First World War, although they are not definitively established, is the most obvious quantitative guide to its costs. Expenditure ranks next. However, the calculation of financial cost involves other indices that were and are open to yet greater dispute. The loss of civilian life, the damage to buildings, the pension rights of widows and orphans, the numbers of the disabled—these were calculations that were subject to national variation, different medical practices and even inadequate statistics. At Versailles, the victorious powers used the cost of the war as a tool with which to punish the defeated. In previous wars the conquerors had levied indemnities, but such sums had not been justified on the basis of apparently quantifiable data. As is well known, the scheme for reparations foundered, and in the process it destabilized the settlement itself. Two sets of consequences accrued. The first was peculiar to Germany. The debate about reparations was linked to the hyper-inflation of 1922–23, which undermined the fledgling Weimar government. The second was international. Germany's perception that it had been unfairly treated at Versailles stoked the rise of the Nazis and contributed to the outbreak of the Second World War. Article 231 of the Versailles treaty, which famously—or notoriously—pinned responsibility for the First World War on Germany, was, after all, included not as an end in itself but to justify the extraction of reparations.

Therefore, the financing of the First World War has mattered to historians because of the war's consequences, not because of its effect on the war's conduct. This book is testimony to my belief that that view is mistaken. Many of its wartime effects were indirect rather than direct. The drive for war loans underpinned the bulk of domestic propaganda in the war, as the splendid graphic art of so many war loan posters testifies. The issue of inflation and declining real wages was what underpinned food shortages and therefore compounded the effects of economic war, and especially the Entente's blockade of the Central Powers. But finance also had a direct impact on the waging of the war. It tightened the alliances. German money brought the Ottoman empire into the war, and German gold enabled the war in the Middle East to be sustained into 1918. The Entente powers may not have coordinated their military commands until the last year of the war, but economic and financial cooperation began in February 1915. Britain became the conduit for its allies' credit. In Germany's eyes and in reality, the Entente's need to fund its orders in the United States yoked American shareholders to the allied cause long before the United States entered the war. On 28 November 1916 the Federal Reserve Board warned its member banks against over-investment in foreign treasury bills. Its statement left the Entente unable to fund its war effort from overseas sources in the long term. Germany's adoption of unrestricted U-boat war on 1 February 1917 and its conviction that the United States was already a *de facto* belligerent show both its awareness of economic considerations and its financial insensitivity. By forcing Woodrow Wilson to take up arms against it in April, Germany made clear its belief that the United States was already bankrolling the Entente but at the same time showed its inability to grasp the vulnerability which that dependence had created for the Entente. This book is not an exercise in counter-factual history, but it is worth asking whether the Federal Reserve Board, if it had been left to enforce its line, could have stopped the Entente's transatlantic trade more effectively than unrestricted U-boat warfare.

This edition of material which originally appeared in *To Arms*, the first volume of my history of the First World War which was published in 2001, has an updated bibliography. The most important addition is Martin Horn's *Britain, France and the financing of the First World War* (2002). In going over similar ground, Horn has used a much wider range of unpublished sources and come to different conclusions. For him the Anglo-French alliance could have done better than it did. That is an entirely justifiable proposition, but my view is that such an interpretation sees the glass as half-empty. I would regard it as half-full. However much rancour and distrust permeated the relationship between Britain and France, it was still far more harmonious than pre-war rivalries might have led one to expect, and considerably more sophisticated than that which functioned on the other side of the front line.

The text which follows is largely unchanged, except for one or two intrusions to give context in relation to the outbreak and conduct of the war as a whole. I have, however, made a number of typographical corrections. These mistakes—which occurred with greater frequency in the discussion of finance than anywhere else—were picked up by a number of hawk-eyed readers. I am particularly grateful to Richard J. Collins jr, Jeffrey Friedman, and N.C. Palmer.

CONTENTS

1

INTRODUCTION

Of the two main arms of economic capability in the First World War, industry and finance, current scholarship is far more preoccupied with the former than the latter. It was not always so. Before 1914 the competition in arms had created such abundance that there seemed little need to consider wartime procurement. How the war would be paid for promised to prove much more intractable. And, in the 1920s, the assessment of reparations and the urgent need to understand the sources of inflation—whether it had been generated in the war or in its aftermath—provided the study of wartime finance with a continuing relevance.[1]

The comparative neglect of finance by modern scholars can no doubt be explained by the fact that its administration was not apparently decisive to the outcome of the war. By 1918 goods were running out faster than cash; the maximization of resources was much more important than the management of money. Few had anticipated this. On finance, the banker I. S. Bloch, so often cited as the perceptive but unheard prophet of the true nature of the war, was wrong. Bloch, on the basis of tactical and technological development, correctly anticipated that a future war would be protracted and indecisive. Extrapolating from the evidence on expenditure in earlier European wars and from defence budgets at the end of the

[1] The only recent general treatment of the subject is Hardach, *First World War*, ch. 6. Balderston, *Economic History Review*, 2nd series, XLII (1989), 222–44, is important but focuses on Britain and Germany only. Soutou, *L'Or et le sang*, a work of considerable intelligence, is concerned primarily with war aims. However, his essay, 'Comment a été financé la guerre', in La Gorce (ed.), *La Première Guerre Mondiale*, makes salient observations in a brief compass. Of the older literature, Bogart, *War costs and their financing*, and Knauss, *Die deutsche, englische, und französische Kriegsfinanzierung*, are comparative and helpful.

nineteenth century, he anticipated that even the advanced nations would have considerable difficulties in funding this long war; smaller nations would find it unattainable. Bloch's implicit, if optimistic, conclusion was that war between the powers of Europe might now be impossible.[2]

Most of his contemporaries in the world of finance disagreed; they reckoned that a war would occur but that it would be short. Bloch had begun with the tactics and saw that the finance did not fit; they—in so far as they thought through the problem—went the other way, shaping the operational model to the financial imperative. They were more realistic than Bloch, in that they did not think that the probable nature of the war would deter the powers from fighting. They were, of course, wrong about its length. Nonetheless, their pre-war orthodoxy, that the war would be short, continued to shape financial thought well into 1915. At a dinner party on the occasion of Kitchener's visit to France on 1 November 1914, the assembled statesmen and soldiers of the Anglo-French Entente deliberated over the length of the war. Ribot, France's finance minister, cut across Kitchener's pronouncement that Britain would not be fully mobilized for another year by saying that finance would determine the war's duration, and that it would end by July 1915 because the means to pay for it would have been exhausted. Accordingly, at the beginning of that year, on 30 January, *L'Économiste français* announced that the war would not last longer than another seven months. In May Edgar Crammond opined in the *Journal of the Royal Statistical Society* that economic exhaustion would force some belligerents to stop fighting from July.[3]

Crammond was no doubt entitled to feel surprised that poverty did not force states to fall out of the war. Pre-industrial societies like Turkey and Serbia were at war virtually without ceasing from 1912, and yet continued the struggle as long as the major powers. Their prostration by 1918 followed from the depletion of their resources in kind, not from the expenditure of cash. Of the principal belligerents, Russia's early exit in 1917 was not in any direct sense a consequence of its small taxable base or its limited capacity for further borrowing. Financial primitivism did not betoken a lack of military staying-power.

For the perceptive few this point had already been demonstrated by the Balkan wars. Lack of money, Raphael-Georges Levy pointed out in the

---

[2] I. S. Bloch, *Modern weapons*, pp. xliv–xlv, 140–6; Jean de Bloch, *Guerre future*, iv. esp. 321–9.
[3] Brécard, *En Belgique*, 95; Bogart, *War costs*, 52.

Revue des deux mondes in 1912, had never stopped a nation from fighting. Paul Leroy-Beaulieu extended the argument in *L'Économiste français* on 23 August 1913. A major European war could be sustained over a long period despite a shortage of funds. Money was needed before the war for its preparation, and afterwards to settle the consequent debts. But during the war states survived by requisitioning, by price control, and by credit: thus, paying for a war could in large part be postponed until after its conclusion.[4]

Such faith in the flexibility and extendability of credit in wartime ought to have been a logical consequence of the policies of the European states in peacetime. Between 1887 and 1913 France's national debt rose 39 per cent (from an already high base-point), Germany's 153 per cent, and Russia's 137 per cent. However, the burden of borrowing declined in real terms owing to the economic growth of the three powers. Germany's fell from 50 per cent of net national product to 44.4 per cent, and Russia's from 65 per cent to 47.3 per cent. Most of Leroy-Beaulieu's contemporaries were more alarmed by the absolute figures than they were reassured by the net cost. This tendency was encouraged by the example of Britain, which over the same period cut its debt by 5 per cent. In 1913 Britain's public debt was only 27.6 per cent of net national product, and a bare 10 per cent of total expenditure was allocated to its service.[5]

Britain's intolerance of debt, intensified by the burdens of the Napoleonic wars, had been reinforced by the costs of the war in South Africa. In reality, the message of that conflict was reassuring; a cavalry captain, R. S. Hamilton-Grace, writing on finance and war in 1910, observed that two-thirds of its costs had been funded by borrowing and one-third by taxation, exactly the same proportions as those of Britain's wars between 1688 and 1785. Hamilton-Grace's conclusion was unequivocal: borrowing in wartime was easy, and Britain in particular was well placed to do it. Moreover, he argued, in contradistinction to Bloch, 'it is improbable that any nation with reasonable chances of victory will be deterred from declaring war owing to lack of funds'.[6]

Nonetheless, the Gladstonian orthodoxy persisted: war should be paid for out of current income. Thus, British economists tended to underesti-

---

[4] Charbonnet, *Politique financière*, 9–10.

[5] Ferguson, *Pity of war*, 126–30; Ferguson's focus is Anglo-German, but he is unique among recent writers in integrating war finance with a general account of the war.

[6] Hamilton-Grace, *Finance and war*, 43, 53, 57, 62, 71–2.

mate the resilience of credit. In the autumn of 1914 J. M. Keynes predicted that Germany's use of credit would give rise to inflation, and that Britain would be better able to stand the strain of a long war. Not until September 1915 did Keynes clearly articulate the argument that note inflation itself would not bring the war to an early end. 'As long as there are goods and labour in the country the government can buy them with banknotes; and if the people try to spend the notes, an increase in their real consumption is immediately checked by a corresponding rise of prices.' What would determine Germany's eventual economic exhaustion, therefore, was not financial catastrophe but the depletion of commodity stocks. However, the bogey of credit inflation was not laid to rest; it was simply reassigned. In Keynes's analysis the power which it now endangered was Britain, which through the importing of resources and the subsidy of allies was spending far more lavishly than Germany.[7]

Keynes was not necessarily wrong in his analysis of the economic effects. But he exaggerated their impact on strategy. The problem with his warnings about inflation was that their focus was on the long term. Financial theory looked to the post-war world more than to the winning of the war itself. In the short term the war put into reverse most nostrums about economic behaviour. The tempo of the war economy was set by consumption, not by production. Thus, worries about overproduction were no longer a concern. Capital investment was nonetheless limited to the satisfaction of immediate needs. The primary purchaser of the goods that resulted was the state rather than the private sector. Therefore the state replaced the individual in requiring credit. Most perverse of all, a nation's standing could depend, not on its solvency or its financial prudence or even its international trading position, but on its military performance. Victory, after all, was the pay-off for a war economy. 'Success', Lloyd George instructed the cabinet in 1916, 'means credit: financiers never hesitate to lend to a prosperous concern.'[8] The position of the German mark on the New York exchange proved his point. In October 1917 100 marks bought $13.73; by April 1918, after Russia's humiliation at Brest-Litovsk and Ludendorff's offensives in the west, 100 marks stood at $19.58.[9] Short-term military outcomes, not long-term economic management, could determine foreign financial confidence.

---

[7] Johnson (ed.), *Collected writings of Keynes*, xvi. 23, 39, 123–5.
[8] Skidelsky, *Keynes*, i. 334.   [9] Roesler, *Finanzpolitik des Deutschen Reiches*, 229.

2

THE GOLD
STANDARD

What shaped the distant perspectives of economists was faith in the gold standard—belief that it had regulated international finance before the war, that it continued to operate after a fashion during the war, and that it would be fully restored when the war was over.

By July 1914 fifty-nine countries were on the gold standard.[1] In other words, they used gold coin or backed their paper money with a set percentage of gold, and they determined a gold value for their currency and guaranteed its convertibility. Domestically, this discipline was believed to check inflation since it regulated the money supply. Internationally, the gold standard maintained the balance of payments. If one country had an adverse trade balance, it would pay out in gold. The process might be corrected spontaneously, as the weakened exchange rate would encourage owners of foreign funds to speculate on the gains to be made when the losses were stopped. Ultimately, the central bank could raise interest rates, so sucking back into the country the gold that had emigrated. If this happened, prices rose and the demand for imported goods fell. Thus, the balance of payments was restored by adjusting the balance of trade. The system was therefore deeply inimical to the requirements of a war economy: it limited note issue, it pivoted around international commerce, and it normally stabilized the economy without active government intervention.

---

[1] Ally, *Journal of Southern African Studies*, XVII (1991), 222.

But for all its overt commitment to international finance, the gold standard in practice was shot through with national considerations. Only active co-operation between the central banks enabled the system to cope with major crises, and the experience of those crises could encourage the hoarding of gold, even in normal times. In 1903 a third of the world's gold was either in domestic circulation or held by the Banque de France. In 1914 two-thirds of France's holdings of gold, a total of 4,104 million francs against a note circulation of 5,911 million, were in the bank: 475 million francs were added in the first six months of the year.[2] Gold, therefore, acted as its own protection without frequent changes in French interest rates. In 1907 both the Banque de France and the German Reichsbank had to draw on their reserves in order to support the Bank of England, caught by heavy American borrowing. In November 1907 the Reichsbank's interest rate, which had stood at 4.5 per cent in 1906, reached 7.5 per cent: the flow of gold to the United States was still not checked. By 1910 31 per cent of the world's official gold reserves were held in the United States, but much of it was immobilized in the Treasury, and America still financed its trade through London. Almost 60 per cent of the world's gold money supply had now been appropriated for official reserves, as op-posed to 31 per cent in 1889.[3] The Germans, therefore, concluded that they too should increase their holdings of gold, so as to use it in the same manner as the French. Their resolve was hardened by the 1911 Moroccan crisis. In 1909 the Reichsbank's purchases of gold totalled 155,241,225 marks; in 1913 they reached 317,450,056 marks.[4] This 'monetary national-ism'[5] carried clear implications for the financial management of all types of crisis, that of war as well as those of peace.

Britain alone did not build up its reserves. The Bank of England's holdings of gold rarely exceeded £40 million, as opposed to £120 million in France.[6] It helped that three of the world's principal sources of gold, South Africa, Australia, and the Klondike in Canada, lay within the empire; furthermore, India's favourable balance of trade buttressed the market against the seasonal highs and lows of American demands.

---

[2] Eichengreen, *Golden fetters*, 52; Knauss, *Kriegsfinanzierung*, 21.
[3] de Cecco, *International gold standard*, 115–21.
[4] Zilch, *Reichsbank*, 40–59, 124; Knauss, *Kriegsfinanzierung*, 21.
[5] de Cecco, *International gold standard*, unpaginated preface.
[6] Eichengreen, *Golden fetters*, 49.

The Bank of England, therefore, argued that gold was a commodity to be used, and that, because London's money market was the world's largest, its manipulation of interest rates was more effective than would have been French or German use of the same policy. The fact that foreign bankers kept their sterling balances in London meant that a balance of payments' deficit did not necessarily draw on the Bank's own reserves. London's strength was its liquidity. In appearance, therefore, the gold standard worked because it was 'essentially a sterling exchange system';[7] in reality, it did so only because of the collusion of the other central banks. As the Bank of England ensured stability and harmony in normal times, so the central banks of other nations supported it in times of crisis.[8]

The Committee of Imperial Defence did consider the imbalance between Britain's gold reserves and its national wealth, but was content to accept the Treasury's assurances that in the short term interest rates could be used to check a run on gold, and that in the long term a free market for gold would ensure the continuance of trade through London. The clearing banks were less confident. They, and not the Bank of England, held an increasing proportion of the country's gold reserves, and yet the Bank was their lender of last resort. In a crisis the Bank of England would be pulled in two directions: as a central bank it had to increase interest rates to draw in gold, but such action would run counter to its obligations as a commercial bank providing services to its clients. Two dangers confronted the Bank. One was that the joint-stock banks had power without responsibility, since they were under no formal obligation to make their reserves available for patriotic purposes in the event of a crisis. The second was the ability of a foreign power to create a run on British gold; many British merchant banks (or acceptance houses) were heavily implicated in German overseas trade, which was paid for by bills drawn on account in London. At the beginning of 1914 the clearing banks lobbied for a royal commission on the country's gold reserves. They noted that the existing reserves of forty-six banks in England and Wales represented only 4.04 per cent of their deposits: 5 per cent was their recommended target. They anticipated two pressures on gold. The first, an external one, would come from foreign powers anxious to exchange their bills. The second would be domestic—a desire from the British public to hoard cash. They

[7] Brown, *Gold standard*, xiii.   [8] Eichengreen, *Golden fetters*, 3–9, 29–66.

therefore proposed that in an emergency the Bank of England should produce additional currency for the clearing banks, secured as deposits by the banks of one-third gold and two-thirds bills. Thus, the Bank of England would increase its holdings of gold and the public would get its money. Neither the Bank of England, still a private not a government institution, nor the Treasury was supportive of this suggestion. Rather than a royal commission, the banks were fobbed off with a Treasury memorandum affirming the status quo. External calls for gold would be met by increased interest rates, and excessive domestic demand would result in a suspension of the 1844 Bank act (which fixed the ratio between gold and the Bank's note issue). Therefore the most likely initial outcome of a war would be an increase, not a reduction, in Britain's gold reserves. The memorandum made the obvious point that, if such optimism proved unfounded, no gold reserves, however large, would be sufficient to prevent the suspension of cash payments: 'regarded as a preparation for war, our Gold Reserves are either adequate in amount or else are incapable of being raised to a figure which would make them more adequate.'[9]

The Treasury reported on 15 May 1914. Already the beginnings of the run on gold could be detected. Demand for short-term securities in London grew throughout May and June, as an economic downturn created pressure to have assets liquid and available. From 24 July, the day after the Austrian ultimatum to Serbia, the continental powers called in their assets via London. Foreign capital applications in London totalled over £150 million in 1914, almost all of them before August: France alone withdrew £1,358,000 in the last week of July. Selling became so general as to threaten a collapse in the price of securities. Between 18 July and 1 August, when Germany declared war on Russia and France ordered general mobilisation, Russian 4 per-cent government bonds fell 8.7 per cent, French 3 per-cent bonds 7.8 per-cent, and German 3 per-cent bonds 4 per cent.[10] The pressure on London increased as stock exchanges elsewhere closed, beginning with Vienna on 25 July. On 30 July only London, Paris, and New York were functioning, and on 31 July Paris

    [9] R. S. Sayers, *Bank of England*, ii. 19; see generally i. 60–3; ii. 3–30. Seabourne, 'Summer of 1914', 79–82, puts the banks' case, and de Cecco, *International gold standard*, 132–41, 191–3, is critical. See also Paul Kennedy, 'Great Britain before 1914', in E. R. May (ed.), *Knowing one's enemies*, 200–1; Johnson (ed.), *Collected writings of Keynes*, xvi. 4–6; D. French, *British economic and strategic planning*, 16–18, 67–70.

    [10] Ferguson, *Pity of war*, 192.

announced it was postponing settlement for a month. At 10 a.m. on the same day, for the first time in its history, the London stock exchange closed its doors.

The problem for sterling was London's inability to meet new demands for capital. Most foreign balances were already committed to current trade. The loss of business from the continent meant that new funds were not forthcoming. Government-imposed moratoriums left foreign debts unpaid; of £350 million outstanding in bills of exchange, £120 million was owed either by the Central Powers or by Russia, and was therefore unlikely to be recovered even when the moratoriums were lifted. All foreign exchange rates, except France's, moved in favour of London, increasing the reluctance to settle debts. Shipping had all but halted. Payments in gold were suspended by the Russian state bank on 27 July; the other central banks followed suit early in August.[11] Catastrophe confronted the London commercial banks. Representatives of twenty-one merchant banks met on 5 August, the day after Britain had declared war on Germany, and reckoned that over £60 million in acceptances was owed them by enemy firms, but that their own capital was only £20 million.[12] The practice of acceptance houses was to rediscount bills when they neared maturity with the clearing banks. The clearing banks' room for manoeuvre was restricted by the closure of the stock exchanges, and by their own refusal to extend credit.

On 30 July the Bank of England advanced £14 million to the discount market and a comparable sum to the banks.[13] But having gone some way to fulfilling its function as the lender of last resort, it then had to protect its own reserves in its capacity as a central bank. It raised the interest rate from 3 per cent to 4 per cent on 30 July, to 8 per cent on 31 July, and to 10 per cent on 1 August. The rate was excessive. The problems on the external market were generated less by the policy of the Bank than by the hoarding instincts of the central banks of other nations. Foreign firms trying to remit to London were being prevented by their governments from doing so. Nonetheless, the last week of July showed a net influx of gold from abroad of £1.4 million. At the same time the Bank's holdings of securities

[11] The main accounts of the crisis used here are Brown, *Gold standard*, 1–23; Morgan, *British financial policy*, 1–32; Seabourne, 'Summer of 1914'.

[12] Roberts, *Schröders*, 153.

[13] Ferguson, *Pity of war*, 197.

and stocks recovered, but its gold reserves fell from £29.3 million to under £10 million. The pressure was now more internal than external.

The fall in the stock exchanges had wiped out the margins on securities used by stockbrokers as collateral for bank advances. The banks had called in their loans, so forcing further selling of shares and further reductions in the margins on collateral. The closure of the stock exchange had then rendered any remaining shares non-negotiable. The bill brokers, under pressure from the clearing banks, rediscounted bills with the Bank of England, so increasing the Bank's deposits but reducing its gold. The banks, anticipating the storm from the acceptance houses, also drew on the Bank's gold. Simultaneously, however, they refused to give the public payments in gold, and insisted they accept the smallest-denomination note, £5, which was too large for normal use. The banks were convinced that their customers wanted to hoard. Their customers were more prag-matic: they wanted cash to cover the impending August bank holiday weekend. They therefore took their notes to the Bank of England to exchange them for coin. Keynes, a severe critic of the clearing banks' instincts for individual self-preservation, observed the collective conse-quence of their actions: 'our system was endangered, not by the public running on the banks, but by the banks running on the Bank of England.'[14]

Not only the clearing banks but also the Treasury—with its refusal to engage in pre-war planning and its lifting of the Bank rate to 10 per cent—had deepened the crisis. All sides now gave themselves breathing-space by adding three extra bank holidays, so that business would not resume until Friday 7 August. The clearing banks had asked the Bank of England to implement its earlier recommendations for creating emer-gency currency; indeed, their hope that their request would be met was an additional factor in their holding gold. Told on 2 August that their suggestion was still not acceptable, they made four demands—that emergency currency be issued nonetheless, that the 1844 Bank act be suspended, that specie payments be halted, and that there should be a general moratorium. All of these proposals were debated at a conference convened by the Treasury on 4 August.

The 1844 Bank act was suspended, but it was not (as the banks had assumed it would be) a necessary corollary of the issue of additional

---

[14] Morgan, *British financial policy*, 30.

notes. The emergency currency (£1 and 10 shilling notes) was issued by the Treasury and not by the Bank of England. This was to ensure its acceptability in Scotland and Ireland. A maximum issue of £225 million (20 per cent of the banks' liabilities) was authorized at the Bank rate of interest. The banks rightly argued that the rate should be reduced. Externally it was not helping as the problems were not of Britain's making, and domestically it was creating panic and depressing business. The Bank of England's commercial concerns helped it accept the clearing banks' case; if the differential between the Bank's rate and that of the clearing banks were too great, then the former's creditors would shift their business to the latter, so enabling the clearing banks to profit from the crisis.[15] The interest rate was reduced to 5 per cent by 8 August. The final issue was convertibility. The banks had assumed that suspension of the Bank act and the issue of emergency currency would oblige the Bank of England to abandon the gold standard.

On 3 August J. M. Keynes, not yet employed by the Treasury but consulted by it, hammered home two vital points. The first was the difference between the internal demand for gold and the external demand. The purpose of the Treasury currency notes was to meet the former—and, although strictly speaking they were convertible, this was not an option likely to be exercised. By easing the domestic calls on gold, the Bank had more gold available for exchange purposes. His second major message, therefore, was the vital importance of continued convertibility. As he reiterated throughout the war, it was 'useless to accumulate gold reserves in times of peace unless it is intended to utilise them in time of danger'. By maintaining convertibility, Britain would sustain its purchasing power in international markets and would retain foreign confidence and therefore foreign balances in London.[16]

At the outset of the conference Lloyd George, the chancellor of the exchequer, had been sufficiently in the thrall of the clearing banks to have been considering the cessation of convertibility. But, as Keynes and the Treasury stressed, the gold which the crisis had siphoned off from the Bank of England had not gone abroad; it had flowed to the clearing banks because of the latter's squeezing of credit and their determination to seize

---

[15] de Cecco, *International gold standard*, 163–5.
[16] Johnson (ed.), *Collected writings of Keynes*, xvi. 7–15; in general, see de Cecco, *International gold standard*, 147–65.

the opportunity which the war offered of fulfilling their pre-war agenda. The only foreign power which could demand gold from Britain was France, a British creditor in July 1914; in general terms the world was Britain's debtor, and London was therefore well able to sustain its overseas purchases. Lloyd George was convinced. Britain stayed on the gold standard. On 6 August a royal proclamation postponing payments on bills of exchange for a month was confirmed by act of parliament. When the banks reopened on 7 August the domestic crisis had passed.

But if the maintenance of convertibility was to have any meaning, it was the exchange market—not domestic confidence—which required reassurance. On 13 August the Bank of England agreed to discount all approved bills accepted before 4 August 1914. The government was to guarantee the Bank against any eventual loss. However, no protection was accorded the acceptance houses, which remained reluctant to undertake new business. Therefore, on 5 September the Bank announced that it would advance funds at 2 per cent above Bank rate to enable the repayment of pre-moratorium bills on maturity; these advances would not be reclaimed until one year after the war's end. By the end of November most of the £120 million's worth of bills discounted by the Bank under its arrangements of 13 August had been redeemed.

The government's handling of the crisis reflected the view that the key to economic management lay in finance, not in industry. Having initially treated the crisis like any other, with the raising of interest rates and the suspension of the Bank act, it had then stepped up a gear to more direct interventionism. Furthermore, it had accomplished this at the urgent behest of that stronghold of free-trade principles, the City of London. Neither the Bank of England nor the clearing banks had cause for complaint. The arrangements for pre-moratorium bills gave the former good business without major risk; the moratorium protected the latter, sandwiched between the absence of overseas remittances and the persistence of domestic demands for payments. One effect, therefore, was to redistribute the pressure generated by the international crisis away from the City to the manufacturers and small traders of Britain. They found themselves subject to a moratorium which starved them of cash but which still required them to pay wages. The government exhorted them to maintain full employment while extending the moratorium for two further months. The fact that the latter was not lifted until 4 November reflected the sway of finance in governmental calculations. The fact that the economic life of Britain continued nonetheless demonstrated the banks' increasingly relaxed attitude to the formal protection which the moratorium provided.[17]

Critics of the government said that it had put itself too much in the hands of the banks. A moratorium on past acceptances and a guarantee of new ones, leaving the banks to hold the debts themselves, would have been sufficient. The measures that were adopted were inflationary. The bills rediscounted by the Bank appeared as 'other deposits' and securities in the Bank's accounts, and thus by a bookkeeping transaction could be the basis for advancing fresh credit. But even if the banks were rewarded with an injection of cash, the resumption of business proved sluggish. Overseas trade had fallen. The stock exchange did not reopen until 4 January 1915, and when it did the Treasury—with a view to giving the government first call on available capital—had to approve all new issues. Between 1915 and 1918 new overseas issues totalled £142 million, as against £159 million in 1914 alone. A merchant bank like Schröders, which had been heavily reliant on German business, limped along for the rest of the war. The Bank of England's arrangements for pre-moratorium bills did not cover all their advances to enemy clients, and their acceptances in 1918 were valued at £1.3 million, as against £11.7 million in 1913. Schröders returned losses in every year until 1919.[18]

The key outcome of the 1914 financial crisis was that Britain remained on the gold standard. From their low of £9,966,000, the Bank of England's gold reserves reached £26,352,000 by the end of August, and £51,804,000 by the end of the year. Freed of the obligation to issue its own notes by the Treasury, and drawing in gold from the clearing banks, its reserves reached 34 per cent of its deposits by 18 November 1914. On the same date the Bank's issue of gold coin and bullion, which had fallen to £26,041,000 on 5 August, peaked at £72,018,000. These were highs not to be repeated for most of the war; for much of the time, and continuously after June 1916, the proportion of reserves to deposits hovered at under 20 per cent, and not until October 1918 did the issue of gold coin again reach its November 1914 figure. But over the war as a whole the gold

[17]   Peters, *Twentieth century British history*, IV (1993), 126–48; see also Skidelsky, *Keynes*, i. 291, for a critical view of the banks.
[18]   Roberts, *Schröders*, 160–4.

reserves of Britain increased by 109 per cent, and by 210 per cent when the currency note reserve was included.[19]

This achievement was set against a decline in the world's production of gold. Russian output fell from 146,470 pounds (weight) in 1914 to 66,960 pounds in 1916—the victim of a loss of labour, increased production costs, and transport problems. Payments to the producers, which had been fixed at a profit of 30 per cent in November 1915, were increased to a 45 per-cent profit in November 1916, but with negligible results on output.[20]

Output in the British empire, which reached almost £60 million in 1916, fell thereafter.[21] Australia imposed an embargo on the export of gold in 1915; designed to ensure sufficient cover for the commonwealth's expanding note issue (by 1918 the note issue had risen from £9.5 million to £52.5 million, but the gold reserve had only fallen from 42.9 per cent to 33.6 per cent), the embargo depressed the price of Australian gold in international terms. Australia's output, which had totalled £8.7 million in value in 1914, fell to just over £5 million in the last year of the war.[22] But more important than any decision in Australia was the Bank of England's fixing of the gold price. Two-thirds of Britain's imperial gold came from South Africa. On 14 August 1914 the Bank of England secured an exclusive agreement with the mining companies of the Union, which fixed the official rate of gold at £3. 17s. 9d. per standard ounce. Given the wartime problems of freight and insurance, the Bank's terms were attractive as 97 per cent of the purchase price would be advanced before shipment. Similar arrangements were concluded with Australia. The gold could therefore remain in the Dominions without incurring the risk of loss at sea, and the advances made by London could go towards the issue of Dominion notes to fund the imperial war effort. But as mining costs rose, so the companies' profits fell. Britain was able to buy gold at a fixed rate and sell it on to neutrals at the market price. The quantity of gold mined fell in 1917 and again in 1918. By then relations between the mines and London were fraught.[23]

[19] Seabourne, 'Summer of 1914', 94–5; Morgan, *British financial policy*, 160–1; Brown, *Gold standard*, 100, 108–11.

[20] Michelson *et al.*, *Russian public finance*, 393–4, 439–41.

[21] Morgan, *British financial policy*, 335–6.

[22] Scott, *Australia during the war*, 503–7.

[23] Ally, *Journal of Southern African Studies*, XVII (1991), 221–38; Grady, *British war finance*, 41–4.

Initially, a further source of gold was the United States. The outbreak of the war coincided with the period before the autumn sales of corn and cotton, when America was normally in debt to London. Domestic depositors, unable to export their produce, withdrew cash from branch banks, which in turn—fearing a run—drew from the reserve city and central banks. As other stock exchanges across the world closed, dealing concentrated on New York. In the week before its closure on 31 July New York's sales of securities increased sixfold. By 8 August 1914 European withdrawals had reduced the gold reserves of the New York banks by $43 million. By the end of the year short-term debts to the tune of $500 million had been called in by the belligerent powers, and gold exports had totalled almost $105 million. Although share prices recovered sufficiently to enable the New York stock exchange to reopen on 15 December, trading remained restricted until April 1915.

The domestic crisis was surmounted by the use of emergency currency, and by the issue of 'clearing house loan certificates' to permit banks with unfavourable clearing balances to pay other banks. Externally, New York was determined to remain on the gold standard. But the exchange rate with sterling began to approach $7 to the £, when par was $4.87. With short-term bills falling due, further gold would have to be shipped abroad to hold the exchange rate. American companies placed the value of their stock held abroad at $2,400 million. The closure of the stock exchange forestalled the immediate danger of these holdings being redeemed, but it did not obviate the possibility of other debts being called in. The US Treasury reckoned that $450 million would mature in London by 1 January 1915, and a further $80 million was owed by the city of New York to London and Paris. Given that the crisis would be circumvented once American exports began to move, and given New York's desire that the United States hold its gold, the preferred solution of the banks was for their overseas stockholders to accept credits in New York. This Britain refused to do, insisting on the shipment of gold. Britain's stance confronted the United States with a choice. Either it declared a moratorium or it maintained payments in gold. By opting for the latter, New York sustained its financial prestige in international markets. Furthermore, it signalled to the world that other countries' floating capital would be safe in the United States. In the event, it achieved this at minimal cost to itself. The clearing houses established a gold fund of $100 million, to which

$108 million was actually subscribed, and of which $104 million was earmarked for deposit at par in Ottawa on the Bank of England's account. The resumption of American exports meant that the dollar was back to par by November 1914, and in December the United States achieved a net import balance of almost $4 million in gold. Only $10 million, therefore, was actually deposited in Ottawa.[24]

Britain's final source of overseas gold was its Entente allies. By the end of the year Entente orders to the United States were stimulating a revival in American exports: in December sterling was already 1 cent below par on the New York exchange. In 1915 British imports from the United States would be 68 per cent higher than they had been in 1913. The fall in the pound was therefore a reflection of Britain's need for foreign exchange to pay for American goods, and the weaker the pound the more expensive they would be. By June 1915 the pound stood at $4.77.[25]

London channelled orders to the United States not only on its own account but also on those of its allies. Its status as the world's financial capital persisted despite the war. It did so, the Treasury argued, because it remained on the gold standard, and therefore its allies France and Russia, which had not, had an obligation to help keep it there. Crudely put, Britain required its co-belligerents to ship gold to London, overtly to pay for munitions in America, indirectly to keep the sterling–dollar exchange in equilibrium.

Initially the Russians proved more co-operative than the French. In October 1914 the Treasury agreed a loan of £20 million secured by the issue in London of Russian treasury bonds valued at £12 million and the shipment of £8 million in gold bullion. But when the Russians came back for a second loan in December, provisionally pitched at £100 million, they baulked at the Treasury's insistence that they should support it with a further shipment of gold.[26] Simultaneously the French began negotiations for a loan of £10 million. They had opened an account with the Bank of England at the beginning of the war to fund purchases which passed through London; by the end of the year £9.3 million had been paid

[24] Gilbert, *American financing*, 14–18; Burk, *Britain, America and the sinews of war*, 55–62; Brown, *Gold standard*, 16–21; Morgan, *British financial policy*, 21–2; Noyes, *American finance*, 60–1, 82–8; Chandler, *Strong*, 55–60.

[25] Burk, *Britain, America*, 61–2.

[26] Neilson, *Strategy and supply*, 54–7, 65–6.

out of this account, and expenditure was beginning to run away from income. The Bank of England demanded that the loan be secured with gold. The French refused.[27]

France had abandoned international convertibility precisely in order to buttress the franc domestically; the spectre of the *assignat*, which had promoted galloping inflation in the wars of the French Revolution, promoted conservatism in relation to gold in the war of 1914–18. By December 1915 the Banque de France had added a further 1,000 million francs to its gold reserves, thus prompting the British to see its governor, Georges Pallain, as obstinate and stupid. But Pallain also represented an alternative approach to war finance: by abandoning peacetime norms, France was confident of its ability to restore them once the war was over. In the interim finance would be the servant of war, not an objective in itself. France's only concession was to agree to spend the loan exclusively in Britain.[28]

Keynes had little truck with the French or Russian attitudes. In a memorandum prepared for a meeting of the three powers' financial ministers in February 1915, he came back to his arguments of August 1914. Gold was to be used, not hoarded. '*They* think that we want their gold for the same sort of reason that influences them in retaining it namely to strengthen the Bank of England's position on paper. And our *real* reason, namely the possibility of our having actually to export their gold and so *use* it, they look on as little better than a pretext.'[29] Increasingly the British aim was less the gold standard per se, and more a gold-exchange standard.[30] The French were nonetheless right to observe the long-term intention, the maintenance of British international credit in the post-war world. Octave Homberg, advising the French government before the same conference, reported that the British aim was to increase their gold stock, and that they intended to remain the clearing house for the world, not just during the war but after it as well.[31]

[27] Petit, *Finances extérieures de la France*, 59, 181–6.
[28] Horn, *Guerres mondiales et conflits contemporains*, 180, (1995), 11–13; Horn, *International History Review*, XVII (1995), 52–4, 56–8.
[29] Johnson (ed.), *Collected works of Keynes*, xvi. 72.
[30] Soutou, *L'Or et le sang*, 224; for a development of this theme, see Soutou, in La Gorce (ed.), *La Première Guerre Mondiale*, 286–8.
[31] Soutou, *L'Or et le sang*, 222–3.

The French saw a potential symmetry, rather than clash, of interests. The French had the gold, the British had the international credit. Therefore when the representatives of the three powers met in Paris on 2 February 1915, Alexandre Ribot, the French finance minister, proposed the issue of a joint allied loan of perhaps £800 million. The British opposed, arguing in part that the total sum would be so large that the issue would fail. Privately they felt that such an arrangement would suit the French and Russians, who would get the loan more cheaply than they would on their own, but that British credit would be undermined by its association with its allies. The outcome was that Britain and France supported Russia, the former to the tune of £25 million and the latter with 625 million francs. In exchange, Britain's allies agreed that if the Bank of England's reserves fell by more than £10 million in the next six months—in other words, below £80 million—the Banque de France and the Russian State Bank would each advance in equal proportions £6 million in gold, to be reimbursed within a year. The French reserved the right to use American dollars for this purpose.[32]

Mutual mistrust persisted. The Anglo-French exchange rate, although now approaching par, had been in France's favour thus far in the war. Ribot was sure the Bank of England was withholding credit with the aim of getting the pound to rise against the franc, and so oblige France to consign gold to Britain.[33] This would have happened anyway. In the first quarter of 1915 the French deficit in Anglo-French trade rose to 400 million francs per month, and Ribot reckoned he needed a credit of up to £12 million per month to cover French purchases in the United States and Britain. The French could not obtain credits in America. So, at the end of April Ribot asked Lloyd George for £62 million to cover French orders over the next six months. The French agreed that two-fifths of their American expenses payable in sterling would be backed by gold sent to the Bank of England.[34]

France remained a reluctant and obstructive disgorger of its gold. It stuck to the principle established in February, that it would not grant the gold but lend to the Bank of England in exchange for British credits to the French government. By the end of the war France's gold reserves had

[32] Michelson *et al.* (eds.), *Russian public finance*, 294.   [33] Ribot, *Letters to a friend*, 90.
[34] Petit, *Finances extérieures*, 62, 71, 196–7.

nominally increased 56 per cent, but the reserves actually held in France had fallen by 2 per cent.[35] The gold was effectively being used twice over, by the French to support their currency, and by the British to support their interpretation of the gold standard.

The Treasury did two things with the gold. First, it prepared the US stock market for eventual allied borrowing by flushing American business with cash and keeping American interest rates low. Secondly, and relatedly, it exported gold to hold the sterling–dollar exchange steady. The French pooh-poohed the first objective, recognizing that the scale of allied credit operations was likely to outstrip the ameliorative effects of comparatively small consignments of gold. By 1916 their expectations were proved well founded. But the export of gold did fulfil the Treasury's second aim, albeit in desperate circumstances.

In November 1915, after the pound had fallen to $4.56, the chancellor of the exchequer appointed an exchange committee formed of representatives of the Treasury and the Bank of England. Using an account in New York in the name of the Bank of England, underwritten by the Treasury, the committee purchased sterling for dollars in order to peg the exchange rate. Between 1915/16 and 1918/19 this account disbursed $2,021 million on exchange, compared with $5,932 million on supplies.[36] Furthermore, although the French never fought as hard to control their exchange rate, they derived benefit from the stability imparted to the sterling–dollar rate. If France had bought abroad without credit from Britain, French exchange on London would have been weakened, without any effects on the sterling–dollar or franc–dollar exchanges. The opportunity for profit through the sale of francs for dollars, dollars for pounds, and pounds for francs would have further depreciated the franc.[37] By the end of March 1916 the franc, for which par was 25.22, stood at 28.50 to the pound. Negotiations initiated by the central banks of the two powers, designed to get credit for French companies to buoy French exchange, and to secure gold for Britain, concluded that Britain should provide a credit of £120 million, a third of which was to be secured in gold. Ribot wanted more; Reginald McKenna, Lloyd George's successor in London, much less. He feared that fresh advances to France would hit the British

---

[35] Brown, *Gold standard*, 100.
[36] Morgan, *British financial policy*, 356–7; Sayers, *Bank of England*, i. 89–91.
[37] Brown, *Gold standard*, 75–6.

exchange in the United States. The outcome of their meeting was that France received only £60 million, with a third still secured in gold. But, most importantly, the agreement was to be suspended if the pound fell below 27 francs. The effect, therefore, was not only to stabilize the sterling–franc exchange, but also to hitch France to the Anglo-American financial nexus.[38]

Overtly, the surprising aspect of this reconstruction of foreign exchanges was the co-operation of the United States. The European currencies did not depreciate against the dollar as fast as European wartime inflation exceeded American inflation. In other words, it was cheaper to buy goods in the United States than to produce them in Europe, because the European exchange rates were pegged at levels that overvalued the pound by 10 per cent (by 1918) and the franc by 35 per cent.[39] The effect was to pass on the price inflation of the belligerents to the neutrals, and so distribute the war's costs.

Voices in the United States objecting to the rise in domestic prices as a consequence of the belligerents' demands made little headway, because by the time the effects were felt the United States was already too deeply implicated. Entente orders had pulled American industry out of recession, and what worried W. B. McAdoo, the US secretary of the Treasury, in August 1915 was that further depreciation of sterling would undermine Britain's ability to pay for its purchases.[40]

McAdoo was not a financier but (in the words of a British Treasury report of June 1917) 'a Wall Street failure with designs on the Presidency'.[41] His political ambitions aside, his long-term objective was to use Europe's indebtedness to the United States to enable the expansion of American business. Outwardly similar were the priorities of Benjamin Strong, governor of the Federal Reserve Bank in New York. Strong was anxious to use the opportunity which the war provided for the United States to prise from London's grasp control of foreign (and especially American) debt, and to establish an acceptance market in dollars, not in sterling. But his policy for doing this was to keep 'our rates as ... the lowest in the world, [and] as ... the steadiest in the world, and make the New York

---

[38] Petit, *Finances extérieures*, 211–16; Ribot, *Letters to a friend*, 104–5.
[39] Eichengreen, *Golden fetters*, 73; Pigou, *Political economy of war*, 184–5.
[40] Nouailhat, *France et États Unis*, 283.
[41] Burk, *Economic History Review*, 2nd series, XXXII (1979), 408.

market so attractive that the business will come willingly'.[42] America had only established a centralized banking structure, the Federal Reserve System, in December 1913, as a consequence of the 1907 crisis. Its purpose, and one which Britain strongly endorsed, was the creation of an agency which would avert or minimize future domestic panics by greater international financial integration. Its sympathies were Republican, and its determination was to establish an identity independent of the US Treasury. In the early part of 1916 Strong toured Europe in order to give the Federal Reserve System a clear profile overseas. His discussions in March with the governor of the Bank of England, Lord Cunliffe, resulted in a memorandum of agreement and Britain's acceptance of the principle of Anglo-American financial equality. The declared aim was joint action to ensure stability in the post-war period; its necessary corollary during the war was America's collusion in the maintenance of British (and French) exchange.

The crunch for America, whether it was to follow McAdoo or Strong, and indeed the crunch for Britain came after the United States's entry to the war, in April 1917. Britain was anxious that the United States should take over its role as Entente financier, but it did not want at the same time to forfeit its international position. McAdoo had to seek the approval of Congress for the legislation which would enable the American government to purchase Entente bonds. Some Congressmen disliked New York bankers as much as the British; furthermore, McAdoo needed Congress's support if he was to advance his political career. He objected to Britain using funds derived from the United States to pay off debts incurred in New York and to sustain sterling on the foreign exchanges. He was prepared to see Britain sell its remaining gold and suspend convertibility. Forced to choose, Keynes was prepared to overturn his previous policy: £305 million in gold had been sent to the United States since the war began in order to peg the rate of exchange, and Keynes now advised that convertibility be suspended before the Bank of England's gold was exhausted. Throughout June 1917 the crisis for Britain's wartime finances deepened, and a suspension of convertibility seemed imminent. Then, on 3 July the US president, Woodrow Wilson, agreed to new American advances, not without conditions but accepting the principle

---

[42] Chandler, *Strong*, 91.

of American support for sterling. Because the American loans were short term, the Treasury continued on a knife-edge for the rest of the war. But the cardinal point was that the United States did not take the opportunity to force Britain off the gold standard.[43]

Strong's commitment to international financial stability did not, however, extend to a British approach to the hoarding of gold. By 1916 many American pundits, observing the neutrals' accumulation of gold as a result of the belligerents' adverse trade balances, favoured not the acquisition of gold but its repulsion. America could have allowed the free export of gold without undermining either the gold cover for its currency or the redeemability of credits based upon gold. However, Strong feared that after the war the gold acquired from Europe during it would be withdrawn, so causing the deflation of domestic credit. On 16 November 1914 the Federal Reserve act, by reducing the reserve requirements of the member banks, had created excess reserves of $465 million. Strong's policy was to promote this trend through the issue of Federal Reserve notes and the withdrawal of gold from public use and from the member banks. He also opposed the Treasury's accumulation of gold, as he felt the government could never redeem paper currency without deepening what would already be a crisis.[44] In 1916 the system held 28 per cent of the nation's gold. By the end of 1918 it controlled 74 per cent. Strong's policy was therefore adopted—albeit not for his reasons. It followed from American belligerency. The export of gold was banned in September 1917, partly so that there was no danger of its falling into German hands, but principally so that it could be a basis for the government's own domestic borrowings to fund its war effort.

This ambivalence about the desirability of gold was evident in the policies of other neutrals. Gold accumulation proved no longer to be a hedge against inflation. The use of gold as a basis for the money supply meant that the latter increased at a greater rate than the stock of purchasable commodities. Even in the United States, whose exports boomed, the growth of business between 1913 and 1918 was only 13 per cent as against a growth of actual money in circulation of 60 per cent and in bank deposits of 94 per cent.[45]

[43] Soutou, *L'Or et le sang*, 120–7, 344–53, 462–3; Burk, *Economic History Review*, 2nd series, XXXII (1979), 405–16.
[44] Chandler, *Strong*, 63, 83–6.
[45] Bogart, *War costs*, 356–7.

By 1916 the response of the Swiss and the Swedes was that they wanted no more of the belligerents' gold. Switzerland, whose gold cover grew from 46.8 per cent in July 1914 to 61.4 in December 1916, reduced it to 41.5 in October 1918. The note issue and the gold supply roughly doubled during the war. Sweden, which enjoyed a gold cover of 45.4 per cent in July 1914, managed to reduce it to 38.2 in April 1918, but still saw its holdings of gold more than double and its note issue triple. The experience of neutrals that were not so firm showed their gold cover increasing to 74 per cent (from 28.1) in the case of Spain and 74.9 (from 38.9) in that of the Netherlands. Both powers, while seeing their gold reserves increase by over 350 per cent, managed to restrict the increase of their note issue— Spain's grew by a third, Holland's by a half.[46]

The neutrals' implicit rejection of the gold standard did place the whole intellectual edifice in jeopardy at the end of 1916. Exchange rates, having been remarkably stable for most of that year, began to wobble as the Entente's trade imbalances with the United States multiplied. American entry to the war was therefore vital for the resilience of the idea of the gold standard. As the erstwhile leading neutral, it set a trend in favour of gold rather than of its rejection. Its own purchases in neutral countries and its embargo on gold exports drove up neutral exchanges; to stop lesser powers from hiving off, the United States (and the other Entente allies using American banking) demanded that the neutrals accord them credits.[47] And it was prepared to support the pivot of British policy, the maintenance of the sterling–dollar exchange. Therefore, while Britain acted as the mainstay of convertibility, America vindicated its judgement.

In the sense of an overarching international financial system, the gold standard did collapse in 1914 into a series of lesser financial units. But the importance of the Anglo-American nexus, and its commitment to a gold exchange system, meant that the basis for the revival of the pre-war gold standard seemed to survive. Pars on the foreign exchanges remained those set before the war, and at the armistice many responded to the expectation that that was the level to which they would return, whatever the financial predicaments of individual countries. The wartime practice changed in order to preserve the peacetime theory; countries went 'off' gold in 1914 precisely in order to be able to go 'on' it again when normality returned.

---

[46] Helfferich, *Money*, 216–17; Brown, *Gold standard*, 46–7, 100, 104–5.
[47] Brown, *Gold standard*, 66–7.

3

FINANCIAL
MOBILIZATION

In Berlin on 2 August 1914 Hans Peter Hanssen, a Reichstag deputy, offered a waiter a 100-mark note. It was refused: the waiter complained that all his customers were proffering large bills and he was running out of change. The following day Hanssen tried to pay for a meal with a 20-mark note. On this occasion the waiter grumbled, saying he would prefer silver, and went away to get change. Fifteen minutes later he returned empty-handed. Hanssen's solution was to ask for an extension of credit.[1]

In August 1914 such trials were not confined to Reichstag deputies in Berlin; they were commonplace throughout Europe. Only in Britain had cheques begun to replace cash in private transactions (it required the war to popularize them in France and Germany). Two pressures produced a shortage of cash. The first of these was hoarding by private citizens. As in Britain, it was more often the banks or their governments which—by a sudden rise in interest rates or by the threat of a moratorium—created the panic. Thus, a run on the banks was as likely to be a pre-emptive response to pressure not to withdraw money as a considered initiative in the face of international crisis. The second constraint, however, was real enough. As the armies of Europe mobilized, their need for ready money to buy horses and to secure fodder and provisions sapped the liquidity of the states they were defending.

---

[1] Hanssen, *Diary of a dying empire*, 14, 17–18.

Germany, with its commitment to rapid deployment and swift victory, was not unmindful of this aspect of its military preparations. But in some respects its response remained extraordinarily rudimentary, rooted in the experiences of 1870–1 and a desire to avoid their repetition.[2]

Frederick the Great's conservative economics had included the accumulation of bullion in a war chest to finance future conflict. In 1871, after the defeat of France, Germany used the indemnity it received to establish a Reich war chest of 120 million marks in the Julius Tower at Spandau. This sum remained unchanged until the 1913 army law, which doubled it to 240 million gold marks, and threw in 120 million in silver for good measure. By 1914 205 million marks had been raised towards the new total. The arrangement was doubly absurd. In peacetime it tied up money unproductively, so that it neither earned interest nor was a basis for note issue. In war, the provision was too limited for even the most optimistic of short-war advocates. The Reichsbank in 1913 concluded that mobilization alone would cost 1,800 million marks; actual expenditure in the month of August 1914 totalled 2,047 million marks.[3]

German estimates of total war costs varied so wildly as to be meaningless. In 1905 the optimistic General Blume suggested between 4,680 million marks and 5,760 million; four years earlier J. Renauld had reckoned on an annual requirement of 22,000 million a year. In 1913 the general staff put its campaigning costs at 10,000 to 11,000 million marks a year. In the event, Germany's annual expenditure during the war averaged 45,700 million marks.[4] However, most official calculations were confined to the period of mobilization only. In 1891 Johannes von Miquel, the Prussian finance minister, managed to establish an annual review by the minister of war of the financial resources available for the first thirty days of hostilities. This, it was felt, would take the war up to the first German

---

[2] Reichsarchiv, *Der Weltkrieg: Kriegsrüstung und Kriegwirtschaft*, i. 417; see, in general, i. 417–79, and documents in app., 293–354.

[3] Burchardt, *Friedenswirtschaft und Kriegsvorsorge*, 8; Helfferich, *Weltkrieg*, 211. On German financial preparations and mobilization in general, see Roesler, *Finanzpolitik*, 18–54; Lotz, *Deutsche Staatsfinanzwirtschaft*, 16–26; Zilch, *Reichsbank*, 83–141. There are also important observations in Holtfrerich, *German inflation*, 102–16.

[4] Burchardt, *Friedenswirtschaft*, 8; Roesler, *Finanzpolitik*, 24; Reichsarchiv, *Weltkrieg: Kriegsrüstung*, i. 464.

victory, after which—as in 1870—German credit would be secure on the foreign exchanges.[5]

To bridge the gap between the holdings of the state (the war chest plus other cash balances) and the anticipated mobilization costs, the government planned to turn to the Reichsbank for credit. Founded in 1875, not least with the needs of war in mind, the bank was independent of the state but obliged by law to provide it with services free of charge. The bank was required to cover at least a third of its note issue with gold, coin, or treasury bills. This—the gold standard—was the rock on which the Reichsbank's proposals for war foundered. In 1891 the bank wanted to issue smaller-denomination notes in peacetime so as to wean the public gradually from its reliance on coin, and to make preparations to suspend convertibility. Miquel opposed: notes, he argued, should not have the character of money. The smallest note in circulation remained 100 marks. All that could be agreed on was the maximum compatible with the maintenance of the gold standard: on the outbreak of hostilities the issue of short-term treasury bills should be increased, and these, together with the war chest and other government balances, should be transferred to the Reichsbank to form the basis for an expanded note issue.

However, in the decade immediately before 1914 the policy of the Reichsbank changed sufficiently to make it far better prepared for war. This shift of direction could be taken as evidence of Germany's role in the war's origins. Certainly, the need to cope with the crisis of mobilization was part of the argument for change. But in 1904, when a law to suspend convertibility in time of war was drafted, the potential needs of an economy at war did not override the immediate desiderata of an economy at peace. Proposals to increase the war chest and to introduce smaller-denomination notes were both rejected. Twenty-mark and 50-mark notes were at last authorized at a crown council in February 1906. Two hundred million marks' worth were for immediate circulation, and 800 million were to be held in reserve. The basis for this decision was the revelation that 2,500 million marks would be needed for the first three months of hostilities (1,300 million in the first thirty days), and that

[5] Bartholdy, *The war and German society*, 63–6; Reichsarchiv, *Weltkrieg: Kriegsrüstung*, i. 434–5.

the Reichsbank had neither enough gold nor enough notes to cover this. But the problems thereby addressed show the interaction between the possible but distant requirements of war and the immediate difficulties of German finance, and that it was the urgency of the latter which gave direction to the solution of the former.

The expansion of German business was constrained by a lack of liquidity. And in 1907 the Reichsbank's support of the Bank of England reduced its gold cover to 41.3 per cent of note issue, perilously close to the 33 per cent legal requirement. The response of the bank's governor, Rudolf Havenstein, was to create a buffer against future crises by withdrawing gold from circulation, and by expanding alternative types of currency. In 1909 the 20- and 50-mark notes were made legal tender, and the use of cheques as exchange and the introduction of postal orders were both designed to reduce the demand for coin. Between 1908 and 1913 the Reichsbank's note issue increased from 1,951 million marks to 2,574 million. In addition, the circulation of treasury notes (*Reichs-kassenscheine*) more than doubled, from 62 million marks to 148 million. Clearing accounts handled cashless transactions worth 163,632 million marks in 1908 and 379,157 million in 1913. One inflationary trend was in place before the war.[6]

More striking evidence of the relative balance between the priorities of peacetime finance and those of wartime is provided by the attitude of the German Treasury. Given the widespread contemporary recognition of the problems of financial mobilization, the Treasury's neglect of the issue was remarkable—and was commented on even at the time. The second Morocco crisis caused major falls on the Berlin stock exchange in September 1911, and the banks said they could not finance a war without borrowing; the French exploited the situation by withdrawing short-term funds and so causing a liquidity crisis.[7] But the Treasury spurned a call in 1911 for a financial general staff; its profile in the standing committee on the economic problems of mobilization, established in December 1912 by the minister of the interior, was low.[8] Indeed, its behaviour provides further evidence of the limited impact of the resolutions of the so-called 'war council' of that month. Adolf Wermuth,

[6] Feldman, *Great disorder*, 28.   [7] Stevenson, *Armaments and the coming of war*, 193.
[8] Zilch, *Reichsbank*, 83–8; Burchardt, *Friedenswirtschaft*, 74; C. von Delbrück, *Wirtschaftliche Mobilmachung*, 64, 77.

secretary of state for the Treasury from July 1909 to March 1912, was more preoccupied with restraining the pressure of defence spending on the current budget than in making future provision. Wermuth lost his battle, but the financial significance of the 1913 army law resided in its projected impact on Reich expenditure over five years of peace. The law did rather less to address the finances of a Reich at war. It doubled the war chest, and it increased the circulation of short-term treasury bills by 120 million marks. But Havenstein reckoned that, in view of the public's hoarding of gold in the 1911 Moroccan crisis, 3,500 million marks would now be needed to cover the period of mobilization.[9]

His worries were increased by the growth of the German credit banks. Deposits tripled and acceptances almost doubled in the decade before the war. This expansion was predicated almost entirely on the banks' close relationship with German business; they were not in the practice of holding either treasury bills or other reserves to cover their own obligations. Havenstein was therefore concerned that in a crisis the banks would deplete the Reichsbank's gold reserves precisely when it itself needed them to fulfil the purposes of the government. Although on 10 June 1914 the Berlin bankers rejected Havenstein's suggestion that they should accept a 10 per-cent liquidity requirement, they saw the wisdom of permitting the Reichsbank to act as a controlling authority. Therefore, it was the Reichsbank and not the credit banks which dictated policy in late July.[10]

Financial circles were made aware of the possibility of mobilization on, or soon after, 18 July 1914.[11] The July crisis did not gather momentum until 23 July, when Austria-Hungary delivered its ultimatum to Serbia. As in Britain, therefore, any sense of crisis began with the banks more than with their customers. The banks' resolve to persuade their clients to deal in paper fostered the clients' determination to do the opposite. The emergency (and unauthorized) issue of 5- and 10-mark notes deepened fears more than it eased circulation. Paper currency was exchanged at a 10 per cent discount, and was refused even by large institutions like the railways. Small savers stormed the banks on 27 July. About 7,000 depositors in Berlin withdrew 935,000 marks, and the totals were only slightly

[9] Zilch, *Reichsbank*, 126–7.
[10] Gall *et al.*, *Deutsche Bank*, 130–3; de Cecco, *International gold standard*, 110; Ferguson, *Pity of war*, 33.
[11] Ferguson, *Paper and iron*, 99.

lower on the following day: between 27 July and 8 November 1914 11 million marks were withdrawn but only 2.5 million paid in.[12]

The pressure was, however, almost entirely domestic. Being comparatively isolated, the German money market was spared the flurry of foreign withdrawals. Between 23 July and 31 July 1914 the Reichsbank's holdings of gold only fell from 1,356.9 million marks to 1,253.2 million.[13] To check withdrawals, commercial interest rates rose from 1.5 per cent to 4.5 per cent by 1 August, and the Reichsbank's discount rate was fixed at 6 per cent on 31 July. By 7 August, partly through the addition of the war chest, the gold losses of the last week of July had been nominally recovered. Gold reserves rose 225 million marks in August as a whole.

On 4 August, with Germany now at war with Russia, France and Britain, the Reichstag approved a package of proposals, including a short-term credit of 5,000 million marks secured on treasury bills lodged in the Reichsbank. The convertibility of both notes and treasury bills was suspended: it was argued that the international element in the gold standard was temporarily redundant, and that domestic confidence could be sustained by an enhancement of the status of the Reichsbank and by the knowledge that the one-third cover for notes still pertained. One of the symbols of this changed relationship between the Reichsbank and the government was the bank's release from the tax on any uncovered notes. Treasury bills and treasury bonds were both declared secondary reserves against note issue. In addition, the task of providing credit to the private sector was delegated to loan banks, *Darlehenskassen*, created specially for the purpose.

The *Darlehenskassen* were another symbol of the continuity in German thinking on war finance. Prussia had used them in 1848, 1866, and 1870. Their purpose was to ensure liquidity so that business and local government could continue without adding to the demands on the collateral of the Reichsbank. They were authorized to give loans of up to 50 per cent of the value of goods, and up to 75 per cent on stocks and shares. Their interest rate was fixed to fall above that of the discount banks and below that of the Reichsbank. They were authorized to issue their own bills, *Darlehenskassenscheinen*, 550 million marks-worth of which had been

---

[12] Verhey, 'The "spirit of 1914"', 132, 135, 187–8; also Raithel, *Das 'Wunder' der inneren Einheit*, 225; Mai, *Das Ende des Kaiserreichs*, 10.
[13] Zilch, *Reichsbank*, 139–41.

printed in preparation for the possibility of war in 1912.[14] While not legal tender, they were exchangeable for notes (but not, of course, for gold) at the Reichsbank. Their initial circulation was fixed at 1,500 million marks, but the Bundesrat was empowered to raise this—which it did. The *Darlehenskassen* proved as attractive to the communes and states of Germany as to the business world. Cut out from the normal loan market by the Reich's needs, they could now get credit and at a rate lower than that of the Reichsbank. The effect was indirectly to draw their reserves, from whose exploitation the Reichsbank would otherwise have been excluded, into the base for an increase in note issue. The Reichsbank could substitute *Darlehenskassenscheinen* (as well as treasury bills) for bullion in the one-third reserve for its notes. Moreover, in practice if not in theory, the *Darlehenskassenscheinen* themselves became currency. Their low denominations (initially down to 5-mark notes, and from 31 August 1914 1- and 2-mark notes) filled the need for small change which had so preoccupied Hanssen and his waiters at the beginning of the month.[15]

The *Darlehenskassen* were a device to help bridge the shift from peacetime finance to wartime finance. Germany played down the significance of this shift. Alone of the major belligerents, it eschewed the declaration of a general moratorium. But this was more of a gesture to boost confidence and ensure credit than it was a reality. Individual states were allowed to take their own decisions. The law of 4 August permitted the postponement of payments, and on 6 August the settlement of bills and cheques was extended to thirty days. Pre-war debts could be put off for between three and six months. The stock exchange, which closed on 30 July, was subject to a moratorium on 14 August which was not lifted until November 1915. Officially, the stock exchange never reopened—although in practice trading, particularly in the shares of arms firms, persisted.[16]

The process of German mobilization had worked a more fundamental revolution in the mechanism of German credit than was realized at the

---

[14] Ferguson, *Paper and iron*, 117.

[15] Holtfrerich, *German inflation*, 115; Roesler, *Finanzpolitik*, 41–3; Knauss, *Kriegsfinanzierung*, 54–5, 57.

[16] Knauss, *Kriegsfinanzierung*, 33–4, 56–7; Dix, *Wirtschaftskrieg*, 213–15; C. von Delbrück, *Wirtschaftliche Mobilmachung*, 109–10, 118–19.

time. The Reichsbank's reserves were increased through treasury bills and *Darlehenskassenscheinen*. On 7 July, against a note circulation of 2,192 million marks were entered 1,626 million marks in gold and 1,025 million marks in treasury bills and other forms of security. On 31 August a note circulation of 4,235 million marks was covered by 1,606 million marks in gold and 4,897 million marks in treasury bills, *Darlehenskassenscheinen*, and exchange bills. The bills served as the basis for the growth in currency, but were themselves not subject to restriction. The supply of money had become effectively autonomous. Total German circulation of all types rose from 5,893 million marks in May 1914 to 8,436 million in September.

Currency inflation was indeed the simplest and most effective means of shifting to a war economy. Britain had incorporated elements of the same approach, particularly in the issue of treasury notes. But in Germany the possibility of the quantity of money itself creating inflation was not seriously entertained. Inflation, in German theory, could only be the consequence of a shortage of commodities, which would generate rising prices. The control of inflation could therefore be managed by the control of prices. And the law of 4 August included the power to fix prices.[17]

Inflation also played an important role in the financial mobilization of Germany's principal ally, Austria-Hungary. And yet the overt manifestations were different, as the shortage of small change was much more persistent. The army's need for cash was a clear lesson of the partial mobilization during the Bosnian crisis, but no preparations were made to meet the sudden demand for currency in August 1914. Although temporary use of 20- and 10-crown notes had been permitted on occasion, the smallest note in normal circulation was 50 crowns. A decision on 14 August to issue notes in denominations of 5 crowns, 2 crowns, and 1 crown was never fully implemented. The 2-crown note was available on 18 August 1914, but so hurried had been its printing that the Hungarian version had mistakes. The 5-crown note was not produced. In May 1915, to meet the demand for coin, a 'new silver' coin (in reality 50 per cent copper, 40 per cent zinc, and 10 per cent nickel) was minted, but the supply of copper began to run out in 1916. From March of that year small coins were fashioned from iron. Finally, in December 1916 the 1-crown

[17] Krohn, 'Geldtheorien in Deutschland', 44–5; Roesler, *Finanzpolitik*, 46–8, 52, 216.

note made its belated appearance. Only now was the need for small-denomination currency fully satisfied.[18]

Ironically, rather than help Austro-Hungarian financial preparedness for war, the crisis over the annexation of Bosnia-Herzegovina undermined it. In 1908 Austria-Hungary was feeling the benefits of five years of industrial growth. Interest rates were set at 4 per cent in March, and in 1909 gold cover averaged 70 per cent of note issue. But, despite their best intentions, the finance ministers of Austria and Hungary found themselves unable to pay for the partial mobilization of 1909 out of tax income, and had to resort to treasury bills and an increase in the national debt. The spurt in arms spending which followed meant that by 1912 the state owed 541 million crowns in government stocks, against an average of 149 million in the decade up to 1909. Capital became increasingly hard to find, especially as the government's needs competed with those of industry. Interest rates rose to 6 per cent in November 1912, and liquidity problems either dampened business expansion or encouraged a search for funds overseas, so contributing to Austria's balance of payments' deficit. Then the 1911 Moroccan crisis and the 1912 Balkan war took their toll. Foreign (particularly French) capital departed, and the confidence of domestic investors was shaken, leading them to place their capital overseas. The Austro-Hungarian Bank had to sell gold abroad to defend the exchange rate. In 1912 its gold cover averaged 45 per cent, and by the year's end had fallen to 1,210 million crowns against a note issue of 2,816 million. Military mobilization was clearly a costly exercise—and, some argued, war itself could not be more damaging.[19] One of the strongest exponents of this view was the common finance minister of the empire as a whole, Bilinski; for him, finance had become the servant of war even while peace still prevailed.[20]

The task of funding mobilization had been given to the Austro-Hungarian Bank in 1887. The bank was a private company, although its governor was appointed by the emperor on ministerial advice, and the board included representatives of the two monarchies. It was obliged to maintain a cover of two-fifths of its note issue, although this could include

[18] Popovics, *Geldwesen*, 34, 56, 94–8; Müller, *Finanzielle Mobilmachung*, 28–30. These are the principal sources on Austro-Hungarian war finance, together with März, *Austrian banking*.
[19] Williamson, *Austria-Hungary*, 157–9; März, *Austrian banking*, 27–32, 99–100; Popovics, *Geldwesen*, 27–9, 39.
[20] Leslie, *Wiener Beiträge*, XX (1993), 360, 363, 367.

up to 60 million crowns in British, French, and German deposits. The effect of the run on gold was that by 1912 the bank could not fund mobilization and adhere to the terms of the Bank act. The requirement for two-fifths cover reduced the possible additional note issue to 950 million crowns. The cost of the first three months of mobilization was estimated at 1,850 million crowns, without any allowance for an intervening increase in prices.[21]

The fact that war would require the suspension of the Bank act was emphasized by the governor, Alexander Popovics, at a conference of the banks and of representatives of the finance ministries in Budapest in November 1912. The conference thought that the normal credit machinery—existing cash, the placing of loans at home and abroad—could produce 800 million crowns for the first eight days, and that thereafter 1,700 million crowns could be borrowed from the clearing banks (*Notenbanken*). But the talk remained general. No draft laws or regulations were prepared. And consideration was given only to the first three months of war.[22] Privately, the finance ministries thought that the empire could not fund hostilities for more than one or two months.[23]

Austro-Hungarian accounts showed some signs of stabilization in 1913–14. Gold reserves picked up, and the interest rate was reduced to 4 per cent in March 1914. But Popovics had had insufficient time to reduce Austria's overseas holdings or to win back domestic capital. Furthermore, the response of the Austro-Hungarian Bank in the course of the July crisis was always late and inadequate. Popovics's problem was that of Austria-Hungary writ small: he did not know whether he should be anticipating partial mobilization, general mobilization, or war, and he was subject to a timetable that was constantly foreshortened rather than lengthened.

On 19 July he was warned that an ultimatum would be delivered to Serbia, but was told that this would happen on 25 July. On 20 July he learnt that the deadline for the ultimatum was now 23 July, and that he should anticipate the mobilization of eight corps. As a result of his experience in the earlier crises he knew that this could not be achieved by normal credit operations. Nonetheless, the easier conditions in the money market encouraged the banks to accept that the message should

---

[21] Popovics, *Geldwesen*, 23–5, 32, 39–40.   [22] Ibid. 34–7.
[23] Regele, *Conrad*, 155; N. Stone, 'Austria-Hungary', in E. R. May (ed.), *Knowing one's enemies*, 50.

be one of calm and continuity. Foreign withdrawals of gold had begun after Franz Ferdinand's assassination. The bank raised the interest rate to 5 per cent on 26 July, but still the withdrawals continued. Its holdings of gold and foreign exchange fell by 148 million crowns in the last week of July. Nonetheless, Popovics had room for manoeuvre. He had actually reduced liquidity in the first three weeks of the month—total circulation had fallen by about 200 million crowns[24]—and therefore a decision to print 400 million crowns on 23 July to meet the army's cash needs still left a cover—despite the outflow of gold—of 58 per cent on 26 July.[25]

Then, on 30 July, the ground shifted again. General mobilization was ordered for 31 July. So far provision had been made to cover the costs of partial mobilization for fifteen days from existing sources. The finance ministers of the two monarchies had begun discussions with a view to borrowing 600 million crowns from an Austrian banking consortium and 340 million from a Hungarian consortium in the event of partial mobilization running beyond fifteen days. The governments planned to borrow at a rate of 5 per cent and repay their debt on 1 February 1917. Now 2,000 million crowns, 1,272 million from Austria and 728 million from Hungary, were required; the state would pay interest at 1 per cent and the Austro-Hungarian Bank, through whom the loan would be channelled, was relieved of the burden of tax payments on note circulation.

On 31 July the interest rate was raised to 6 per cent, and on 2 August, following the Bank of England's rise to 10 per cent, to 8 per cent. But Austria-Hungary's only real protection from the run on gold was to come off the gold standard. On 5 August the policy settled between the finance ministers and the bank reserved gold for military and state use; foreign payments were banned. On the previous day the Bank act was suspended, relieving the Austro-Hungarian Bank of the need for its 40 per cent gold cover. The security on the bank's note circulation now became the loans which the bank provided the government to enable it to wage the war. By the year's end the money in circulation had increased 91 per cent on its 31 July figure.[26] When current account deposits are included and the comparison shifted back to 23 July, the total circulation had grown from under 2,500 million crowns to over 6,500 million.[27]

[24] Müller, *Finanzielle Mobilmachung*, 25–6.   [25] März, *Austrian banking*, 130.
[26] Gratz and Schüller, *Wirtschaftliche Zusammenbruch*, 181.
[27] März, *Austrian banking*, 141; the key account of the crisis as a whole is Popovics, *Geldwesen*, 41–58.

The confusion of Austria-Hungary's financial mobilization was compounded by its use of the moratorium, first imposed on private transactions for a two-week period on 31 July. It created panic and contributed to
the shortage of small change. But it was then extended to 30 September,
to allow people to accustom themselves to the new economic conditions.
By the time of the third extension, on 27 September to 30 November,
creditors were becoming restive. The moratorium was therefore partial,
providing for the settlement of 25 per cent of a debt after 15 October. At
the same time the legal machinery was set up to protect small businesses
which had valid reasons for not satisfying their creditors; the effect was to
allow enterprises that would not have been viable in peace to limp on in
war. Up to 31 August 1917 2,552 concerns became subject to this legislation, but of 1,885 cases actually referred to the courts only 110 resulted in
bankruptcy. The moratorium itself was extended three more times, on
25 November 1914, 25 January 1915, and 22 December 1915, each extension
permitting settlement of further tranches of debt (normally 25 per cent of
a demand at a time). The moratorium was not fully lifted until 31 December 1916. Inflation over this period meant that many debts were effectively
wiped out by the time they fell due.[28]

The impact of the moratorium on private credit had national reper-
cussions. Savings banks, deposits having been withdrawn in the period up
to 31 July 1914, could not win them back again until 1915. The government,
having moved to credit operations at the outset, found that the banks
could not unlock their deposits, and—after securing its first advance—
had to turn directly to the Austro-Hungarian Bank for funds. By the same
token, loans could not be floated for public subscription.

Partly in order to meet this last need, but principally to finance
business, Austria-Hungary aped its German ally and set up *Kriegsdarlehenskassen* on 20 September 1914. The aim was to meet the demand for
cash and at the same time to furnish credit against exports whose markets
had been cut off by the war. However, the shortage of goods in relation to
purchasing power meant that commodities tended to find a domestic
market: sugar was the only major product to be mortgaged in quantity.
More significant in the books of the *Kriegsdarlehenskassen* were shares (by

the end of 1915 they had accounted in Austria for advances of 140.77 million crowns, as against 18.7 million in goods and 0.96 million in book credits). With the empire's stock exchanges having closed after 24 July,[29] assets had become frozen at an early stage in the crisis. Initially the *Kriegsdarlehenskassen* would only take over the rather conservative range of stocks admitted as security by the banks before the war, but the list of negotiable shares was gradually extended. The *Kriegsdarlehenskassen* issued in exchange non-interest-bearing treasury notes, which were effectively treated as money and were exchangeable for cash at the Austro-Hungarian Bank. However, the *Kriegsdarlehenskassen* did not have the inflationary effects of their German prototypes. The maximum issue was set at 500 million crowns for Austria and 290 million for Hungary. By the end of 1915 231.27 million crowns had been disbursed in Austria, but only 105.36 million was still in circulation. In Hungary the peak demand of 22 million crowns had already fallen to 16 million by the end of 1915. As liquidity returned and the moratorium eased, and as savings banks' deposits recovered, so the *Kriegsdarlehenskassen* became redundant and their loans were repaid. In 1916 only 62 million crowns were issued in Austria. The quantity of notes in circulation never even approached the legal maximum until the final collapse of the empire in October 1918.[30]

In Germany and Austria-Hungary the establishment of the *Darlehens-kassen* relieved the central banks of the day-to-day deposit business, thus enabling them to concentrate on a much closer relationship with the state. In neither Russia nor France was this the case. In the two Entente powers the central banks simultaneously funded their states' mobilization needs and supported the continuation of commerce.

Nonetheless, when considering Austria-Hungary's mobilization, Popovics—even in 1925—could look ruefully across to the comparatively greater financial preparedness of his country's major foe in 1914, Russia.[31] In the run-up to the outbreak of the war Austria was struggling to recoup its gold reserves, while Russia's monetary base looked impressively strong. On 29 July 1914 2,357 million roubles were in issue: 1,633.4 million of them

---

[29] Most histories, e.g. Popovics, *Geldwesen*, 46–7, and Reichsarchiv, *Weltkrieg: Kriegsrüs-tung*, i. 478, give 27 July. However, März, *Austrian banking*, 141–2, says the stock exchanges were closed on 24 July for three days: 25 and 26 July fell on Saturday and Sunday.

[30] Müller, *Finanzielle Mobilmachung*, 72–5; Popovics, *Geldwesen*, 86–90; März, *Austrian banking*, 154–5.

[31] Popovics, *Geldwesen*, 40–1.

were in notes, and 48.2 per cent of those were in small denominations. Only 463.7 million roubles in gold were circulating, and 260 million in other metal. Most of Russia's gold was in the bank: 1,603.8 million roubles were held in the State Bank at home and 140.7 million abroad or in foreign drafts.[32] The note cover was thus approximately 100 per cent.

Like Germany in 1870–1 and Austria-Hungary in 1908–9, Russia had an experience of financial mobilization on which to draw. On 14 January 1906, as a consequence of the Russo-Japanese War and the 1905 revolution, Russia's gold reserve was reduced to 700 million roubles against a note issue of 1,207.5 million. But Russia was not forced off the gold standard. Foreign loan stock boosted the gold reserves back up to 1,190.6 million roubles within a year, as against a note issue of 1,194.5 million. Russia paid over the odds for its foreign money (as it kept interest rates high), and it needed a lot of it; therefore, despite its grain exports, it had a balance of payments deficit. In addition, the costs of military re-equipment and re-expansion after 1905 pushed the budget into deficit, even if the size of the deficit was obscured.

Russia was financially more ready for war in 1914 than this recent history might suggest. The pace of its economic growth was reducing its burden of debt in real terms. In 1913 increased state revenues and a good harvest meant that the surplus on the ordinary account wiped out the debt on the extraordinary account. Moreover, its response to the confrontations and mobilizations in the Balkans was not the hawkishness of Bilinski but renewed caution. On 27 March 1914 Peter Bark, the finance minister, declared that 'at the present time we are far less prepared for war than ten years ago'.[33] He was wrong, but it was this conservative approach to monetary matters which determined Russia's pecuniary preparedness in 1914.

Russia's international credit was of short duration and its fiduciary reputation slender. Witte had established a gold standard in 1897 far more rigorous than that applied elsewhere: foreign confidence was essential if Russia was to attract foreign investment. Thus, the State Bank was required to maintain a minimum gold cover of half its note circulation; if the latter exceeded 600 million roubles, then the cover for the excess

[32] Michelson et al., Russian public finance, 364.
[33] Spring, Slavonic and East European Review, LXVI (1988), 570.

was to be of equal value. The greatest demand for notes fell in the autumn, when the crops were harvested but before overseas remittances were received. Therefore the gradual increase in the State Bank's gold reserves in the first half of 1914 reflected its desired annual cycle.[34]

The determination with which Russia cleaved to the gold standard displayed a greater awareness than was necessarily shown elsewhere of its two distinct functions—its external as opposed to its internal role. On 5 August Russia suspended specie payments, thus making its notes unconvertible. But the State Bank's own holdings of gold only dipped slightly, to 1,558 million roubles in January 1915, and by 14 January 1916 had reached a high of 1,613 million. During 1916 gold reserves fell, to 90 million roubles in May, but domestic production brought them back up to 1,474 million in January 1917. What forced Russia finally to abandon the international gold standard in March 1917 was the domestic depreciation of the rouble, not an inability to export gold abroad.

On 5 August 1914 the State Bank was authorized to issue 1,200 million roubles above the legal maximum. The Treasury, with cash balances of only 580 million roubles in hand, was, therefore, turning to the State Bank to fund mobilization. In return, the bank discounted short-term treasury bills, but never to the same value as the notes required by the Treasury. Thus, on 1 January 1915 the State Bank held 656 million roubles in treasury bills, but the note circulation had increased by 1,171 million roubles.[35]

In addition to its role as a central bank tied to a close relationship with the government, the State Bank was also the linchpin in commercial credit. Therefore, the peacetime official rate of interest was—unusually for a central bank—below the market rate: in 1912 the State Bank's rate was already 5 per cent, and the market rate was 6 or 6.5 per cent. With rates set deliberately high to attract foreign funds, an increase in the official rate to 6 per cent on 29 July was not unsettling. The message of the State Bank was calm and continuity. The moratorium was limited and brief. Its only major sign was the closure of the stock exchange on 29 July. As the government feared a flood of redeemed Russian securities from abroad it remained closed, except for a limited period in February 1917.

---

[34] Michelson *et al.*, *Russian public finance*, 342–66.
[35] Claus, *Kriegswirtschaft Russlands*, 16; also more generally 14–19.

However, in the five years before 1914 Russian commercial banking had expanded significantly. In 1908 2,969 million roubles were held in deposits and current accounts; by 1913 the total was 5,228 million. In 1909 the share capital of the thirty-one commercial banks was 236.6 million roubles. In 1910 eleven of these banks increased their capital by 70 million roubles, and in 1911 thirteen banks increased theirs by 80 million and in 1912 by 100 million. In 1912 there were 776 credit houses, of which 172 had been founded in 1911: their capital totalled 120 million roubles as against deposits of 500 million roubles. This rapid growth relieved the State Bank of much of its commercial business, but it underlined its role as banker to the banks. The expansion relied on the State Bank for credit, and in 1912 the government slowed its pace by insisting that new banks pay between 25 and 50 per cent of their original capital to the State Bank.

The outbreak of the war prompted a massive withdrawal of deposits.[36] Thus the State Bank, while simultaneously addressing the needs of the Treasury, was also required to support the commercial banks. Some of the deposits withdrawn from the credit houses were reinvested in the State Bank. But in the month between 14 July and 14 August the State Bank's accounts showed an increase in bills and other securities from 521.8 million to 963.8 million roubles, 425 million of which were deposited after the outbreak of the war.[37] Thereafter the position stabilized. Funds were reinvested, and by January 1915 deposits were approaching their pre-war levels. But the commercial sector was slow to extend credit to industry. Lending remained below its pre-war level throughout the second half of 1914 and all of 1915. Not until 1916 did this aspect of banking activity revive. Thus, the war industries too turned to the State Bank.

In France, as in Russia, the central bank performed both commercial and state functions. But the burdens on the Banque de France were that much greater than they were on the Russian State Bank, undertaken as they were in the context of overt confusion in public finance, compounded by a particularly fierce moratorium.

However, France was like Germany in one respect. The experience of 1870 determined the obligations imposed on the Banque de France in the

---

[36] The figures given by Claus, *Kriegswirtschaft Russlands*, 41–2, and Michelson *et al.*, *Russian public finance*, 375–6, show the position after it had stabilized. But see, in general, Claus, 39–48, and Bernatzky in Michelson *et al.*, 354–8, 374–6.

[37] Claus, *Kriegswirtschaft Russlands*, 17.

event of another war. Then the bank had been relieved of its obligation to redeem notes for currency, and had made advances to the state in the shape of an increased note issue. On 11 November 1911, in the aftermath of the second Moroccan crisis, Lucien Klotz, the finance minister of the day, put these principles into more concrete form. Convertibility would be suspended. The Banque de France was to advance the government 2,900 million francs. As security, the bank would receive treasury bills, paying 1 per cent interest, with an initial life of three months but renewable. Five hundred million francs of the advance would be immediately distributed throughout the country as credits to fund mobilization. To meet the anticipated demand for small change, the bank prepared a supply of 5-franc and 20-franc notes. On 30 November 1911 a comparable arrangement, this time for an advance of 100 million francs, was reached with the Bank of Algeria.[38]

The end of July 1914 found the Banque de France, unlike the government, in a financially healthy position. Its concentration of gold gave it a 69 per-cent cover on a note issue of 6,800 million francs. France did not require its central bank to have a fixed gold reserve. But public confidence in the bank and its notes was amply justified by a perusal of its accounts. In addition to its 4,141 million francs in gold it held 625 million francs in silver, 1,373 million francs in Paris securities, 1,071 million francs in its branches, and 744 million francs in advances on shares. Its active balances, therefore, totalled 7,954 million francs, against notes actually in circulation of 6,683 million.[39] In addition, France had healthy overseas balances, and further gold—to the tune of 4,500 million francs—in private hands.[40]

The public's faith in the bank, however, was not matched by its faith in the nation's capacity to organize itself for war. Between 27 and 31 July 1,500 million francs were withdrawn from the banks.[41] In Pau savings banks withdrawals rose fourfold on 27 July, sixfold on the 28th, and twentyfold on the 29th.[42] On 30 July the savings banks limited withdrawals to a maximum of 50 francs every fortnight. On 31 July a one-month moratorium was imposed on all trade settlements. The interest rate was

[38] Jèze and Truchy, *War finance of France*, 190, 228–30, 236–7; Klotz, *De la guerre à la paix*, 16–17.
[39] Charbonnet, *Politique financière de la France*, 36; Duroselle, *La France*, 206.
[40] Petit, *Finances extérieures*, 74.
[41] Becker, *1914*, 513–15; Duroselle, *La France*, 217.
[42] Pourcher, *Les Jours de guerre*, 58.

raised from 4 per cent to 6 per cent on the same day. But the banks were complaining that they were rich in paper and poor in specie. So, on 1 August they too became subject to a moratorium. On 5 August convertibility was suspended. On 6 August withdrawals on deposits were limited to a maximum of 250 francs and 5 per cent of the balance. On 9 August the trade and banking moratoriums were combined. On 14 August a moratorium was imposed on rents. Six days later the bank rate was lowered to 5 per cent. But further moratoriums followed. On 30 August all local-government bodies were relieved of the obligation to redeem debt, and on 23 September they no longer had to pay interest or dividends. On 27 September insurance companies became subject to a moratorium, although most had already been postponing premiums for the previous six weeks.[43]

Many of these moratoriums could be justified, at least temporarily, because of the confusion created in financial transactions by the operations of war. Those living in occupied areas could not remit rent to those residing elsewhere in France; war-related damage to property would require assessment and arbitration. And there was the threat to Paris itself. Many banks had decamped, along with the government, and could not be traced by their account-holders. Between 18 August and 3 September 36 million francs in silver, 4,000 million francs in gold, and 14 million francs in share certificates were removed from the capital to the southwest.[44]

But on 24 November 1914, when the situation had stabilized, the government, instead of removing the moratoriums, announced that they would continue until the end of the war. Although that in Algeria was lifted in March 1916,[45] in metropolitan France they persisted until December 1920. Of course there were modifications. On 16 August 1914 war ministry contractors were allowed funds to buy raw materials or to pay wages. However, there was no provision for investment in new plant, and on 29 August their right of withdrawal was modified to the extent that they received advances direct from the state.[46] The same decree on 29 August charged debtors with accrued interest and therefore encouraged them to settle if they could. The maximum withdrawal from a deposit was

---

[43] Knauss, *Kriegsfinanzierung*, 66; Fisk, *French public finance*, 80.
[44] Klotz, *De la guerre*, 18–19.   [45] G. Meynier, *L'Algérie révelée*, 366–7.
[46] Jèze and Truchy, *War finance*, 122–3, 128.

raised to 1,000 francs and 50 per cent of the balance by 27 October. But the net effect remained deadening for industry and for commerce. Employers could not buy raw materials and workers were not paid. Deposits flowed out but not in: the discount portfolio of the Crédit Lyonnais on 31 March 1915 was half its end-of-year total in 1913 (746 million francs as against 1,518 million), and its deposits had fallen from 913 million francs to 620 million. Nationally, all credit houses showed a decline in deposits from 7,500 million francs to 4,270 million in 1914.[47] The total annual house rent that remained unpaid was reckoned to be 1,500 million francs.[48] In the short term landlords confronted bankruptcy, but in the long run the calling in of the accumulated debt threatened tenants with penury.[49] The bad debtor was protected, the creditor was not. The French economy carried an immense burden for the rest of the war.

Gradually the banks and other institutions began to disregard the moratorium. But, particularly in 1914–15, it was the Banque de France that enabled any semblance of economic activity to continue. The bank's commercial portfolio doubled between 27 July and 1 August 1914, from 1,583 million francs to 3,041 million. By 1 October it was carrying 4,476 million francs in deferred bills. This total declined as banks elsewhere defied the moratorium. On 31 December 1915 the figure was 1,838 million francs, and by December 1918 1,028 million.[50] In the rented property market, although the government provided an indemnity for up to 50 per cent of a loss scaled according to the population size of the town, it was again the Banque de France that carried most of the obligations.[51] And it was the bank that provided the kick-start to activity in the share market. The Paris bourse reopened for cash business on 3 August, but then migrated to Bordeaux on 2 September, and did not return until 7 December. It remained closed for business that had been settled in late July 1914, but in September 1915 the Banque de France made 250 million francs available to the Chambre Syndicale des Agents de Change to settle floating commitments. Debtors were required to pay a tenth of their outstanding debt and interest on the remainder: the principal was then paid off in tenths, so that the debt was fully redeemed in July 1916.[52]

[47] Olphe-Galliard, *Histoire économique*, 34.   [48] Knauss, *Kriegsfinanzierung*, 67.

[49] Flood, *France 1914–18*, 47–8.

[50] Olphe-Galliard, *Histoire économique*, 20, 24.   [51] Bogart, *War costs*, 35.

[52] Knauss, *Kriegsfinanzierung*, 65.

In none of this activity did the bank enjoy any form of government guarantee. Thus, while the Bank of England moved from a position of commercial independence to one where it was underwritten by the Treasury, the Banque de France was effectively self-reliant. Alexandre Ribot, who became finance minister on 26 August 1914, made a virtue of the relationship. By keeping the bank's credit separate from that of the government, the bank would act as a restraint on the state's increasing its issue. On 21 September Ribot committed the state to pay 3 per cent interest on the bank's advances after the end of hostilities, rather than the nominal 1 per cent set at the start of the war. This, he believed, would be a symbol of the state's financial self-discipline: the bank could put the extra 2 per cent into a sinking fund to wipe out the debt.[53]

In reality, however, any discipline in the relationship between government and bank would be undermined if there was no necessary internal self-control in the fiscal affairs of either party. On 5 August, when the 1911 agreement came into force and the bank duly advanced the government 2,900 million francs, the authorized note issue was increased to 12,000 million. The bank, with no requirement to maintain a set gold reserve, and now also released from convertibility, effectively had a free hand. Its note issue could be enlarged by decree of the council of state without reference to the assembly. At the same time the latter gave to the council of state the right to open extraordinary credits for the duration of hostilities. Ribot's financial purism on 21 September was set against a request for a further advance from the bank of 3,100 million francs, making 6,000 million in all. When the assembly next reconvened, on 22 December, it found that the government had voted itself 6,441 million francs in extraordinary credits. Thus, the primary pressure to increase the bank's note issue was not to ensure liquidity for the sake of business (this, after all, was effectively curtailed by the moratorium), but to meet the fiscal needs of the government. The enlargement of note circulation was the main method of state borrowing, and would in turn lead to currency inflation, the depreciation of the franc, and rising prices.[54]

France, of course, was not alone in using currency inflation as a means to cover its mobilization costs. Without a rapid increase in available cash

[53] Ribot, *Letters to a friend*, 29–32; see also Charbonnet, *Politique financière*, 107–8.
[54] Bogart, *War costs*, 112; Fisk, *French public finance*, 40–4.

the liquidity necessary for paying suppliers, financing industry, or staving off public panic would have been forfeit. Without it, too, the switch from the requirements of a peacetime economy to those of war would have been much more protracted. The success of these methods is perhaps best rendered in negative terms: none of the major powers, not even Austria-Hungary, was constrained militarily in those first few weeks of 1914 because of financial problems. But the powers were prepared to act as they did, to suspend convertibility and to borrow from their central banks, in response to what they saw as an immediate crisis, not as a long-term situation. The crucial question, therefore, would be how they managed war finance and its inflationary effects over the long term. This would require them to pace themselves, but in a race of whose ultimate length they had no better knowledge than (mostly) over-optimistic guesses.

4

THE LOSS OF
BUDGETARY CONTROL

In January 1917 an Australian division had one officer and fifty men continuously employed in salvage operations.[1] There is no reason to think that they were atypical. But their attentions were concentrated on the items that could be reused, not on those which could not. When visitors toured the battlefields of France and Flanders after the war they saw piles of rubbish—the refuse of industrialized war. Rusting rifles, rent helmets, and spent shell-cases were the obvious signs of fighting. But also there were old tin cans, discarded corrugated iron, and broken bottles, the remnants of the daily needs of millions of men over four years. The First World War was fought with equipment that was both more sophisticated and yet more vulnerable than its predecessors, that proliferated spare parts and spawned its own obsolescence. The destructiveness of its weapons was in part responsible for its wastefulness. But in addition, standards and expectations—of medical care, of rationing, and of creature comforts—were all higher. The litter sprang above all from abundance; lavishness proceeded from lack of financial limitation.

War reversed the relationships between exchequers and their spending departments. The treasuries of Europe saw their task no longer as one of restraint but as one of enablement. Karl Helfferich, an economist, a former director of the Deutsche Bank, and Reich secretary of state for

---

[1] Cutlack, *War letters of Monash*, 160; see also Chapman, *Passionate prodigality*, 266–7; Binding, *Fatalist at war*, 165–6.

finance from February 1915 to May 1916, declared after the war that he had little enthusiasm for thrift. His task, as he saw it, was not to deny departments what they wanted but to work with them. He boasted that he had acceded to every request that the army had made. The watchword in Germany—for all Helfferich's empty efforts to rebut it—was 'money plays no role'.[2] And attitudes were little different among the Entente powers. Lloyd George, as Britain's chancellor of the exchequer on the war's outbreak and prime minister at its conclusion, set the tone. Although chancellor since 1908, he never, in Keynes's view, 'had the faintest idea of the meaning of money'.[3] After resolving the crisis of July 1914, Lloyd George neglected his departmental business for the wider world of the war as a whole. Octave Homberg, meeting him in December, reported to Ribot that he 'seems to know nothing of financial affairs and is above all a politician'. By May 1915 discontent within the Treasury made his continuation there insupportable.[4] His transfer to the government's prime spending department, the Ministry of Munitions, completed the erasure of any instincts for economy he had once possessed. For the rest of the war the only limits on Lloyd George's mobilization of resources for the purposes of victory were those imposed by physical availability, not those suggested by cost.

That governmental restraints on spending were easing was evident— albeit to different degrees—before 1914. The demands of the pre-war arms race had already pushed back the frontiers of financial control. In Britain the quest for 'national efficiency', not least in relation to defence, had forced the Treasury to defer to specialist advice, regardless of financial orthodoxy.[5] Between 1900 and 1913 Britain had the highest defence spending per capita in the world.[6] But Britain could afford it: it also had the highest per capita income. And so it was able to observe two cardinal principles before 1914: expenditure should be paid for out of revenue, and

    [2] Helfferich, *Weltkrieg*, 200–1, 210–14.

    [3] Skidelsky, *Keynes*, i. 300; see also Stamp, *Taxation during the war*, 32–4; Hirst and Allen, *British war budgets*, 44–5, 53.

    [4] Ribot, *Journal*, 23; Gilbert, *Lloyd George 1912–16*, 200–2; David, *Inside Asquith's cabinet*, 182, 230.

    [5] Pugh, *Making of modern British politics*, 103–4.

    [6] Davis and Huttenback, *Mammon and the pursuit of empire*, 160. For an important corrective to Davis's and Huttenback's calculations, see Hobson, *Journal of European Economic History*, XXII (1993), 461–506.

parliament had the ultimate authority to approve the budget. In the other belligerent countries the combination of weak parliamentary systems, ill-developed systems of taxation, and of rising defence budgets at a time of increasing expenditure on social benefits fostered devices and deceits in peace which would flourish and grow in war. Accounting ploys and deficit financing were lessons already well learnt by 1914. Helfferich and Lloyd George might therefore protest that they did no more than preside over trends already in place.

Helfferich's predecessor but one, Adolf Wermuth, finance minister from 1909 to 1912, had argued as a British chancellor of the exchequer would have done. Without a thriving economy and a secure financial base, an enhanced defence capacity would have nothing to protect. Wermuth resigned rather than preside over the 1912 and 1913 army laws. The 1912 budget approved defence expenditure up until 1917 without making clear how it was to be funded; the army, like the navy, was manoeuvring into a position where its growth would be autonomous, independent of Reichstag control. The 1913 budget appropriated 61.8 per cent of its total for military purposes: military spending rose 62.9 per cent from 1910, when it had been 49.1 per cent of the total budget. Thus the Reich's financial arrangements were already being 'militarized' before the war broke out. The Bavarian finance minister said of the tax which resulted, 'in truth it is...a war contribution in advance...not a tax, but a sacrifice, a patriotic gift'.[7]

The new tax, a direct levy on property to run for three years, meant that Germany's 1914 budget—although drawn up in peace—contained an element which suggested that it was appropriate for war. Hermann Kühn, Wermuth's successor, did not see the need to revise the budget when war broke out, and Helfferich followed its outline in 1915 and to some extent in 1916. However, the new principles of the defence tax were overshadowed by a legacy of financial laxity, manifested in two interlocking elements in the budget.

The first of these was the burden of debt. On 31 March 1914 the Reich's total debt was 5,441,897,600 marks, all but 524 million of which was long-term and interest-paying.[8] The second significant continuity was the

[7] Witt, *Finanzpolitik des Deutschen Reiches*, 364; see generally, Kroboth, *Finanzpolitik des Deutschen Reiches*, 127–30, 161–4, 192–4, 301.
[8] Lotz, *Deutsche Staatsfinanzwirtschaft*, 6.

extraordinary budget. Technically this was for capital improvements and was therefore self-amortizing: it was funded by loans, the interest and redemption of which were met by the ordinary budget. But the strain of rising defence costs before the war had eroded the rigour implicit in these arrangements. Loans were being used to meet recurrent expenditure, including not only defence costs but also interest and redemption payments. Furthermore, the expenditure for the redemption of debt appeared as a charge on the ordinary account, but as an income on the extraordinary. Provided ordinary receipts, including new loans, met ordinary outgoings, and provided transfers to the extraordinary account covered that element of the budget's outgoings, the Reich avoided declaring a deficit. Formal deficits or surpluses could appear because it was possible to carry forward extraordinary allocations from the previous year as income for the new year. This rolling over of accounts obscured whether the deficit was real or not—and in any case, even if it were, it could be simply resolved by the contraction of fresh debt.[9]

It was intended in the 1914 budget to break this cycle by balancing the ordinary budget through the defence tax. But with the outbreak of war all the additional military costs created by hostilities were pushed into the extraordinary account, which was funded through credits. In 1915 and subsequently even peacetime defence expenditure was shifted out of the ordinary account, and thus that aspect of the budget was reduced in line with the reduction in the receipts for ordinary income.[10]

The effect was to remove from Reichstag supervision the auditing of the war's financing. The Reichstag's concerns were effectively narrowed to those costs which could not be transferred to the extraordinary budget. Not once throughout the war did it review Germany's financial policy as a whole.[11]

Arguably this would have happened anyway. On 4 August the Reichstag itself voluntarily gave up what oversight it had by empowering the Bundesrat to adopt the financial measures it deemed appropriate. Thereafter, so compelling and immediate were the needs of the war that no nation, including Germany, could manage its funds according to an annual budget: what mattered was the monthly cash flow. In addition,

---

[9] Ibid. 7–8; Williamson, *Helfferich*, 123.   [10] Roesler, *Finanzpolitik*, 67–70.
[11] Ibid. 102, 105, 119, 174; Dix, *Wirtschaftskrieg*, 215.

as elsewhere, proper controls were the casualty of conscription: insufficient men remained to keep tallies and to collect taxes.

Germany's domestic political agenda—the services' battle to be independent of parliamentary control, the Bundesrat's clash with the more liberal and more democratic Reichstag—created the context into which the issues of war finance irrupted. Thus, its experiences were more characteristic of its forms of government than of its military situation. In this it had at least something in common with its main ally Austria-Hungary. Admittedly, the latter's difficulties in central control and accountability, with its finances divided between the two monarchies in war as in peace, were entirely *sui generis*. But, like Germany, the best of the finance ministries' staffs, at the top as well as the bottom, were called to other duties. When Alexander Spitzmüller, who had left the Austrian government's employ to become president of the Creditanstalt bank in 1909, was appointed to head the Austrian finance ministry in December 1916 he found that it had been split into too many departments, that it lacked strong leadership to give it unity, and that it was 'no longer the elite instrument of national and political economy'.[12]

In many ways, however, the more obvious comparison between Germany and its allies was with Bulgaria, which joined the Central Powers in July 1915. Bulgaria, like Germany, used the device of an extraordinary budget to fund its war effort. As a result, its ordinary account showed a surplus in 1917 and 1918. Only in the latter year did the outgoings on the ordinary account increase, by about 41 per cent, and in real terms inflation meant that the expenditure charged to the account was constant. Indeed, the depreciation of the Bulgarian currency, the lev, ensured that by 1918 actual spending on the ordinary account had fallen to 27 per cent of its 1914 value. Even in 1911, the last full year of peace for Bulgaria, 21.7 per cent of the budget was devoted to direct defence spending, and debt charges, many of which arose from the acquisition of military equipment abroad, was responsible for a further 20 per cent. After 1915 all military expenditure, including the peacetime costs of the army, was shifted into the extraordinary account. Beginning in 1916, any attempt at an annual statement was abandoned in favour of monthly credits in twelfths. The extraordinary account duly multiplied by a factor of 14.4 between 1914 and

---

[12] Spitzmüller, *Memoirs*, 158–9.

1918. Again, depreciation limited the real cost, which peaked at a threefold increase on the 1914 figure in 1917, and by 1918 the combined values of both ordinary and extraordinary accounts had declined 45 per cent on their 1914 totals. But the accounts understate the price of Bulgaria's war. About half of wartime expenditure was simply unbudgeted. Using the protocols of the civil and military authorities, the state borrowed from the national bank of Bulgaria, Bulgarska Narodna Banka, without cover or with, at best, the security of provisional receipts or anticipated post-war extraordinary credits. At any one time the Treasury had no idea of its current commitments, let alone its anticipated outgoings.[13]

Of the Entente powers, Russia was most akin to Bulgaria in its practices. Between 1900 and 1913 Russia's state spending rose 93 per cent, but its national income increased only 80 per cent. The finance minister and future chairman of the council of ministers, V. N. Kokovtsov, alarmed by military spending which accounted for 43 per cent of the budget in 1909–10, tried to bring the armed services under control. He did reduce the national debt, from 9,054 million roubles in 1908 to 8,825 million in 1913, so that its cost was 13.7 per cent of the budget as against 16 per cent. Nonetheless, military spending rose over the same period. The navy's expenditure grew 178.4 per cent and the army's 43.1 per cent. Russia's ostensible financial health was confined to its ordinary budget, whose revenue was derived from the state railways, state monopolies, and taxation, and a quarter of whose expenditure was allocated to the services. Its extraordinary budget, funded through loans, was what shouldered spending on railways and on the major arms programme of 1914.[14]

As in Germany, the principle of the extraordinary budget was extended on the outbreak of hostilities. Russia's fundamental laws gave the Tsar the power to authorize additional wartime spending for all government departments, and also to raise state loans to fund it. The war could effectively be financed out of the war fund, and be totally independent of the Duma. The ordinary budget continued as it had before the war— and remained subject to the Duma and to the state council. The absurdity

---

[13] Danaïllow, *Les Effets de la guerre en Bulgarie*, 69–70, 496–512.

[14] Geyer, *Russian imperialism*, 255–7; David Jones, 'Imperial Russia's forces at war', in Millett and Murray (eds.), *Military effectiveness*, i. 258–9; Michelson, 'Revenue and expenditure of the Russian government during the war', in Michelson *et al.*, *Russian public finance during the war*, 15–72.

of this position was clear from even the most superficial glance at the accounts as presented to the Duma. Those for 1914 showed a deficit of 242.7 million roubles on the ordinary and extraordinary budgets; those for 1915 moved into surplus, and for 1914–17 as a whole recorded a favourable balance of 2,190.7 million roubles. Ordinary spending in 1915 was actually recorded as 452 million roubles below that of 1913.

Two things were happening to obscure the true state of Russia's finances. First, into the war's expenditure were transferred not only the additional military costs generated by the fighting but also the normal expenses of the services' peacetime establishment. Secondly, many items of non-military expenditure, particularly spending on state railways, but also other capital projects, were billed to the war. By 1916 10 per cent of all civil outgoings were channelled through the war fund. Between the outbreak of war and August 1917 41,392.7 million roubles had been appropriated for the war fund, 20 per cent of it for government departments other than the army and the navy. Thus, even the apparent health of the ordinary budget was in reality misleading: ordinary revenue was not covering ordinary expenditure. The gravity of the position was further underlined by the fact that much of the revenue in the ordinary budget was generated by the profits of war industry or by customs duties on the services' imports. If the war had ended in 1916 the ordinary budget was likely to have been up to 2,000 million roubles in deficit.

The principal cause of Russia's loss of budgetary control was artifice. The opportunity afforded the Tsar to undermine the Duma made the war fund an instrument in the battle for autocratic control. The Duma protested about the bookkeeping fictions over which it retained oversight, but to little avail. However, incompetence also played its part. Ribot expressed the view of many of his Entente colleagues when he described Peter Bark, a banker and Russia's minister of finance throughout the war, as 'a child who knows nothing, neither of his resources, expenses, nor budget'.[15] Even if Bark had wished to assert control, he probably lacked the machinery to do so. The execution of the 1914 Finance act was the last on which the state audit department was able to report: the growth of the budget and the diminution of the

---

[15] Schmidt, *Ribot*, 125; Keynes was perversely complimentary, see Johnson (ed.), *Collected writings of Keynes*, xvi. 130–3.

department's staff through the demands of military service spelt the end
of any rigour in accounting controls.[16]

France before 1914, like Germany and Russia, paid for the growing
costs of central government, particularly the military ones, by borrowing.
Unlike Germany and Russia, it made rather less effort to disguise the fact.
In 1907 it budgeted for a deficit of 295 million francs, in 1908 for
54 million, in 1909 for 45 million, and in 1910 for 48 million. In 1912
Klotz showed a surplus, but only by an accounting sleight of hand, which
was repeated in 1913. The 1914 budget anticipated a deficit of 794 million
francs, all of it and more generated by the 1913 three-year service law.
Between 1904 and 1914 fresh expenditure totalled 1,777 million francs, but
normal income only netted an additional 800 million francs. France's
consolidated debt in July 1914 was 27,000 million francs, its annual
arrears on that 967 million francs, and all its obligations of whatever
description 34,188 million francs.[17]

Perhaps more surprising than the pre-existing burden of debt which
France carried into the war was the ease with which such a fiercely
republican country could slough off the principles of parliamentary
control. Caught up in the symbolism of 1793, the assembly's authorization of extraordinary credits by decree was a willing delegation of power
to the centre in a time of crisis. Even when parliamentary activity
resumed in December, Ribot was surprised to find that the financial
committee of the senate was only interested in matters of secondary
importance: 'we did not speak of the general financial position and of
the possible means to provide the treasury with the sums it needs.'[18]

The chamber agreed that the government should have provisional
credits, given in twelfths, and in December accorded the government
six twelfths (in other words, cash for six months) to the tune of 9,000
million francs. When, in June 1915, fresh credits were needed the period
was reduced to three months, and there it remained for the rest of the
war. Although in December 1914 the government had drawn up a list of
headings under which the money would be disbursed, the allocations
were not binding and the credits were effectively voted as undivided

---

[16] Michelson *et al.*, *Russian public finance*, esp. 75–8, 119–21, 125, 129, 138, 145, 157, 214, 215.
[17] Charbonnet, *Politique financière de la France*, 21–35; Duroselle, *La France*, 205; Jèze and
Truchy, *War finance*, 187.
[18] Ribot, *Journal*, 24.

blocks. The assembly was authorizing expenditure without any calculation as to income; lacking a firm hold on how the money was meant to be
spent, it possessed no means of monitoring how it had been spent. Its
limited knowledge led it to encourage expenditure without regard to
revenue. The credits voted in 1915 totalled 22,804.5 million francs. They
then rose by approximately 10,000 million francs in each year of the war,
to reach 54,537.1 million in 1918.[19]

In practice, actual spending in France exceeded the credits voted.
Moreover, their global figures did not encompass the special accounts
created at the beginning of the war to ensure food supplies. Technically,
the accounts could show favourable balances, since they sold commodities as well as bought them. The most important embraced wheat, sugar,
petrol, coal, and the merchant marine. Their foreign purchases, as well as
their multiplicity, made proper control problematic—even after the war
had ended. In 1920 30,000 million francs passed through the special
accounts. During the war their adverse balances amounted in all to
10,305 million francs, including 3,904 million in 1916 alone.[20]

What the special accounts highlighted was the difficulty for a country
that was itself a major battlefield in distinguishing between civil and
military expenditure. The voting of lump-sum credits meant that even
without the device of the extraordinary budget France lost control of its
peacetime disbursements as surely as did Germany and Russia. Parliament lacked the information to be able to balance non-military spending
against normal income.

In December 1914 the assembly left itself with two instruments with
which it could scrutinize the government's financial affairs—the budget
committee of the chamber and the finance committee of the senate.
Although passive at first, these two bodies—especially the latter—
became more assertive as the war lengthened. In particular, they tried
to get the ministry of war to justify the credits it requested and to monitor
the disbursements it then made. The ministry's hand was not strong: a
law of 1869 permitted the commander-in-chief at the front to authorize
expenditure. Much of France was a front, and Joffre reasonably protested
that his headquarters had more pressing concerns than the keeping of

[19] Jèze and Truchy, War finance, 22, 160–75; Renouvin, War government in France, 109–11;
Charbonnet, Politique financière de la France, 43–53.
[20] Jèze and Truchy, War finance, 40–7.

accounts. Army commissaries and paymasters-general were requested to produce monthly statements—a request honoured as much in the breach as in the observance. The ministry of finance, under pressure from the two committees of the assembly, tried, somewhat feebly, to get the ministry of war to channel orders through it, and to control prices through the centralization of the competing demands of the service departments.[21]

Ribot's determination to establish control was not strong. His financial advisers, including the same Paul Leroy-Beaulieu who had recognized before the onset of hostilities that a long war could be funded on credit, were unconcerned about the loss of budgetary control. Debt mounted in proportion to the government's existing borrowings, not according to its receipts, which did not even match its normal peacetime outgoings. Ribot defended his position by reference to the military situation: with so much territory under occupation normal fiscal self-discipline was irrelevant. At the end of 1915 he drew up a draft law which aimed to compare total credits with total expenditure, and thus show whether France was in balance or deficit. Nothing came of it. In May 1916 he engaged in a similar exercise when, in order to argue for increased taxation, he tried to match outgoings to income. But the first promise of a proper budget had to wait until June 1917, when Thierry, finance minister in the Painlevé government, projected his expenditure and his receipts for the third quarter of 1917, and announced his intention to produce a proper annual budget in 1918. His aim, minimal as it might seem, was to stabilize France's non-war costs, and to end the system of provisional credits.

It was not fulfilled. When Clemenceau became prime minister in November 1917 France adopted the principles of Lloyd George to the securing of victory. To mix national metaphors, Klotz, who succeeded Thierry as minister of finance, belonged to the Helfferich school. 'He signed cheques', Clemenceau said of him, 'as though he was signing autographs.'[22] After the war Klotz boasted that, while on the chamber's budget committee, he had never obstructed an order placed by the ministry of war—indeed, quite the reverse—and he rationalized his

[21] Ibid. 173–83; Schmidt, *Ribot*, 123.
[22] Duroselle, *La Grande Guerre des français*, 157. See also Martin, *Les Finances publiques de la France*, 132–5, 140; Martin, *La Situation financière de la France*, 216–22.

position—as Helfferich did—by saying that the payment by a defeated enemy of an indemnity would solve the problem of accumulated debt. Ribot's horror at Klotz's ambition to be minister of finance proved well founded.[23]

Klotz kept the provisional twelfths for war credits. He followed Thierry in announcing his intention to meet the costs of civil administration and of servicing the debt from ordinary income, but he did not achieve it. France in 1918 was still budgeting for a deficit in its ordinary accounts. But at least parliamentary control was reasserted to the point where on 29 June 1918 the first budget of the war was approved.[24]

Perhaps Thierry need not have worried. Britain had a budget for every year of the war, but parliament still lost control of expenditure. The chancellor of the exchequer dutifully informed the House of Commons what he anticipated the country's disbursements would be in the coming year, and how he proposed to fund them. But when the cost of war exceeded its budgeted figure, the government supplemented its receipts with emergency votes of credit. On 12 February 1917, for example, the House of Commons voted £350 million to see the government through until the end of May. But on 9 May Bonar Law, the chancellor since December 1916, was back asking for £500 million. Furthermore, he told the House that the average daily cost of the war was £7.45 million, when only a week before he had declared it to be £5.5 million. These were extremes, but in such circumstances it was impossible for Members of Parliament to grasp the full financial picture.[25]

The British annual budget, nonetheless, served three principal functions. First, the debate which it engendered showed that, except during the chancellorship of Reginald McKenna (May 1915 to December 1916), the House was inclined to greater financial radicalism than the government. Thus, the cabinet was not held back from potentially unpopular taxation for fear of its political effects. Secondly, the appearance of parliamentary accountability and of financial rigour was enormously important in sustaining domestic confidence and foreign credit. And thirdly, the effective result was that Britain, alone of all the European belligerents, continued to cover its peacetime expenditure through

[23] Klotz, *De la guerre*, 43–6; Ribot, *Journal*, 28–9, 46–7.
[24] Knauss, *Kriegsfinanzierung*, 129–34.   [25] Hirst and Allen, *British war budgets*, 186.

income. A calculation that aggregated revenue through taxation and then deducted interest charges and the pre-war civil budget showed that over the war years Britain generated a surplus of $5,396 million. By contrast, Germany showed a deficit of $4,180 million, Russia (to 1917) of $1,142 million, France of $3,346 million, Austria-Hungary of $401 million, and Italy of $787 million.[26]

The controls that Britain lost were specifically over war costs. Furthermore, they were willingly forfeited. Neither the War Office nor the Admiralty was used to ordering without restraint. It required Lloyd George to tell the War Office in October 1914 not to come to the Treasury for approval for orders.[27] Even then the culture of penny-pinching was sufficiently ingrained for the chancellor to have to continue hectoring, and eventually—as minister of munitions—to take over the job of spending himself. In other words, in Britain civilian government deliberately loosened the reins rather than having them prised from its grasp.

Responsibility for their daily handling lay, of course, not with parliament but with the Treasury. But in 1914 the Treasury was ill-prepared to supervise the expenditure of an empire in a world war. It mustered thirty-three officials in its administrative class.[28] It then found itself neglected and humiliated by its political head. Keynes reflected the Treasury's disillusionment. Lloyd George 'soon got bored with' Sir George Paish, one of his principal financial advisers, 'and stopped reading his lengthy memoranda. [Paish] was, however, given a good salary and an exalted title...and...a room set at a considerable distance.'[29]

McKenna, when he succeeded Lloyd George in May 1915, found 'hopeless financial disorder at the Exchequer, so great indeed that we could not have carried on for another three months'.[30] He himself had served as financial secretary a decade before, so he ought to have known what he was talking about. But, somewhat surprisingly, that was not the prevailing view. His own financial secretary, Edwin Montagu, agreed with him that the department was in confusion, but on little else. His political colleagues felt that he was simply keeping the seat warm for Lloyd

[26] Bogart, *War costs*, 316–18.
[27] Kathleen Burk, 'The Treasury: from impotence to power', in Burk (ed.), *War and the state*, 91.
[28] Ibid. 85.
[29] Skidelsky, *Keynes*, i. 299.
[30] David, *Inside Asquith's cabinet*, 247; see also Farr, 'McKenna', 57, 70–1, 154, 238.

George, and that therefore calls for fiscal rectitude ill behoved him. On
finance itself, E. C. Grenfell of Morgan Grenfell characterized him 'as a
very ignorant man ... [who is] inclined to try to appear wise'.[31]

Some, at least, of McKenna's problems derived from the fact that by the
time he assumed office the new culture had taken hold in the departments
of disbursement. In a memorandum of February 1916 Keynes showed how
munitions orders were being increased. The War Office added a margin
over what it reckoned it needed, and the Ministry of Munitions then made
a similar supplement to the War Office's already inflated request: thus, a
scheme for 3,404 guns had been elevated to one for 4,362.[32] McKenna
complained that Lloyd George was not only ordering more munitions
than he could use but that, in the process, he was actually impeding
output rather than promoting it. A retrenchment committee was created
in July 1915, and in November McKenna secured an undertaking that all
contracts worth more than £500,000 would be referred to the Treasury.[33]

For the Treasury, the key issue was whether finance should be the
regulator of British policy or its servant. One traditional interpretation of
British strategy contended, in the words of Austen Chamberlain in 1903,
that 'Our defensive strength rests upon our financial not less than upon
our military and naval resources'.[34] Britain's determination to cling to its
international convertibility in 1914 reflected its commitment to this
approach. But the actual experience of major war injected pragmatism
into its formulation, not least for McKenna. Outwardly, his policies
seemed to accommodate the needs of the City of London. He was, for
example, loath to use compulsion when securing control of American
securities, not because of any political commitment to Liberal principles,
but because he feared that foreign investors would withdraw their deposits. His ultimate objective, therefore, was not to prop up the City but
to preserve Britain's liquidity.[35] And it was this pragmatism which made
him a shifty and even uncongenial ally for any one camp. McKenna saw
funds not as an end in themselves but as the means to purchase goods for
the prosecution of the war. Therefore, at bottom he reckoned production, not purchasing power, to be the regulator of British strategy. The key

[31] Burk, 'A merchant bank at war', 162.
[32] Johnson (ed.), *Collected writings of Keynes*, xvi. 173.
[33] French, *British strategy and war aims*, 128.
[34] Neilson, *Britain and the last Tsar*, 129.   [35] Farr, 'McKenna', 186, 211.

issue was the division of manpower between output and military service. If Britain's productive effort was directed to the latter to the detriment of the former, it would have to buy the munitions its armed forces and its allies would need from overseas, and so jeopardize its financial supremacy.[36] Herein was the nub of British strategy. It was a battle which McKenna fought in the cabinet from late 1915 until the early summer of 1916, and lost.

Ultimately, controls on British spending were reimposed not by parliament or by the Treasury, but by the United States. Britain's need for American credit provoked the United States into demanding coordination among its new allies in their overseas purchasing. The scale of British and French orders made the management of the exchange rate a key aspect in regulating their cost. The bankers regarded this as their business, and Lord Cunliffe, the governor of the Bank of England, was convinced that the accumulation of gold and its export when required were the keys to its regulation. By appointing Cunliffe as chairman of the London Exchange Committee McKenna hoped to defuse a fraught situation. Cunliffe was not an easy man: E. C. Grenfell thought the problem was his teeth, and that if he had only seen a dentist all would have been all right.[37] But the underlying difficulty was that neither the Bank nor the London Exchange Committee had real bite. His deputy, Montagu Norman, was as frustrated with the Treasury as Cunliffe: 'one might as well talk to an airball as them.'[38] By 1917 Cunliffe was openly undermining the Treasury's policy in the United States, insisting that Britain should ship gold. In July he challenged the Treasury's increasing intervention in the management of the exchange rate. Bonar Law, as chancellor, told Cunliffe that in war the Bank must be subordinate to the national interest and follow the Treasury. Cunliffe huffed and puffed, was overruled, and resigned in April 1918.[39] The confrontation did more than mark the completion of the process by which the Bank of England became a central state bank. It gave the Treasury the whip hand in the key component of British financial policy: control of foreign dealings became the substitute for the lack of control of domestic disbursements.

---

[36] Farr, 'McKenna', 169–71.   [37] Burk, 'A merchant bank at war', 167.
[38] Norman, 27 June 1916; I am grateful to Dr Martin Farr for this quotation.
[39] Burk, *Historical Journal*, XXII (1979), 361; Sayers, *Bank of England*, i. 99–109.

Some of the same effects could be observed in France. The efforts to reimpose peacetime budgetary procedures in 1917–18 coincided with American pressure on France to reduce its call for American credits. Furthermore, the squeeze which the United States placed on Britain was relayed to Paris in British restrictions on French borrowing through London. The inter-allied purchasing committee forced on the Entente by McAdoo in August 1917 therefore provided the external constraint on France's spending departments which its government had failed to impose internally. The value of its imports fell from over 3,000 million francs to under 2,000 million in the autumn of 1917. In 1918 France found it was underspending on the credits afforded it in the United States, and in the summer the franc rose against the pound and the dollar.[40]

The United States thus imposed some discipline on its allies. But it too found that domestically the control of the war's costs was not necessarily easier for a democratic power than an autocratic one. Like Britain, it sustained the outward form of public accountability. However, its spending on the war far exceeded that of any other nation, averaging $42.8 million per day between 1 July 1917 and 30 June 1919. That of each of the other major belligerents hovered around $32 million over the same period. Federal expenditure rose 2,454 per cent between 1916 and 1919.[41]

The contrast in financial management between the United States and, say, Austria-Hungary was therefore much less striking than the difference in their political structures might have suggested. Austria did not even consult its parliament between 1914 and 1916. But its principal fiscal problem, that of controlling the army's expenditure, was a difference of degree rather than of substance. The complaints of the Austrian finance minister[42]—that the army paid for its needs without regard to the market rate, that efforts to control costs in the higher administration of the army were undermined by independent commanders in the field, that civilian procedures had been usurped by military necessity—found echoes throughout the nations. Whatever their nominal controls, all powers were operating some form of arrears to fund their war efforts. Britain's wartime budget deficit, if calculated in current prices, was 60.6 per cent of its pre-war national income; Germany's, at 64 per cent, was little higher.[43]

[40] Petit, *Finances extérieures*, 101–7, 133–47, 248–52, 282–303, 433–6, 446–69, 477–93, 497–8.
[41] Gilbert, *American financing*, 65, 221–3.   [42] Popovics, *Geldwesen*, 167.
[43] Balderston, *Economic History Review*, 2nd series, XLII (1989), 229.

All powers, therefore, ended up borrowing. The crucial questions were how they managed that borrowing, and how they juxtaposed it with taxation.

5

TAXATION

The choice between taxation and borrowing as means to finance the war was at bottom a choice between taxation now or taxation in the future. Loans contracted during the war would have to be repaid on maturity through tax receipts. They could, of course, be postponed by contracting fresh debt, but even if the state thereby retained the principal over a longer period taxation would still be required to pay the interest.

Servicing the debt made loans more expensive than taxation. But it did not follow that the state should therefore tax heavily in order to pay for as much of the war as possible out of current income. Part of the case against such a policy rested on the principle of equity. Those fighting the war were making sufficient sacrifices for the future well-being of their societies for it to be reasonable to expect not them but their successors to meet the financial costs. In addition there was an economic argument. The taxable capacity of a country was a reflection not simply of the money in circulation but also of the goods and services for which the money was the means of exchange. Waging the war depressed both commerce and those industries which were not war-related. Peace would revive normal business. Thus, a higher tax burden would be easier to sustain after the war than during it.

The problem of post-war reconstruction was therefore a material consideration in the development of intra-war taxation. But it was one which split both ways. The easing of taxation after the war would boost consumer spending and so help reactivate peacetime markets. This, then, was a case for a short, sharp shock—heavy taxation in the war. The opponents of such an approach contended that excessive taxation during

hostilities would erode individual savings. Consequently, potential consumers would be too impoverished to be able to buy goods when they
were once again available.

The real difficulty with not taxing heavily during the war was that
those whose incomes were left relatively untouched could not be relied
upon to save the money they earned. Inflation eroded the real value of
capital. Goods seemed a securer investment. But because the state was
increasingly taking over the means of production for the needs of the war,
goods were in short supply. The consequent monetary overhang—the
problem of too much money chasing too few commodities—prompted
price inflation. An effective system of wartime taxation which reduced
the purchasing power of the consumer was therefore an essential element
in the armoury of price control in particular, and of inflation control in
general. Because there were few goods to buy, heavy taxation was unlikely
to curb actual consumption any more than it was already depressed by
the war. And since the war made the state the most important arbiter in
the investment of capital (as well as the most significant consumer of its
products), there seemed little short-term case for saying that taking such
decisions out of private hands restricted industrial growth.

Government policy, therefore, had to strike a balance between on the
one hand actively dampening consumer activity over the short term and
on the other securing immediate and, above all, future capital investment. The result was a taxation pattern that in its final form inverted
peacetime priorities. Broadly speaking, taxation ceased to be socially
progressive. It needed to shore up the wealth of the rich, since this
might be invested in goods and services over the long term, and it needed
to reduce the disposable income of the less affluent, which would otherwise contribute to price inflation.

The most striking illustration of this process was the declining significance of inheritance tax. Death duties had generated major constitutional struggles in Britain in 1909–10 and in Germany in 1906–13. In
both cases expenditure on armaments had been the prime motor for
change. But during the war the egalitarian argument for the direct
taxation of large estates was offset by a desire not to penalize patriotism.
The deaths of heirs in action threatened families with payments in unex-
pectedly rapid succession. Britain in 1914 granted relief to those estates
where war casualties resulted in the ownership changing more than once.

A single transfer caused by a war-related death could be offset by deferring payment until three years after the war's conclusion.[1] Thus, yields rose only marginally and then stabilized. No alternative emerged, despite pressure from the Trades Union Congress in September 1916. Sidney Webb called for a levy on accumulated wealth to reduce government debt and as an alternative to higher rates of income tax. He argued that interest payments would fall, with the result that the profits of rentiers would slump and investment in production rise. But the Treasury rejected the idea for fear that property sales to release cash would cause a slump in values, and that individuals would therefore borrow to pay the levy rather than invest in government bonds.[2] In France the return on inheritance tax averaged 100 million francs less than the 1913 total in each of 1914, 1915, and 1916. Only in Germany did the annual income on death duties rise progressively—from 47.1 million marks in 1913 to 77.8 million in 1918.[3] And even here the increase was not proportional to the growth in direct taxation in general.

The declining significance of inheritance tax was, above all, relative. In Britain it accounted for 13.8 per cent of all direct taxation at the war's outset, and 3.4 per cent at its conclusion.[4] Other forms of direct taxation, therefore, grew at a much faster rate. In Britain the most important was income tax, which netted £47.2 million in 1913, £205 million in 1916, and £291.1 million in 1918. None of the other major belligerents possessed an effective form of income tax in 1914. Nor did they develop one during the war. Their major revenue producer, a tax also introduced in Britain, was a duty on excess profits arising from or during the war. Delays in its introduction and problems in its assessment meant that the duty varied in its application from country to country, and that it only made an effective contribution in 1917 and 1918. But by the last year of the war it provided France with just under a quarter of its direct taxation, Britain with nearly a half, and Germany with almost all.

A major question in relation to excess profits duty was the identity of the ultimate payer. Ideally the burden would be shifted onto the consumer. Levies on excess profits would therefore constitute a form of indirect tax, and could depress consumer demand.[5] But such theorizing

---

[1] Stamp, *Taxation*, 143.   [2] Daunton, *English Historical Review*, CXI (1996), 890–1.
[3] Knauss, *Kriegsfinanzierung*, 135–6.   [4] Ibid. 136.
[5] Gilbert, *American financing*, 62–3.

harboured a logical inconsistency. The industries making large profits in wartime were doing so out of the war; their principal client was not the public but the state. But the state's spending was not easily curbed. Thus, if the war profits tax was borne by the prime consumer it would not inhibit inflation but promote it. The tax would drive up prices which the state could only then pay by further taxation (and a further increase in prices) or by borrowing. The corollary of an excess profits duty, if it was not to stoke credit inflation, was an effective policy of price control.

The crux of the debate between state and business over war profits was, therefore, the question of what constituted a reasonable return on capital. Firms argued that a radical reduction in their profits would inhibit reinvestment and reduce the plant devoted to war production. Taking the average of pre-war profits as a basis for comparison, which is what most states did, had the disadvantage that firms producing war goods reckoned on a high level of profits during the course of hostilities to sustain them in peacetime when orders were slack. On the other hand, the three years before 1914 were marked by unwonted activity in the armaments industries of Europe. The distinction between war and peace might be less immediate in terms of war profits than it was in many other areas.

What was clear was that a levy on excess profits could only reduce the demand for goods where peace industries flourished alongside war industries. In these circumstances the duty would act in the same way as indirect taxation. This argument was advanced in the United States. But there, as elsewhere, the nominal returns on indirect taxation fell. In 1916 excise duty accounted for 47.6 per cent of federal revenue; in 1918, 17.9 per cent. Customs receipts declined from 27.2 per cent to 4.4 per cent over the same period.[6] In Germany indirect taxation fell from 81.3 per cent of ordinary receipts in 1913 to 47.9 per cent in 1918; in Britain from 46 per cent to 21.2 per cent; and in France from 53.5 per cent to 43.1 per cent.[7] The goods were simply not available in sufficient quantity to produce the cash required. Industry's production for public consumption was pared to essentials. Imports of luxuries and non-essentials were limited in order to maximize shipping space and foreign purchasing power for war goods.

---

[6] Gilbert, *American financing*, 76.

[7] Knauss, *Kriegsfinanzierung*, 148; Daunton, *English Historical Review*, CXI (1996), 896, gives the British figures as 42.5% in 1913–14 and 20.4% in 1918–19.

Much of the increase in direct taxation was therefore no more than relative—a response to a decline in absolute yields elsewhere. Germany between 1913 and 1918 increased its direct tax from 3.5 per cent of its ordinary receipts to 47.9 per cent without establishing a proper Reich income tax. The growth looked so dramatic because, for example, customs, responsible for raising 679.3 million marks in 1913, fell, under the impact of the blockade, to 133 million marks in 1918.[8]

Falling real levels of indirect taxation meant that direct taxation was the only effective tool with which to control consumer-led inflation. The major potential change in taxation policy was that which made income tax a burden on all wage-earners and not just on the wealthy. But the belief that the principal aim in war finance should be the securing of cash, not the curbing of consumption, died hard. Even in 1921 a distinguished British economist, A. C. Pigou, observed that a man who paid his income tax by reducing his consumption might manage—because he would avoid indirect taxes on goods—to pay less tax, not more. Pigou's attention was on the need to raise money to cover the real costs of the war.[9] But in practice the function of wartime taxation was less important to this than to the reduction of the monetary overhang created by credit inflation.

In these terms, no power, not even Britain, taxed as heavily as it needed to or could have done. But, arguably, the possibility of harsher regimes became more evident after the war and with hindsight than it was at the time. Taxation itself was a cumbersome instrument of economic control, in that its burdens were slow to take effect. New areas of liquidity became evident in retrospect; new taxation was applied in future. The time-lag between cause and result was therefore at least a year. The war, however long, presented rapidly changing economic conditions, but conditions whose longevity was of uncertain duration. Pacing the financial effort and retaining a system which would enable a swift change to peace were both factors inhibiting innovation. The taxation systems of most belligerents, therefore, changed little and late. Those states that taxed most efficiently were those that had the appropriate taxes already in place when the war began.

In Britain income tax was first adopted, in 1799, specifically as a war tax. It was the engine by which the nation harnessed its commercial

[8] Knauss, *Kriegsfinanzierung*, 142, 148.   [9] Pigou, *Political economy of war*, 48.

strength to military applications. But in 1842 Sir Robert Peel employed the tax in peacetime, albeit still on a temporary basis, to enable a reduction in indirect taxes in his bid to stimulate the expansion of commerce and consumption through free trade. So apparently successful was this policy that Gladstone felt consistently able to promise its abolition. But in reality the burdens of colonial defence made the financial distinction between peace and war increasingly irrelevant. Gladstone's logic, that Britain would be unlikely to go to war if income tax resumed its primary status as a war tax, and if—broadly speaking—liability for the tax correlated with the parliamentary franchise, proved unfounded. The rebuilding of the Royal Navy under the pressure of competition with France raised the basic rate from 5d. to 8d. in the £ in 1885. The Boer War pushed it up to 1s. 3d. in 1902–3, and in the five years before 1914 it stabilized at 1s. 2d. In 1900–14 the average tax burden per person per year in the United Kingdom was £3.44, about £1 more than in the other developed countries of the world.[10] Britons avoided the necessity of conscription by virtue of their dependence on the navy for primary defence. But they paid for the privilege in cash.

The result was that in 1914 Britain possessed, as no other nation did, the basis for a system of war finance. It had developed the machinery which enabled it to draw on the nation's liquid assets. The Dreadnought revolution was funded not through loans, as was half of Germany's spending, but through income. Britain's lead over Germany was not only naval but also fiscal. Therefore, unlike Germany or France, its stock market was not already encumbered with a superfluity of government stocks. Indeed, in 1914 Britain budgeted for a surplus which was to be applied to the reduction of the national debt.[11]

Pre-war opponents of the naval programme argued that the revenue implications were eroding Britain's fiscal base—that the wealth required in the event of war was being spent before the war broke out.[12] In reality income tax, despite its high rate compared with other countries, had plenty of spare capacity. Real earnings per worker rose 36 per cent between 1875/6 and 1889–1900, and yet most did not become liable for direct taxation. In 1913–14 only 1.13 million of the country's electorate of

[10] Davis and Huttenback, *Mammon and the pursuit of empire*, 225–6.
[11] Sumida, *In defence of naval supremacy*, 196, 336.
[12] French, *British economic and strategic planning*, 14–15.

8 million were paying direct taxes. The political acceptability of the 'people's budget' of 1909 resided in the fact that its principal burden fell on 11,000 payers of supertax and on the heirs of estates valued at £20,000 or more. With allowances for children and reduced rates on small earned incomes, it exempted most working-class and many married middle-class men. Those taxes which did affect the working class, indirect duties, fell from 70 per cent to 55 per cent of the total tax yield; the cost of customs and excise per head of the population rose a mere 2 per cent. The bulk of the British population, therefore, was encumbered with taxation that was no more than nominal. The country, the supporters of Liberal defence policies contended, was getting financially stronger, not weaker; the total wealth not taken by taxation was put at £1,747 million in 1904–5 and £2,020 million in 1914.[13]

The advice of the Treasury to the chancellor of the exchequer on the war's outbreak, therefore, was that he should increase income tax. By November 1914 Britain's liquidity was rising as the government spent the money it had borrowed to pay for the war. But Lloyd George's budget of that month, the first of the war, was, by common consent, not as fierce as the circumstances demanded or as parliament was prepared to accept. On the advice of Austen Chamberlain (speaking for the Conservatives) he did not expand the levying of direct taxation to embrace all income-earners. Liability remained confined to those earning £160 or more per annum, and Lloyd George restricted himself to doubling the basic rate from 9d. in the £ to 1s. 6d. and to proportional increases in the higher rates. To compensate for his feebleness over direct taxation, the chancellor increased the duty on tea from 5d. to 8d. in the £, and on beer from 7s. 9d. to 25s. per barrel. But as he aimed to reduce consumption of the latter by 35 per cent through restricting the hours of opening of licensees, the total increase from both sources in the first full year of operation, 1915–16, was reckoned to be about £20 million. Lloyd George's arrangements increased the revenue for the year 1914–15 from its peacetime target of £207 million to an actual figure of £226.7 million. And yet he was anticipating expenditure of £555.4 million, of which £348.5 would be attributable to the war. One of his parliamentary critics, Thomas

---

[13] Balderston, *Economic History Review*, 2nd series, XLII (1989), 231–3; Stamp, *Taxation*, 11–12; Daunton, *English Historical Review*, CXI (1996), 885–6.

Lough, pointed out that six-elevenths of the costs of the Crimean War
were covered by tax, and two-fifths of those of the Boer War, but on
present reckoning only one-seventy-fifth of the current war.[14]

The shortfall between Lloyd George's rhetoric and the financial substance continued into his second war budget, in May 1915. In the first he
had warned of a long war. In February 1915 he continued in a similar vein,
calling for Britain to be fully mobilized for total war by 1916.[15] But in his
budget speech he projected two alternatives—a war lasting until the end
of September 1915 and one continuing until March 1916. He put the cost of
the latter at £1,136.4 million, but then said that most of that sum would be
spent on the army and the navy and would be covered by votes of credit.
He acknowledged a probable deficit of £800 million without explaining
how he would cover it. He observed the growing liquidity of Britain,
prompted by government spending; he noted the rise in earnings; he
adumbrated the possibility of an excess profits duty. But the budget
contained no increases in direct taxation. When tackled on these points,
the chancellor replied 'with a speech full of taxing precepts, but no
taxes'.[16]

What really concerned Lloyd George was his political position—his
status as the representative of radical nonconformity and of its preoccupation with temperance. Growing individual incomes were manifesting
themselves in the consumption of spirits, which in turn contributed to
gains in the yield on customs and excise. In December 1914 beer-drinking
fell 38 per cent, in response to the augmentation in duty, but spirit sales
increased 3 per cent. In January spirit sales rose 6 per cent, in February
15 per cent, and in March 26 per cent. Lloyd George attributed falling
productivity in war industries to drink. At the beginning of April thirty-
three Special Branch men in plain clothes investigated the shipyards, and
reported that the problem was local and specific: Clydebank was more
affected than Plymouth, and riveters were the principal offenders, especially on Mondays. The king, under Lloyd George's influence, was persuaded to take the pledge for the rest of the war, but the cabinet decided it
would be inexpedient to extend prohibition to his subjects. It also

---

[14] Hirst and Allen, *British war budgets*, 22–35; Morgan, *British financial policy*, 89–90; Stamp,
Taxation, 24–8; Gilbert, *David Lloyd George*, 139.
[15] French, *British strategy and war aims*, 92.
[16] 'F. W. H.' in *The Economist*, 8 Apr. 1916, cited in Hirst and Allen, *British war budgets*, 135.

rejected, after somewhat greater deliberation, the notion of a national monopoly. Finally, five days before the budget itself, Lloyd George proposed a doubling of the duty on spirits to 29s. 6d. per gallon, and an addition of 12s. per barrel on strong beers and of 15s. per gallon on sparkling wines. Increases in indirect taxation were to substitute for the failure to grasp the nettle of direct taxation.

The effect was to threaten simultaneously two props of Asquith's tottering Liberal government. The Conservatives, on whose tacit support the cabinet relied in order to be able to offset its own radicals, were the traditional spokesmen of the drink interest. Even more seriously, the Irish MPs saw the new duties as an attack on the only major manufacture of southern Ireland. Arthur Henderson, for the Labour party, added his voice to the protest: Lloyd George's assumptions about its drinking habits were a gross calumny on the working class. On 29 April 1915 the government withdrew its proposed increases in duty, and confined itself to a restriction on immature spirits and to local regulation under the Defence of the Realm act. By failing to take the whole matter of excise within the budget proper, it prevented a full discussion of the financial provision for the coming year.[17]

Thus, when Reginald McKenna became chancellor later in the same month he inherited a catalogue of missed opportunities, a Treasury anxious to tax more fiercely, and a parliament predisposed to accept its advice. Moreover, in a memorandum of 9 September 1915 Keynes alerted his political superior to the fact that the issue was not simply that of financing the war but of controlling inflation. The war had diverted 'a greater part of the income of the nation than ever before into the hands of those classes of the population which are not much affected by direct taxation and are not accustomed, or likely at any time, to subscribe largely to Government loans'. In a crude calculation, Keynes reckoned that half the industrial population was employed directly or indirectly by the state, but much less than half its money income was being appropriated by the government.[18]

McKenna raised income tax by 40 per cent in his first budget (the third of the war), in September 1915. He lowered the threshold from £160 per

[17] Hirst and Allen, *British war budgets*, 36–50; Gilbert, *David Lloyd George*, 159–71; Grigg, *Lloyd George 1912–1916*, 230–7.

[18] Johnson (ed.), *Collected writings of Keynes*, xvi. 117–19.

annum to £130. Given the rise in nominal wages, McKenna's measure
was the vital step in expanding the number of taxpayers. At a stroke,
their number was all but doubled. Furthermore, inflation made the effect
progressive. Two million wage-earners became taxpayers between 1916/17
and 1918/19. Arguably, those on lower incomes were still spared at the
expense of those with higher earnings. Farmers were to be assessed on
their whole rental, not on one-third as in the past. Rates on incomes over
£8,000 were increased to 2s. 8d. in the £, and the scale thereafter rose
in three further steps, so that an income of £100,000 or more was taxed
at 6s. 10d.

But McKenna's approach was two-pronged. He doubled duties on tea,
tobacco, coffee, cocoa, chicory, and dried fruits, and increased the levy on
sugar from 1s. 10d. per hundredweight to 9s. 4d. Imported luxuries were
subject to a tax of one-third of their value. McKenna's motivations were
pragmatic. He wanted to depress consumption, to free shipping space for
goods vital to the war effort, and to husband Britain's foreign exchange.
He was not a Liberal betraying the party's cardinal principle of free trade.
But inevitably his critics, and particularly the radical opponents of the
war policies of Asquithian Liberalism, saw the new tariffs as a sell-out to
the Conservatives and to protectionism. Their fears were justified, not by
the principle but by the practice: the universal applicability of free trade
had been breached.[19]

Import duties may have generated the major controversy, but the real
innovation of McKenna's budget lay elsewhere. A duty of 50 per cent was
to be levied on all profits earned during the war which were in excess of
peacetime norms. In most cases assessments were based on the best two of
the three trading years before 1914. For business as a whole, 1912 and
particularly 1913 had been highly successful. Therefore this method, not
least because it eliminated from the calculation the effects of low profits in
any one pre-war year, mitigated the effects of profits made during the war.
Big firms making big profits before the war could continue to make
comparable gains during it without showing any growth in profit.
McKenna himself made the point that no firm would pay anything unless
during the whole of the three years 1914 to 1917 it had made an average
profit equal to that of the best two out of the three years preceding the

---

[19] Soutou, *L'Or et le sang*, 205–8.

war.[20] Those companies which still felt themselves harshly treated because they had suffered a more sustained depression could ask to be assessed on the best four years of the six preceding the war. Firms for whom capital formation was relatively more significant (particularly, therefore, those businesses commencing activity or undergoing expansion just before the war) were permitted to base the calculation on a percentage of capital invested. The norm was 6 per cent on 5 August 1914, but private firms were allowed 7 per cent, and a prima facie case for a greater proportion could be made to the Inland Revenue for arbitration by a board of referees. Allowances under this head were particularly frequent in small businesses where capital was necessarily at stake or in larger concerns where the case for capitalizing the profits was linked to such factors as the rapid depreciation of equipment or the expansion of war production. Under the first head, West End theatres were permitted 15 per cent, and under the second aircraft construction was also granted 15 per cent, mining 14.5 per cent, and the iron and steel industries 8.9 per cent.[21]

Ironically, therefore, the initial impact of the excess profits duty was not on firms directly engaged in weapons production, not on the profits arising from warfare itself, but on profits made during the war through unwarlike activities. McKenna himself said that the issue was not that of profits from war production per se, 'but that during the war persons are enjoying profits more than the average'.[22] Indeed, the arms manufacturers were specifically exempted under the terms of the Munitions of War act of June 1915. This act gave the government the power to take over control of the arms firms, fixing their wages and salary scales, and setting their profits at 20 per cent of the average of the last two pre-war years. The wartime profits which had drawn the attention of the public and of the Treasury were those generated in grain and food production, in the manufacture of boots and clothes, and in the chemical and soap industries. Profits were generated through the creation of new markets for war services; through the curtailment of supplies from overseas, and particularly from belligerents; through population movements within Britain itself; and through the rapid working up to a proper return on new fixed capital unrelated to the war. The Treasury's survey showed that those

[20] Hirst and Allen, *British war budgets*, 114.
[21] Grady, *British war finance*, 111–12; Stamp, *Taxation*, 170–8.
[22] Public Record Office T 170/212; I am grateful to Dr Martin Farr for this reference.

industries which were doing well were doing very well, with profits in excess of 10 per cent of capital.[23]

One principal attraction of excess profits duty to the Treasury was its simplicity. In 1916/17 56,430 firms were assessed, and the collection of the tax could have proved extraordinarily complex. But its calculation was based on data which the Inland Revenue already possessed. And it operated through self-assessment, relieving the Revenue of the principal onus at a time when it was short of manpower. But the corollary was the possibility of evasion. In a sense this was recognized in legislation that condoned laxity. The state appropriated no statutory powers to examine the books of companies. Many concerns escaped entirely. Agriculture was exempted—partly because it had already been hit by the new assessment of rentals, partly because of its importance to the war effort, but princi-pally because many farmers failed to keep proper accounts. More con-troversially, shipping also escaped: the formal explanation was that the Admiralty had already commandeered much British-registered tonnage, and that it was now hard to distinguish between the contributions of British vessels and of neutral ships in the transport of British trade.[24] The tax was levied on firms, not individuals: thus, for example, a lawyer whose income increased through war-related business would escape the duty, but a small business which had been struggling to make its way before the war would be hit with disproportionate severity.

Business critics elevated their opposition to a high moral plane by talk of principles. They objected to the principle of retrospectivity; they pointed out that the first year of assessment included months in 1914 when Britain was not at war. Neither criticism recognized the two fundamental objections to the tax. First, it failed to distinguish between profits derived from speculation and profits generated through hard work and increased productivity (both desirable elements in a war, as in any other, economy). The duty effectively penalized good manage-ment; cash was capitalized for the development of production but diverted into direct taxation; wastefulness, in so far as it was reflected in low profit margins, was rewarded. As a corollary, new businesses with low profits before the war but which became established during it were hit harder than pre-existing large and over-capitalized firms.[25] Secondly,

[23] Stamp, *Taxation*, 146–9.   [24] Farr, 'McKenna', 262.
[25] Daunton, *English Historical Review*, CXI (1996), 898.

firms were not prevented, particularly in the early stages of the duty's operation, from setting prices to include the tax element. The government was therefore creating profits through its own contracts which it then clawed back again in taxes. Even one of its principal architects, Josiah Stamp, was tempted to conclude that the whole exercise might have been an illusion.[26] In so far as the cash gained represented goods and services, he may have been right. But in the struggle to soak up the liquid money supply the excess profits duty became an important, if imperfect, weapon in the government's armoury.

McKenna tackled the most obvious anomaly, the simultaneous continuation of both the munitions levy and the excess profits duty, in his second wartime budget of April 1916. The arms firms maintained that their agreement with the Ministry of Munitions exempted them from liability to the new tax. McKenna accepted rates of depreciation which would write off the extra capital invested in new plant within the period of the war. But he insisted that the administration of the munitions levy should be in the hands of the Inland Revenue. The first 20 per cent of the new profit was made liable for excess profits duty; any profit beyond that was forfeited to the munitions levy. The merger of the two taxes was completed in January 1918.

In other respects the budget of April 1916 contained no major innovations. It was, however, widely seen as an assault on the rich. The rate of excess profits duty was raised to 60 per cent; income tax was increased to 5s. in the £ on earned incomes above £2,500 and on unearned incomes over £2,000. Those liable to excess profits duty, surtax, and income tax could find themselves liable to pay joint rates of 77 per cent. The growth in income tax yield was anticipated to be £43.5 million, roughly double that budgeted for in additional customs and excise.[27]

McKenna's tenure of the chancellorship earned the praise of the *Economist*: 'The public credit stands unshaken,' F. W. Hirst averred on 8 April 1916, 'thanks to the principle of providing new taxes in advance sufficient to cover both interest and a liberal Sinking Fund on the new debt.'[28] Presumably the Gladstonian ring of sound financial management in these precepts compensated for the sin of McKenna's challenge to free trade. In addition, the chancellor had spurned the apparent attractions of

---

[26] Stamp, *Taxation*, 216; also 118. [27] Hirst and Allen, *British war budgets*, 129–33.
[28] Hirst and Allen, *British war budgets*, 136.

many small taxes, costly to assess and complex to collect. Instead, in embracing the excess profits duty, he had established before any other power one of the principal revenue producers of the war. He anticipated a yield, admittedly highly speculative, of £30 million in its first full year of operation. In practice only £140,000 was netted in the half financial year to March 1916.[29] But in 1916/17 the tax totalled £140 million against an expected £86 million.[30] By 1918/19 it was budgeted to produce £300 million, putting it on a par with income tax, and thus contributing almost half of Britain's direct tax and over a third of its total revenue.

McKenna's credentials were those of Liberal economic orthodoxy, even if his operation of them was stamped with pragmatism. He stood for a strategy built on sound finance. He was therefore a necessary casualty of Lloyd George's accession to the premiership in December 1916. Bonar Law, the Conservative leader, succeeded him at the Treasury.

Law was less bound by the legacy of free trade than McKenna. He was therefore able to introduce an increase in duty from 3.5 per cent to 5 per cent on Lancashire cotton goods imported to India. The package was reciprocal; it included a contribution to the costs of the war of £100 million from the Government of India, to be funded not only by the new import duty but also by a war loan. The Lancashire Liberals saw the tax as a protectionist assault on free trade and expected McKenna and Walter Runciman, the former president of the Board of Trade, to lead the attack from the opposition front bench. They did not do so. For them the issues were not those of Liberalism or of free trade, but of effective government, both in Britain and in India.[31]

McKenna's respect for Law's position was well founded. His successor added nothing to the principles which he had established, and indeed consulted him regularly on financial issues and retained Keynes as his advisor. Law's priorities were to manage his party, to deputize for Lloyd George, and to lead the House of Commons. The Treasury spared him the accusation of neglect. But it was surprised that his reputation as a practical businessman did not transform itself into consistency of purpose and firmness of execution.[32]

---

[29] Ibid. 84; Morgan, *British financial policy*, 92.

[30] Hirst and Allen, *British war budgets*, 128.

[31] Rumbold, *Watershed in India*, 65–6; Turner, *British politics*, 188–90, 346.

[32] Stamp, *Taxation*, 107–8; also Hirst and Allen, *British war budgets*, 199; Farr, 'McKenna', 236.

His first budget, the fifth of the war, in May 1917 was widely criticized
for its failure to increase income tax. He raised the duties on tobacco and
entertainments. But in doing so he netted only £26.1 million, or sufficient
to fund five days of the war.[33] Even his fierceness over the excess profits
duty, boosted to 80 per cent, was moderated by concessions. Assessments
on the basis of capital were raised from a profit of 6 per cent to 9 per cent
(or from 7 to 11 per cent in the case of private companies).

Law went some way to meeting his critics in the final budget of the war,
that of April 1918. The standard rate of income tax was increased to 6s. in
the £. The maximum rate of supertax was raised to 4s. 6d., and the
income threshold for the tax was lowered from £3,000 to £2,500. Farmers,
whose exemption from the excess profits duty aroused controversy, were
assessed on double their annual rental. Indirect taxes targeted luxuries,
and the duties on beer and spirits were doubled. In increasing the tax on
tobacco to 8s. 2d. in the £, Law justified its use of shipping space by saying
that 'in importing tobacco we are almost importing money'.[34]

Law failed to note the implication of his claim. If the consumption of
alcohol and cigarettes continued despite high levels of duty, taxation
generally was making insufficient inroads into the fiscal base of the
country. In each of the previous two financial years, 1916/17 and 1917/18,
excess profits duty and income tax had brought in yields over budget. The
chancellor's tax provision was not keeping pace with the growth of the
money supply. In 1913/14 the gross income of the nation for tax purposes
was estimated at £1,167 million; tax was received on £791 million. In 1917/
18 the gross income was put at £1,967 million but tax was received on only
£1,083 million.[35] Income tax peaked as a percentage of the total tax yield in
1915/16; by 1918/19 it had fallen from 38.10 per cent to 32.75 per cent.[36] The
government response, that the excess profits duty over the same period
climbed from 0.04 per cent of the tax yield to 32.06 per cent, assumed that
that tax was a direct tax on income. That was the view of business, and as
its consent was central to the tax's collection the exchequer tended to
share its view. But most of the government's critics argued that it was an
indirect tax passed on to the consumer, and that in consequence the
increase in direct taxation claimed by the government, as well as the
corresponding fall in indirect tax, were exaggerated. On their calculations

[33] Knauss, *Kriegsfinanzierung*, 115.   [34] Hirst and Allen, *British war budgets*, 211.
[35] Ibid. 176.   [36] Grady, *British war finance*, 78.

the excess profits duty increased wages and inflated credit, thus multiply-
ing, rather than reducing, the need for harsher income tax.[37]

During the war the income tax yield rose six times. This was the
multiple by which a typical supertax payer saw his tax burden grow.
Somebody earning £50,000 a year paid tax at 8.4 per cent at the beginning
of the war but 50.6 per cent at its conclusion. But the numbers earning
such large incomes were small, and did not grow as much as war-inflated
incomes might have led one to expect. Those in Britain with annual
incomes of £75,000 to £100,000 increased from sixty-five to ninety-eight
over the whole war. In 1913/14 13,664 individuals were assessed for supertax. This total had already jumped to 30,211 in 1914/15, and it actually fell
in 1915/16 and 1916/17. It rose to 35,564 in 1917/18 and 46,107 in 1918/19.

The attention to the affairs of the wealthy led to an underestimation of
the tax's impact on the waged. The government seems to have imagined
that it was more lenient than in practice it was with those on lower
incomes. A person already paying tax at the bottom end of the scale in
1914 saw his tax burden increase twofold during the war to 9 per cent.
However, the more realistic picture was not of somebody on a small fixed
salary but somebody on a low but increasing wage. The 2.4 million
taxpayers who entered the system during the war constituted two-thirds
of all taxpayers by 1918/19. The contributions of a waged member of the
working class multiplied 3.7 times. The pre-war system of income tax had
been a means by which to bind the working classes to the state; wartime
levels threatened to undermine this consent.[38] But protests were surprisingly muted. Many Labour leaders felt that direct taxation would incul-
cate political awareness in the working class, and were, accordingly, not
opposed to the trend. A perverse proof of their argument was provided in
March 1918 when the desperate situation on the western front prompted
the Scottish miners to shelve their opposition to income tax on patriotic
grounds. But the amenability of the miners also suggests that the collective phenomenon was more significant than the individual burden. In
1919 only 4 per cent of the total revenue from income tax was derived
from the direct taxation of wage-earners. The system of allowances
removed the liability of many men who were eligible in terms of gross

[37] Kirkaldy, *British finance*, 204–6.
[38] Daunton, *English Historical Review*, CXI (1996), 887, 903, 915.

earnings. In 1914 allowances for children were doubled for those on incomes of less than £500, and in 1918 extended to incomes below £800 (and for larger families below £1,000). In the latter year allowances for wives or other adult dependants were introduced. Thus, only 25 per cent of wage-earners earning between £130 and £160 per annum actually paid income tax in 1916/17. Although the reliefs did not keep pace with the money supply, the proportion had only risen to 32 per cent in 1918/19. Of 5.75 million people with incomes in excess of £130 per annum, 2.2 million were exempted by virtue of the system of allowances.[39] Not for nothing did the working class dub income tax the bachelor's or spinster's tax.

This did not mean that the breadwinners in working-class families escaped tax; they just paid it indirectly. The 2.6-fold increase in customs and excise and the possible operation of the excess profits duty as an indirect tax hit the low wage-earner with several mouths to feed proportionally harder. In 1919 a married man with three children earning £200 a year was not liable for income tax but still paid 10 per cent or more of his income to the Inland Revenue. Indirect taxes, however, were less visible and caused less grumbling. The fact that different taxes hit the working classes in variable ways fragmented possible opposition. And the net effect was to leave taxation operating rather more as Keynes wished it to: it was reducing the consumptive capacity of the bulk of the population.[40]

What mattered as much as anything else was the perception that Britain was taxing effectively. It was important for the control of domestic inflation; it reassured international credit. The belief that Britain had got it right, primarily through its income tax but also through the excess profits duty, acted as a benchmark for the other belligerents.

In practice, only the United States followed the lead. The incidence, distribution, and yield of federal taxes were all transformed by the war, and because the period of active American belligerency was so short it is not unreasonable to call the effects revolutionary. Nonetheless, as in the British case, the practice fell short of the declared intentions. In April 1917 McAdoo announced his belief that taxation was the main method to finance war, and that he hoped in this way to cover half the war's costs.

[39] Ibid. 889.
[40] Whiting, *Historical Journal*, XXXIII (1990), 895–916; Balderston, *Economic History Review*, 2nd series, LXII (1989), 235–6; Grady, *British war finance*, 75–83, 95–9, 102; Stamp, *Taxation*, 219; Hirst and Allen, *British war budgets*, 176.

So vociferous was the response from those who argued that such rates would reduce the incentives to investment that McAdoo reduced his target to one-third. Moreover, he was too optimistic with regard to outgoings. He budgeted for total expenditure of $8,400 million in 1917/18; in reality federal spending was $13,000 million, and in 1918/19 it reached $18,515 million, twenty-four times its 1916/17 level.[41] The ratio of budgeted war revenue to war expenditure fell continuously between 1917 and 1919, averaging below 29 per cent. The actual ratio of war revenue to war expenditure was only 23.3 per cent.[42]

In 1916 74.8 per cent of total revenue was raised through customs and excise. The latter, increased by the Emergency Revenue act of October 1914 to compensate for the loss of the former, accounted for 47.6 per cent of the whole. By contrast, only 16 per cent was derived from taxes on incomes and profits. Income tax, levied on net receipts over $3,000 per annum or $4,000 for a married person, supertax, which began on incomes over $20,000, and corporation income tax, charged on net profits over $5,000, were all introduced in 1913 at a rate of 1 per cent. Supertax rose to 6 per cent on incomes over $500,000, producing a maximum combined rate of 7 per cent. There was therefore plenty of slack in the system.[43]

Although in 1915 the new excise duties only produced $52 million against an anticipated $100 million, Wilson's initial preference was to increase them rather than to move to direct taxation. Congress disagreed. Therefore, the Revenue act of 8 September 1916, designed to cover the defence programmes of that year, marked a significant shift in principle. Income tax and corporation tax were raised to 2 per cent. The top rate of supertax was set at 13 per cent (i.e. 15 per cent when combined with income tax) on incomes over $2 million per annum. Inheritance tax, hitherto levied by forty-two states, was appropriated for federal purposes. Beginning on estates of over $50,000, it was charged on a scale rising from 1 per cent to 10 per cent on $5 million or more. The final major innovation was a form of excess profits duty, a tax on munitions' manufacturers of 12.5 per cent of the entire profit for 1916. In aggregate, federal receipts were increased 70 per cent and exceeded the budget

---

[41] Chandler, *Strong*, 99–101.   [42] Gilbert, *American financing*, 74, 82–91, 221–3.
[43] Gilbert, *American financing*, 26–7, 54–5, 76; Bogart, *War costs*, 264–7. These constitute the principal sources for what follows; see Gilbert, *American financing*, 70–114; Bogart, *War costs*, 264–95.

forecast of $975.5 million by $142.4 million. But their incidence was borne chiefly by the wealthy, and (in the case of the munitions levy) the Entente. In 1913 49.7 per cent of the tax yield was paid for by those whose incomes exceeded $20,000. Under the terms of the 1916 act this same group paid 95.4 per cent of the yield. The government was therefore appropriating savings, not purchasing-power, and so failing to deter consumption.

On the other hand, the United States had made effective the two major taxes of war finance, income tax and excess profits duty, in advance of its actual entry to the war. The Revenue act of 3 March 1917 never became operational, but it serves to underline the point. It proposed a duty on the excess profits of all companies, at a rate of 8 per cent on profits of over 8 per cent.

Not until 3 October 1917 was the United State's first War Revenue act passed, six months after its entry and at a stage when the monthly deficit was already over $400 million. The delay was less attributable to the fact that the system of war finance had been anticipated before April 1917, and more due to the pleading of special interests. The casualty was the rate of excess profits duty, which, although a great fiscal success ($2,227.6 million was raised in the year ending 30 June 1918), was insufficiently severe. Net profits equal to between 7 and 9 per cent of the capital invested in 1911, 1912, and 1913 were exempt. Thereafter 20 per cent was payable on the first 15 per cent of profits, 25 per cent on the next 5 per cent, 35 per cent on the next 5 per cent, 45 per cent on the next 7 per cent, and 60 per cent on the remainder. The tax on munitions' manufacturers was reduced to 10 per cent, and this, together with a generous depreciation policy, halved its yield in 1918.

That McAdoo's taxes were failing to anticipate new areas of liquidity was reflected, as in Britain, by yields over budget. The year ended 30 June 1918 showed a surplus of nearly $300 million on a budget of $3,400 million. Furthermore the taxes lacked simplicity. Their temporary nature was emphasized by dubbing each of the new direct levies a war tax, and they operated alongside the existing bands. Thus, the war income tax was superimposed on the prevailing income tax. The new threshold was fixed at $1,000 for a single person and $2,000 for a married person, and was charged at 2 per cent. The surtax liability was also lowered, beginning at $5,000, not $20,000. The initial rate remained 1 per cent, but those earning $20,000 or more were liable to pay a rate of 8 per cent. Somebody earning $2 million paid 13 per cent under the old surtax arrangements plus 50 per cent under the new. A war estate tax was added to the existing inheritance tax to give a maximum rate of 25 per cent on estates over $10 million, but estates worth under $50,000 were exempt from the old duty and paid only the new one at a rate of 2 per cent.

The combined effect was to continue to load the burden onto the rich and so to tax savings rather than purchasing power. Seventy-seven per cent of taxpayers earned less than $3,000 per year, but they contributed only 3.6 per cent of income tax. Indirect taxes targeted luxuries, including cars, jewellery, cameras, cosmetics, and boats, not major consumer items. By 1918 customs and excise contributed 22.3 per cent of federal revenue, as against 67.8 per cent generated by incomes and profits.

McAdoo's proposals for 1918 included increased taxes on lower incomes and a maximum rate of 80 per cent on war profits. If the latter had been passed on to consumers it could have operated to curb demand and so check inflation. But Congress was more worried about the elections impending in November 1918, and preferred to meet a deficit—accumulating at over a $1,000 million a month by July—through reducing expenditure. The debate dragged on in the Senate until February 1919, and the War Revenue act of 1918 was therefore not effective until 1920.

Thus, even though the United States swung the balance of its revenue from indirect to direct taxation during the war, it found itself unable to effect major changes during the period of its active belligerence. An addition to the principles on which taxation rested proved extraordinarily difficult in wartime. No country demonstrated this more graphically than the third major financial power of the Entente—France.

In June 1914 France was poised to introduce individual income tax. For the radicals it was the denouement to a struggle begun by Caillaux in 1909 but prolonged by the recourse of successive governments to loans and deficit financing. In 1913 Barthou had promised income tax as the corollary of the deeply divisive law establishing three-year service in the army. He then did nothing. The success of the left in the 1914 elections put the three-year law under sufficient threat to make tax reform the quid pro quo of its retention. However, what followed was a feeble response to the length and depth of the debate. Eligibility for the tax, introduced on 15 July 1914, began with incomes of over 5,000 francs, but allowances for spouses of 2,000 francs and for each child of 1,000 francs raised the practical threshold to that comparable with supertax across the Channel. The full rate of 2 per cent was only applicable to incomes over 25,000 francs. Moreover, the opportunity to overhaul the existing tax structure was spurned. Four taxes—the ground tax, the door and window tax, the personal furniture tax, and the business tax—dated from the Revolution and were to a large extent dependent on regional variations in property values. They rested on the principle of equality of incidence rather than on social progressivism. Although a fifth, taxing the income on capital, had been added in 1872, whole areas of wealth and actual incomes were untouched.[44]

Almost immediately, the entire economic life of France was thrown into disarray. The implementation of a new tax seemed impossible when so many tax collectors were ordered to report for military service. Those that remained were instructed not to prosecute the families of servicemen. Tax collection never recovered from the initial disruption of invasion and mobilization. In 1913 10 million Frenchmen paid personal taxes, however low and however antiquated. During the war only 557,000 paid income tax. About 2.5 million were taxed on industrial and commercial profits in 1913, but only 1 million between 1914 and 1919. Certain classes were almost entirely exempt: only 120,000 farmers paid tax and only 32,000 members of the liberal professions (of four times that number practising) paid duty on their profits.[45]

Administrative confusion was not the only cause of falling revenue. Military service and the loss of north-eastern France also reduced France's fiscal base. The moratorium cut off rental income, rendering landlords unable to pay taxes. Import duties on foodstuffs were suspended. The return on customs, which had increased sixfold between 1870 and 1913 to produce a total of 777.9 million francs, fell to 548.3 million francs in 1914. Between August and November 1914 yields on indirect taxes and monopolies were 43 per cent below their total for the first six months of the year; they were still 35 per cent down in December and only recovered to 22.21 per cent below in the first half of 1915. Indirect taxes did not rise significantly above their 1914 total until 1916, and monopolies not until

[44] Krumeich, *Armaments and politics*, 138–40, 213; Knauss, *Kriegsfinanzierung*, 36–40; Ferguson, *Pity of war*, 120–1.
[45] Charbonnet, *Politique financière*, 347; Eichengreen, *Golden fetters*, 75–6.

the following year. In fact 1917 was the first year in which the revenue raised through France's existing taxes exceeded its pre-war level.[46]

The appointment of Alexandre Ribot as finance minister on 26 August 1914 was not calculated to reassure the radicals. An opponent of income tax, he proposed to delay its introduction from 1 January 1915 to 1 January 1916. The practical impediments to change gave legitimacy to his argument that France had more than enough problems to cope with. His preference was to wait until economic activity had recovered sufficiently to enable the new tax to be the basis for a balanced budget. As an interim measure he offered to double existing taxes. But the budget commission of the chamber was concerned that by doing so he would entrench the old system and provide an excuse for further procrastination on the new. France went into 1915 without any significant increase in its rates of tax.[47]

The problem for both Ribot and the budget commission was that the situation was no more settled by the end of the next year. In December 1915 Ribot proposed once again to postpone the introduction of income tax. This time he argued that the yield would be too low to warrant the trouble of change, as the richest part of France remained in enemy hands. He was voted down in the chamber. In response, Ribot not only introduced income tax, albeit at the low rate of 2 per cent and at the unnecessarily high starting point of 7,000 francs for a married man, but he also promised a war profits tax.[48]

Ribot modelled his war profits tax on Britain's. As on the other side of the Channel, agriculture was excluded. But France's tax, unlike its ally's, made some effort to target the profits of individuals as well as those of companies. The average of the last three years of peace was to form the basis for judging the profits gained between 1 August 1914 and 31 December 1915. Those who refused to supply information to enable assessment were to have their normal profits assessed as thirty times the yield of the business tax. The first 5,000 francs of profit were to be exempt.[49] In practice, the spectacular yields on the war profits tax were retrospective. A law of 1920 providing for the revision of all contracts formed during the

---

[46] Olphe-Galliard, *Histoire économique*, 161; Knauss, *Kriegsfinanzierung*, 41–2, 142; Jèze and Truchy, *War finance*, 192; Fisk, *French public finance*, 72, 186.
[47] Charbonnet, *Politique financière*, 63; Duroselle, *La France*, 208–10; Schmidt, *Ribot*, 117.
[48] Schmidt, *Ribot*, 133; Knauss, *Kriegsfinanzierung*, 120–1.
[49] Ribot, *Letters to a friend*, 62; Knauss, *Kriegsfinanzierung*, 122.

war, and establishing 10 per cent as a reasonable profit, netted 2,937 million francs in 1920 and 3,313 million in 1921.[50] But in the war itself 10 per cent was the effective rate of the tax. Fear of the moratorium's effect on banking activity and the latter's support for business were partly to blame. The government was too fearful of reducing output by removing the profit incentive. Thus Citröen, who showed a profit of 6.1 million francs between 1914 and 1917, paid only 60,000 francs in tax.[51] Fiscal lag did the rest. The tax was enacted on 1 July 1916, and produced a mere 192.5 million francs in 1917 and 521.5 million in 1918.[52]

In May 1916 Ribot sounded a more robust note. He proposed to double all the existing direct taxes, except the door and window tax, and to increase income tax to 5 per cent. Although an attempt at last to recognize the mismatch between France's outgoings and its declining revenues, the positive effects on revenue would have been minimal and the fiscal implications regressive. The inadequate levels of new taxation were being compensated for by the perpetuation of the old. As a result, the system was becoming more complex at a time when the tax authorities were understaffed, and individually each tax was producing a return too small for the effort required to collect it.

The law of 30 December 1916, therefore, seemed a better answer to the problem. Income tax was raised to 10 per cent, and liability was to begin on incomes of 3,000 francs. Furthermore, the rates were progressive, rising in steps of 10 per cent so that all income over 150,000 francs was forfeit. A war tax, modelled on that adopted by Napoleon, carried a further 25 per cent surcharge on income tax (or a flat rate of 12 francs per annum for those not liable for income tax) payable by men of military age not in the services. The war profits tax was raised to 60 per cent of profits over 500,000 francs. But total receipts in 1916 did little more than match those of 1913, and even in 1917 the yield on direct taxes only exceeded its 1914 total by a third. The effect of the new rates of income tax was moderated by exemptions. Duties on consumption—on

[50] Jèze and Truchy, War finance, 152–8.

[51] Gerd Hardach, 'Industrial mobilization in 1914–1918', in Fridenson (ed.), French home front 1914–1918, 77–8; also Alain Hennebicque, 'Albert Thomas and the war industries', in ibid. 110–12.

[52] Jèze and Truchy, War finance, 152; Fisk, French public finance, 186, has radically different figures—634 million francs for 1917 and 1,780 million for 1918. Knauss, Kriegsfinanzierung, 136, gives 363.7 million for 1917 and 350.2 million for 1918.

beverages, sugar, alcoholic drinks, and tobacco—were raised and an entertainments tax introduced. Therefore, of the extra revenue for 1917 206.5 million francs derived from direct taxation and 379.6 million from indirect.

The fundamental reform of direct taxation, repeatedly postponed since 1914, was finally effected by Thierry on 31 July 1917. Thierry established seven schedules which combined to levy taxes on capital (on property and mobile capital), on capital and income combined (on business and agriculture), and on income (pensions, wages, and profits on trade). By including farming, Thierry closed the obvious loophole for evasion. But the rates, although progressive, were not high. Agriculture was assessed on half the annual rental; rates in other areas began at 3.75 per cent over 3,000 francs or 4.5 per cent over 5,000 francs, with reductions for income below these levels and exemptions according to the size of family. The new taxes, which came into force on 1 January 1918, brought in 411 million francs of additional revenue. But, as the old system was finally abandoned, income of 325 million francs was simultaneously forfeited.

France, therefore, entered the final year of the war at last possessed of a machinery for taxation appropriate to the undertaking. But the levels of tax were still low. Thierry anticipated increasing the rates of income tax, making the war profits tax truly progressive, and introducing a turnover tax. Klotz, his successor, was reluctant to increase income tax. However, in February he raised the rate from 12.5 per cent to 14 per cent. In December 1917 he adopted an estate tax and increased rates of inheritance tax. But France's preoccupation with its declining birth rate once again moderated a tax into virtual ineffectiveness. Only an owner of an estate of over 50 million francs with no children faced a significant burden, fixed at 24 per cent. The owner of a similar estate but with three children paid only 3 per cent. A comparable fate overtook Thierry's plan for war profits, which Klotz also accepted. He established a rate of 50 per cent on profits under 100,000 francs, rising to 80 per cent on those over 500,000 francs. But he then introduced lower rates for newly established war industries, for businesses in war areas, and for companies in which workers held up to a quarter of the total capital. Postponements of the tax were so freely given that of 720 million francs owed up to November 1918 only 24 per cent had been collected.[53]

---

[53] Knauss, *Kriegsfinanzierung*, 123–35; Charbonnet, *Politique financière*, 77–81.

Thus Klotz, like his predecessors, could not escape an excessive reliance on indirect taxation. A turnover tax of 2 per cent was charged on all payments of more than 10 francs if a receipt was issued, and of more than 150 francs if not. Luxuries, including first-class hotels and restaurants, were subject to a 10 per-cent levy. The tax was pointless. In wartime the yield was small: by definition, luxuries found few markets in the conditions of 1918. In peacetime, industrial interests argued, the duty would hamper France's post-war recovery, since French exports were led by luxury products.[54]

Therefore, the profile of French taxation during the war changed remarkably little. It was still heavily weighted towards indirect duties. In 1913 27.8 per cent of taxation was direct, in 1918 39.1 per cent; indirect taxation stood at 53.5 per cent in 1913 and 43.1 per cent in 1918. Income tax raised less than 1,000 million francs by the war's end.[55] A distinctive feature of France was the relatively high burden of trade taxes (including the post and railways), which, at 18.7 per cent of the whole in 1913 and 17.8 per cent in 1918, remained virtually unchanged.[56]

After the war France's defenders would argue that the taxes on consumption and the registration and stamp duties constituted not-ineffective substitutes for income tax.[57] The former depressed the demand generated by rising nominal incomes; the latter represented a levy on cash as it circulated. If the population of France was characterized by a mass of small-income earners, rather than by great concentrations of wealth, and if the retrospective purpose of war taxation was the control of inflation, not the covering of war costs, then French policy was not as ill-conceived as its critics sometimes maintain. But the problem for France after the war remained that of paying for the war. France spent 223,000 million francs in the years 1914–19. It raised 32,000 million through taxation: this was not enough to cover its normal peacetime budget, let alone the servicing of the war debt. By November 1918 France had yet to pay for a single centime of its direct war costs.[58]

---

[54] Olphe-Galliard, *Histoire économique*, 430–1.
[55] Duroselle, *La Grande Guerre des français*, 155.
[56] Knauss, *Kriegsfinanzierung*, 148–9.
[57] Jèze and Truchy, *War finance*, 218–19, 223–5.
[58] Georges-Henri Soutou, 'Comment a été financée la guerre', in La Gorce (ed.), *La Première Guerre Mondiale*, 284; Knauss, *Kriegsfinanzierung*, 175.

France's problems were more those of forwardness than of backward-ness. Its old tax structure, hallowed by the triumphs of the Revolution and of Napoleon, was the product of a transformation in the power of the state over a hundred years earlier. Administrative innovation had there-fore preceded rapid economic growth. Its principal continental ally, Russia, confronted a range of issues that superficially were similar. Like France, Russia was considering the introduction of income tax in 1914; like France, Russia saw its tax yield decline in 1914/15; and, like France, it planned major reforms, embracing income tax and a war profits tax, in 1916/17. But there was a cardinal difference. Russia was backward, in an administrative as well as in a fiscal sense. It lacked the developed eco-nomic base possessed by its major Entente partners. It then compounded its weakness by decisions calculated to worsen its position. By the time of the Bolshevik revolution, it had—again like France—failed to cover any of its war costs, including the servicing of its debt, through taxation.

In 1911 76.8 per cent of Russia's revenue was derived from indirect taxation, and only 13.7 per cent from direct. By 1913 the latter figure had fallen to 8 per cent.[59] The principal sums were raised through excise rather than customs, the latter being designed principally to protect Russia's nascent industries rather than to contribute to the exchequer. Of 1,606.9 million roubles generated by customs and excise in 1913, only 352.9 million came from customs. The impact of the war on overseas trade was therefore less burdensome than for other powers. The main sources of excise duty were sugar, beer, tobacco, petrol, matches, and—above all—spirits. In 1912 the combination of the duty on spirits and the state's monopoly of their sale produced net profits of 626.3 million roubles, or about a quarter of all state revenue.

Direct tax was levied on land, on urban property, and on commerce and industry. The yield of all three doubled between 1903 and 1913. But the total, 272.4 million roubles, remained low. Russia was too predomin-antly agricultural for the increases in commercial and industrial taxation arising from urbanization to have significant effect. Land values were falling. Estate duties, levied on the transfer of land, including death,

---

[59] Michelson et al., *Russian public finance*, 24, 47. Michelson remains the only English-language source on the subject; some additional comments can be found in Claus, *Kriegs-wirtschaft Russlands*, 31–6.

were minimal: the top rate was 12 per cent and the bottom (for a widower or for children) only 1.5 per cent.

A bill for the introduction of income tax was drafted in 1905 and introduced in 1907. In 1914 it still languished in committee. The case against its implementation in peace was real enough. Russia was not a rich country; its geographical size and its population density would make assessment and collection complex. A low threshold would therefore be difficult to administer and possibly not very productive. A high threshold (the 1907 bill planned to exempt incomes below 1,000 roubles per annum) would discourage the accumulation of capital and its subsequent investment. Thus, the possible net returns on income tax were murky. Moreover, Russia before the war did not need direct taxation to soak up surplus cash. During the war it did.

On 28 July 1914 the state liquor shops were closed as a temporary measure to expedite mobilization. On 3 September the Duma extended the closure for the duration of the war, and a month later authorized local governments to intensify the ban. Temperance, it was hoped, would help the war effort by raising standards of public health and boosting industrial productivity. But it had two fiscal disadvantages. First, it contributed to monetary overhang, increasing the quantity of unspent cash in private pockets. Secondly, it diverted the trade in alcohol into illicit channels, so passing profits from the state to speculators. The gross loss to governmental revenues was 432 million roubles in 1914 and 791.8 million in 1915.

Even without such self-administered wounds, the war eroded Russia's fiscal base. Loss of territory accounted for a decline in revenue of 69 million roubles in 1914 and 226.7 million in 1915. Customs receipts were hit by the closure of the western land frontier and of the Dardanelles. Railway traffic in the combat zone fell by two-thirds (and by a quarter elsewhere), so reducing returns on the railway tax. The budget of June 1914 had assumed an income for that year of 3,585.5 million roubles. In practice it sank to 2,898.1 million, and receipts for the second half of 1914 totalled 1,130.5 million roubles as against 1,804.8 million for the comparable period in the previous year. Revenue for 1915 continued at a similar level, 2,827.6 million roubles, when a rise to 3,132 million had been forecast.

The growth in income budgeted for 1915 rested on increases in almost all Russia's existing taxes in 1914. The most contentious of these was the railway tax, whose abolition had been anticipated as part of an effort to encourage trade. As a result of its intensification, it became cheaper to move cargo on passenger trains and humans on freight trains. The only significant innovation of 1914 was a tax on the carriage of goods. Calculated by weight, it was particularly designed to restrict the movement of raw materials, so curbing demand which was exceeding supply. In practice, both the railway tax and the duty on the carriage of goods formed the beginnings of a vicious circle in which the government levied taxes on itself. The increase in military transport more than compensated for the loss in volume of civilian railway traffic; the ministry of war therefore paid the railway tax, albeit at half rates. The carriage of goods tax fell on materials destined for the production of munitions, and its burden was therefore passed on by industry in the price paid by the government for the finished article. A related point could be made about customs duties, which were revised in February 1915: 25 per cent of customs were paid by the Ministry of Finance for imports for military purposes.

The full force of this bogus income was revealed in the 1916 budget. Only minor changes were made to taxation in 1915, and the revenue anticipated for 1916 was 2,914 million roubles, a level comparable with the previous year. In the event, receipts totalled 3,974.5 million. The depreciation of the rouble played its part in creating a nominal increase. But that, in its turn, was partly fostered by the government's taxation policy which was stoking cash inflation. About 70 per cent of the total revenue for 1916 was contributed by the state itself.

The 1916 budget, unlike that of 1915, did, however, recognize the need to plan for a long war followed by a sustained period of post-war recovery. The burden of indirect taxation had been significantly reduced by the ending of the monopoly on spirits, and it was proposed to continue the trend to direct taxation by the establishment of progressive income tax and of an increased tax on industrial profits. The target was not only to cover Russia's ordinary expenditure during the war, but also to establish its taxation system on a new permanent basis appropriate to peace.

In the event, less was achieved than Bark's ambitious programme promised. He wanted to exempt incomes below 700 roubles, recognizing that Russia's population was becoming increasingly wealthy in nominal terms, and was being spared a significant burden of indirect tax. The Duma, arguing that Russian workers were poor and their cost of living high, was more concerned with the social than the inflationary implications. Its members pushed for a threshold of 1,000 or even 1,500 roubles. A compromise was struck at 850 roubles. Depreciation did mean that this level embraced about half the households of Russia, and its progressive effects put the top level of taxation higher than that of any other European country except Britain. But the tax was not to come into force until 1917. And the yield budgeted for that year, 178 million roubles, was still small alongside the forfeited spirit revenue.

The same point could be made in even stronger terms in relation to the new levels of tax on industrial profits, scheduled to produce only 55 million roubles in 1917. Companies whose profits exceeded 8 per cent of their invested capital and of their average profits for 1913/14 were liable for tax on sums over 2,000 roubles. Individuals were taxed on emoluments over 500 roubles. The bottom rate of tax was 20 per cent; the top rate, including the existing direct tax and income tax, was not to exceed 50 per cent.

In many ways the fiscal policy of the Provisional Government of March 1917 built on the programme developed by the Tsar's ministers in the previous year. Nor was what it proposed dissimilar to the thinking displayed by the other Liberal governments of the Entente at this stage of the war. It planned to increase rates of income tax, setting a combined top level of 90 per cent. As the assessment was based on 1916 incomes, which in some cases had fallen in 1917, the new taxes could in theory have exhausted a taxpayer's total salary. The war profits tax was to be subject to progressive rates, so that individuals were liable to a maximum of 60 per cent and publicly audited companies to one of 80 per cent. The maximum combined level of tax on businesses was again 90 per cent. Speculators and middlemen, who had effectively escaped the 1916 legislation, were liable to be taxed on income rather than on profits from capital. Plans were also afoot to increase indirect taxes and establish new state monopolies.

But the Provisional Government was the victim of its predecessors' weaknesses, of fiscal lag, and of its own flabby-mindedness. It increased salaries and allowances, promising to pay them out of its tax reforms. But taxation was too slow in its effects. In the short term it could only do so through monetary inflation. Between January 1917 and the Bolshevik revolution in November Russia's note issue doubled. Little of this additional cash could be soaked up by the fiscal structure inherited from the Tsarist government. Thus the Provisional Government contributed to the very process which its harsh fiscal policy was designed to check. Inflation was not the least of the factors making Russia ungovernable in the autumn of 1917.

Russia had only a limited fiscal base. The increased money supply generated by the war, therefore, bore less and less relationship to the availability of goods and services. But a limited fiscal base did not mean that a state had to wave farewell to an efficient system of war finance. Good administration could in theory—by tight control of the money supply and by severe taxation—compensate for limited wealth. During the war and after the commentators of the major economic powers of the Entente, including Keynes, remarked approvingly on the performance of Italy. In 1914 Italian taxation drew off a higher proportion (about 10 per cent) of the gross national product than that of any other major European power.[60] Throughout the war, Italy made, it was maintained, a real effort to service its war-related borrowings from current revenue. Some thought it had succeeded.[61] It had not, but E. L. Bogart's 1921 calculation of Italy's deficit on normal expenditure plus interest charges for the war, $786.5 million, compared favourably with his reckonings for France ($3,346 million) and Germany ($4,180 million).[62]

Economic growth had enabled Italy to generate budget surpluses between the financial years 1897–8 and 1910–11. But the invasion of Libya in 1911 combined with Giolitti's social reforms to push the national account into deficit. Although Italy did not join the Entente until April 1915, the burden created by military expenditure was exacerbated by preparations for war from 1914. Thus, Italy had been living with some of the features of a war economy for three years before it commenced active belligerence. Like France and Germany, it entered hostilities with an exchequer already encumbered by pre-war debt.

The period of budget surplus was, with hindsight, an ideal opportunity to restructure Italy's taxation system. Taxes were levied under three heads—direct taxes on land, buildings, and mobile capital; transaction

---

[60] Forsyth, *Crisis of Liberal Italy*, 3, 326; what follows relies almost exclusively on Forsyth, whose work revises Luigi Einaudi, *La guerra e il sistema tributario italiano* (Bari, 1927).

[61] Teillard, *Les Emprunts de guerre*, 73, 127; Forsyth, *Crisis of Liberal Italy*, 69.

[62] Bogart, *War costs*, 317–18.

taxes (including inheritance duty); and consumption taxes. In 1913 only 27 per cent of Italy's revenue was generated through direct taxation, as opposed to over 40 per cent in the 1870s. Fifty-eight per cent derived from the taxes on consumption, and 15 per cent from transaction taxes. Personal income tax was advocated, but as a measure of social justice, not as a means to increase revenue.

Italy's tax structure remained unreformed in 1914. Its post-war critics would accuse it of inflexibility. But as serious as its increasingly anti-quated structure was the fact that its stringency was more apparent than real. A powerful argument against personal income tax and in favour of the high rate of indirect tax was the relative poverty of Italy compared with its western European neighbours. The difficulties generated by relatively low incomes and high rates of taxation were resolved by the Ministry of Finance in a series of personal negotiations between individuals and the state as to their commitments. Published rates, therefore, did not reflect actual payments. Nor was the system of assessment only unfair, it was also inefficient. The direct tax on land was levied on the basis of an incomplete land register. Italy had voted to draw up a national register in 1886. Those provinces which expected their assessments to fall as a result co-operated in its establishment; the majority did not. Thus the yields on land tax fell. Thus too the tax on mobile capital became a proportionally greater element of direct taxation. However, this latter tax assessed each source of income separately, rather than considering each person's total holdings. A taxpayer who divided his wealth over several heads therefore paid less on the same income than a taxpayer who concentrated his investments.[63]

Italy entered the war with much trumpeting about fiscal rectitude. Unable to claim that its purpose was defensive, it could harbour no latent hopes for an indemnity, and had therefore to confront its own capacity to pay for what it was about. But by the end of the war the structure of its taxation was little changed. In 1917/18 direct taxes still only contributed 36 per cent of total revenue, transaction taxes remained virtually constant at 14 per cent, and consumption taxes had yet to fall below 50 per cent. By the same year the burden of taxation, expressed as a proportion of gross national product, showed no more than a marginal increase

[63] Forsyth, *Crisis of Liberal Italy*, 5, 28–33.

to 10.9 per cent (expenditure rose from 11.2 per cent in 1913/14 to 36.7 in 1917/18).[64] The accusation of inflexibility was justified.

The rates of direct tax were, of course, increased. Indeed, the three permanent direct taxes carried a 5 per-cent surcharge from October 1914, and a 10 per-cent increase followed in December of the same year. But these rises were low compared with the increased liquidity created by the war. Efforts to introduce progressive taxation, in November 1916 and September 1917, foundered on the illogicalities of the basic structure. Property in different regions continued to be assessed separately; distinctions as to earned, unearned, and mixed income persisted; investments in different businesses were not aggregated. Evasion was simple. Like France, Italy fell into the trap of an excessively diverse structure, complex and confusing in its administration, and with each tax generating only small returns. Like France, these pinpricks included a levy on those of military age not in the services (introduced in November 1916), and taxes on luxuries that were in limited demand.

Italy's reputation for fiscal prudence was, nonetheless, sustained by its early introduction of a war profits tax. Indeed, the Italian duty actually became law in November 1915, ahead of the British scheme. Its basic structure aped the British proposal. Profits over 8 per cent of invested capital were defined as excessive, unless firms could prove that they had made higher profits in the three years preceding the war. The basic rate of tax was 20 per cent, rising to 60 per cent on profits over 20 per cent. As at first in Britain, the duty was not accompanied by a policy of price controls. Potentially, therefore, the tax operated not as direct tax on industry but as an indirect tax on the consumer. But, unlike Britain, the profits subject to assessment were not all the profits generated during the war but only those profits derived from the war. The excess profits duty adopted by Westminster did not have the munitions firms as its primary target; that embraced by Rome did. Therefore, the consumer which would bear the indirect burden would be the state. In Britain the excess profits duty had at least some impact in the battle to absorb private purchasing power. In Italy it did not.

A tax regime favourable to heavy industry was justified on strategic grounds and by Italy's need to compensate for its economic backward-

---

[64] Ibid. 326, 327; also 93–4.

ness by an accelerated programme of investment. War profits were therefore seen as an opportunity to write off debts and to develop fresh plant. State controls on industry were reduced, not tightened. Fiscal privileges were extended to equipment which did not necessarily need to be written off during the war but which could be used for peacetime purposes. To achieve all this, the state took, in the form of increased prices for war goods, the burden of its own excess profits duty. Similarly, a tax on all payments of the state to private parties (the *centesimi della guerra* introduced at 1 cent in November 1915, and then raised to 2 cents in July 1916, and 3 in June 1918) could be reflected back in the form of prices. The Italian exchequer's creation of fictitious revenue bore at least a passing resemblance to that of Russia.[65]

Italy's failure to control costs meant that, although during the war 23 per cent of its expenditure was nominally covered by revenue, the wholesale price index stood at 364 in 1919, if 1913 is taken as 100.[66] But what, of course, is surprising in the Italian story is the reputation for fiscal rigour, not the fact of post-war inflation. The Liberal government of Italy was weak, its foreign policy misguided and unpopular, and its economy ill-developed. Italy was the least of the great powers of Europe in 1914.

Much more complex, and much more alluring to scholars in the 1920s and ever since, was the failure of Germany to manage its war finances. In 1919 its wholesale price index was 415, and it would quintuple by the end of 1922. Germany was not only the mainstay of the Triple Alliance, it was also, in economic as well as in military terms, the greatest of the continental powers. And yet, if the existing deficit in 1914 is included, German revenue between 1914 and 1918 met only 13.57 per cent of expenditure.[67] Its total tax yield from all sources throughout the war was less than Britain's revenue from its excess profits duty alone.[68] It thus failed to cover not only the servicing of its war-related debt but also its ordinary peacetime outgoings.

Self-evidently, Germany's difficulty with taxation was not primarily the consequence of insufficient wealth (however illiquid much of it might be, compared, say, with France). It did not begin the war, as Russia and Italy did, with an already limited fiscal base. The problem was

[65] Forsyth, *Crisis of Liberal Italy*, 7–9, 64–5, 70–99.   [66] Ibid. 76.
[67] Lotz, *Deutsche Staatsfinanzwirtschaft*, 105.
[68] Balderston, *Economic History Review*, 2nd series, XLII (1989), 230.

political: it was in origin the consequence of the circumstances of the Reich's foundation.

Broadly speaking, Bismarck had left the power of direct taxation to the individual states. To the Reich he had appropriated indirect taxation, and particularly stamp duty and customs and excise. In the circumstances of 1871 the Reich and not the states possessed the major producer of revenue. Furthermore, the states were obliged to contribute to the running of the Reich at a level set by the Reichstag. These two elements, Reich customs duty and the states' *Matrikularbeiträge*, were set in an interlocking relationship in 1879. The Centre party agreed to support Bismarck's programme of tariffs, on condition that when the yield on customs exceeded 130 million marks the excess would go to the states. The ceiling set on the Reich's share was sufficiently low to necessitate the survival of the *Matrikularbeiträge*. The arrangement worked to the Reich's advantage until the end of the century. Thereafter it did not. Central government activity expanded faster than the consumption of the population. Between 1875 and 1913 the Reich's net expenses grew five times, but its population only increased by 57 per cent.[69] The fact that the per capita income of that population was also rising meant little when the Reich had no constitutional right to tax it. Nor did the *Matrikularbeiträge* provide the flexibility Germany required. They were a head tax, not an income tax: thus their burden on the poorer classes in the more impoverished states of Germany was already heavy. Indeed, the population of Germany, when it aggregated the taxation levied by Reich, state (*Land*), and commune (*Gemeinde*), considered itself hard pressed. The exemption level in Prussia was set at the equivalent of £45 (as opposed to £160 in Britain), and by 1903 there were already 3.9 million taxpayers in Germany. In 1913 local authorities (including the states) were responsible for 66.9 per cent of government spending, the Reich for only 33.1 per cent, and 22.6 per cent of the total was funded by income tax.[70]

Between 1906 and 1913 the Reich was locked in battle with the states in an effort to appropriate some element of direct taxation, and so cover its increasing expenditure on the armed forces. However, this struggle was

---

[69] Knauss, *Kriegsfinanzierung*, 30; see also 24–30; Roesler, *Finanzpolitik*, 13–17; Carl-Ludwig Holtfrerich, 'The modernisation of the tax system in the First World War and the Great Inflation, 1914–23', in Witt (ed.), *Wealth and taxation*, 126–8.

[70] Roesler, *Finanzpolitik*, 134; Daunton, *English Historical Review*, CXI (1996), 886.

not simply an issue of governmental centralization; it was also a matter of party politics. The Socialists were in favour of progressive direct taxation; they were prepared even to support a larger army and navy to achieve that aim. The Conservatives were opposed to duties on property, particularly on land, but were compromised by their wish to strengthen the services. The objective of Bethmann Hollweg, in particular, was as much to secure an ongoing majority in the Reichstag as it was to reform Germany's finances.

The Conservatives' alarm at the implications of *Weltpolitik* seemed justified in 1906 itself, when a Reich inheritance tax was imposed. Their opposition rendered it a tax without teeth. In 1911 Wermuth proposed to make death duties effective in order to end the Reich's deficits. Bethmann Hollweg sought a solution that would be less offensive to the Conservatives. By taxing all property, he hoped to draw more on the wealth of industry. But the opposition of the states to an inheritance tax prompted Wermuth to resign in March 1912. The subsequent budget did no more than adjust indirect taxation, although the Reichstag budget commission required the government to formulate a new universal property tax by 1913. The Conservatives and the Centre party hoped this would be a duty on mobile capital, and wanted it raised by the states; the Progressives and the SPD advocated a central tax on all property.

Wermuth's successor at the Treasury, Hermann Kühn, planned a tax on capital gains. By not appropriating any of the states' taxes, by leaving existing wealth untouched and yet imposing a levy on all types of property, he produced a workable and sensible compromise. As originally proposed, this *Wehrbeitrag* would have taxed any increase in value of over 2,000 marks on all property worth more than 6,000 marks. As enacted, the thresholds were 10,000 marks and 20,000 marks. Most small tradesmen, skilled craftsmen, and peasant farmers were thereby exempted. The rate was progressive, between 0.75 per cent and 2.5 per cent according to the size of the unearned increment.[71] The right was appeased by two concessions: agricultural land was assessed on its fictional yield value, which was below the real value on sale; and the total package for 1913 still included increases in indirect taxation. But in overall terms the shift in policy between 1906 and 1913 favoured the less

71 Witt, *Finanzpolitik*, 370.

privileged. Consumption taxes over that period rose 19.3 per cent, transport taxes 71.8 per cent, and direct taxes 71.7 per cent. The total Reich yield borne by each of these elements in 1913 was 34 per cent, 9.1 per cent, and 56.8 per cent.[72]

Nonetheless, it is exaggerated to claim that the Reich had made the breakthrough to a system of progressive taxation, which favoured the poor and milked the rich.[73] Such an argument is essentially counterfactual. In 1912/13, at least temporarily, the financial implications of the arms policy created a form of social fusion; that fusion possibly prefigured the liberal Reichstag majority of 1917/18. But the tax that had made this possible was not envisaged as part of the normal peacetime financial arrangements of the Reich. The *Wehrbeitrag* was a one-off contribution to defence, to last three years only. The direct tax levied on each individual was still only half that of Britain, and the total tax burden little more than that.[74] The *Wehrbeitrag* was a reflection of international tension more than a reform of fiscal principles.[75]

Above all, there had been no intellectual shift in the Reich. The acquisition of limited powers of direct taxation did not produce the determination that taxes rather than loans should be the main means of financing a war. Even in peacetime, borrowing was the means by which to finance increased defence spending. This was a principle established by the build-up of the navy, and by 1913/14 65.3 per cent of all Reich debt had been incurred through expenditure on the colonies, the army, and the navy. As a corollary, servicing the debt which the armed forces largely generated itself became a significant element of Reich expenditure— about 11 per cent of the whole in 1913.[76] In an influential text of 1912, *Kriegssteuer oder Kriegsanleihe?*, Heinrich Dietzel argued that war should be paid for out of loans, or in other words, that taxation should be deferred. He anticipated that wartime taxation would reduce consumption and encourage the withdrawal of investments: given a limited understanding of inflation, both consequences seemed to him undesir-

---

[72] Kroboth, *Finanzpolitik*, 302.
[73] Ibid. 284–9, 321; also Holtfrerich, 'The modernisation of the tax system', in Witt (ed.), *Wealth and taxation*, 128; Knauss, *Kriegsfinanzierung*, 28; Witt, *Finanzpolitik*, 372–6; Ferguson, *Historical Journal*, XXXV (1992), 725–52, provides a historiographical survey in English.
[74] Kroboth, *Finanzpolitik*, 304.
[75] Holtfrerich, *German inflation*, 110.
[76] Ferguson, *Historical Journal*, XXXV (1992), 748; also Ferguson, *Pity of war*, 129.

able. Dietzel was anticipating a short war. Taxation, because of the lag in its collection, would be much slower in raising money than the issue of government loans. Finally, Dietzel warned against fostering a divisive political debate just at the point when the nation needed to be united. Dietzel did not go unanswered. Jakob Riesser, a National Liberal and a banker, called for a sound budget resting on direct and indirect taxation in *Finanzielle Kriegsbereitschaft und Kriegführung* (2nd edition, 1913). Riesser advocated what became the orthodox rule of thumb for liberals, that one-third of a war's costs should be met through tax.[77] But it was the writings of Dietzel, not of Riesser, that found reflection in what Helfferich did. The fact that Dietzel's title posited taxation and loans as competing alternatives encouraged the view that one was the replacement for the other; the possibility that both might be required was neglected. Indeed, Helfferich even harboured the hope that the loans would not be redeemed by deferred taxation but by payments from the defeated enemy. When he took over from Kühn at the Treasury on 26 January 1915 he already had behind him the experience of advising the chancellor on appropriate levels of enemy indemnity.[78]

However, Helfferich's major concern as finance minister was not pecuniary but political. The *Burgfrieden* was too recent, too fragile, and too precious for it to be sacrificed on the altar of fiscal rectitude. Any increase in direct taxation would please the left and would augment the power of the Reichstag; therefore it could be calculated to antagonize the right and the *Bundesrat*. Helfferich received clear warning of the limits this imposed on his effective powers in July 1915. The *Bundesstaaten* told the Reich that it would not be allowed to renew the *Wehrbeitrag*.[79]

The German government was therefore caught in a cleft stick. Its traditional source of revenue, indirect taxation, was a wasting asset. The Socialists would only agree to increased duties on consumption if they were accompanied by the taxes on income opposed by the right. But more significant than the political arguments were the falling returns on existing rates of duty because of the war. Customs were eased in an effort

[77] Manfred Ziedler, 'Die deutsche Kriegsfinanzierung 1914 bis 1918 und ihre Folgen', in Michalka (ed.), *Der Erste Weltkrieg*, 418–19.
[78] Hecker, *Rathenau*, 178.
[79] Williamson, *Helfferich*, 129–30; Helfferich, *Weltkrieg*, 224–5; Roesler, *Finanzpolitik*, 71, 104–5.

to attract goods to Germany despite the blockade. In 1913 they had raised 679.3 million marks (or 30.8 per cent of Reich revenue); in 1915 they contributed 359.9 million, and in 1918 133 million. Domestic duties were caught by the decline in national income. Taking 1913 as 100, the most optimistic index shows a fall in national income to 88 by 1918, and the most severe to 57.[80]

Neither the 1914 budget, introduced by Kühn, nor that of March 1915, the first actual war budget and the first proposed by Helfferich, showed any change in the structure or rates of tax. Without the *Wehrbeitrag*— which produced 637.4 million marks in 1914 and 307.8 million in 1915— the position would have been bleak. Receipts under most of the major traditional heads fell. The exception, significantly, was the Reich printing works, busy producing notes for the government, the Reichsbank, and the *Darlehenskassen*. The *Matrikularbeiträge* remained constant (as they did throughout the war) at 51.9 million marks. Total Reich income in 1914 was 2,471.1 million marks (excluding the net profits on postal services and railways); in 1915 it fell to 1,825.2 million marks.

In 1916 the *Wehrbeitrag* would decline to 19.5 million marks. Rebuffed over its renewal, Helfferich had to find a substitute. He suggested a tax on all wartime profits, to be levied on a scale of up to 15 per cent of the increase in value of property or 30 per cent of the income. But inherited property and corporate profits would be excluded, and he did not envisage introducing the tax until after the war. Helfferich found he had struck a chord both with the Bundesrat and with the public. On 30 November 1915 he formally introduced a proposal for a war profits tax.

This time company profits were included. Businesses were to deposit 50 per cent of gains in excess of their pre-war average over five years in a special reserve fund. The tax would be drawn from the fund. The complicated arrangement was designed to forestall the distribution of the profits on the second year of the war before a definitive law had been passed. The proposal and the debate were uncontentious. By building on the principles of the *Wehrbeitrag*, the tax could be construed as a once-and-for-all levy on capital gains accrued in the calendar years 1914, 1915, and 1916. The income which had been consumed or capitalized during this period would be liquidated without the imposition of a direct income tax at a

---

[80] Holtfrerich, *German inflation*, 224–7, on these indexes and their variations.

time when the cost of living was increasing. The Bundesrat was therefore convinced that the states' rights to income tax were unimpinged. Conversely but conveniently, the Socialists—although wanting the tax to be at a higher rate than was the case—were persuaded that the tax was a Reich levy on income. Even the industrialists had little to complain about. At first only public companies were affected, and they—by virtue of Helfferich's notice in July—had had time to take evasive action. Furthermore, they could still draw on the special fund in order to subscribe to war loans. Private companies and individuals remained exempt until June 1916. The Reichsbank alone was severely handled. Its release from the tax on its note issue and the increased circulation of notes had boosted its profits, three-quarters of the excess on which were now diverted from its private shareholders to the government.

Helfferich's budget of March 1916 therefore marked a first attempt to put Germany's war finances on a firmer foundation. The war profits tax was set at a rate of 10 per cent on a 2 per cent excess, rising in steps to 30 per cent on sums above 15 per cent. If average profits were more than 25 per cent of paid-up capital and reserves, then a surcharge of up to 50 per cent was payable.[81] Similarly for individuals, 50 per cent was the maximum rate of tax on the nominal increase in their assets (on an increase of more than 400,000 marks).[82] Property, provided it retained 90 per cent of its value as at 31 December 1913, was taxed at 1 per cent; increased wealth derived from inheritance or from insurance payments was exempt. None of this became law until June, and it had little impact on revenue until 1917.

The remainder of Helfferich's budget rested on more traditional devices. Excise duties began to climb back to their pre-war yield, principally thanks to an increased duty on tobacco; the rates on alcoholic drinks were untouched, and continued to fall. His proposal to impose a stamp duty on almost all transactions was thrown out by the budget committee of the Reichstag, on the grounds that it would inhibit business. Goods tended to change hands many times on the market, and commercial circles therefore preferred a sales tax on finished goods. The

---

[81] Roesler, *Finanzpolitik*, 71–4; Williamson, *Helfferich*, 130–4; Lotz, *Deutsche Staatsfinanzwirtschaft*, 54–5, 60–1; Knauss, *Kriegsfinanzierung*, 97–100; Helfferich, *Weltkrieg*, 229–31.

[82] This follows the table in Roesler, *Finanzpolitik*, 189; Lotz, *Deutsche Staatsfinanzwirtschaft*, 60, gives 50% on an increase of 1 million marks in personal wealth.

budget committee replaced Helfferich's proposed duty with a charge of
one-thousandth on the value of sales in kind, a tax that hit small
shopkeepers more than the powerful figures represented in the chambers
of commerce.[83] Although a potentially powerful generator of revenue, a
value-added tax in prototype, the tax's rate was too low to be of much
short-term significance. The combined outcome was disappointing.
Helfferich had projected revenue of 2,749.2 million marks for 1916,
hoping thus to balance the ordinary budget (including debt charges of
2,308.7 million marks). Actual income was only 2,122.2 million marks,
and ordinary expenditure rose to 3,066.8 million marks.[84]

Helfferich's move to the Ministry of the Interior resulted in the appointment of Graf Siegfried von Roedern as his successor at the Ministry
of Finance on 1 June 1916. Roedern's budget of February 1917, although
apparently harsh, was rightly criticized in the Reichstag for not going far
enough. Roedern announced that he needed an additional 1,250 million
marks to be raised through taxation in order to cover interest payments.
He got 1,473 million. But in 1917 the net debt increased by 36,092.9 million
marks, with the result that the interest payments alone were running at
3,250 million marks on 1 April 1917.

Furthermore, much of the increased revenue was the legacy of Helfferich's 1916 budget, now fully operational. Total receipts for 1917 were
projected at 4,026.7 million marks; in the event 8,010.1 million were
raised. Half of this came from Helfferich's war tax, to which Roedern
added a 20 per cent surcharge. Roedern was also the beneficiary of
Helfferich's budget in the duty on tobacco, whose yield—at 419.5 million
marks for 1917—was double that of 1916 and eight times its pre-war level.
His own principal innovations fell into the trap of creating revenue that
was largely fictitious. Coal was taxed at 20 per cent of its sale price at the
mine. The attractions of the coal tax were its ease of collection (only
about 500 firms were involved) and the possible stimulus to neutral
imports through an increased domestic price. But the principal consumer of coal was ultimately—via the arms industries and its products—
the government. To spare it a double burden, coal was exempted from the
other major new tax, on the transport of goods and individuals.

[83] Ferguson, *Pity of war*, 130–1.
[84] Roesler, *Finanzpolitik*, 68; see also Williamson, *Helfferich*, 133–43.

Reich revenues for 1918 fell to 7,395.2 million marks. Principally, this was because the war profits tax was a one-off arrangement, which required renewal or reconstruction to be effective for 1918. Roedern felt that direct taxation was incompatible with the government's preferred method of war finance, that of loans. Both could be seen as chasing the same wealth, and appropriation through the former might inhibit voluntary subscription to the latter. Furthermore, Roedern still preserved the notion that direct taxation had not become a permanent feature of the Reich's finances: he was prepared to use it only to reduce accumulated debt and not to cover current deficits. Therefore, although his budget of July 1918 contained a dozen new laws, and effectively ten new taxes, it was heavily weighted towards indirect taxation. The war profits tax produced only 791.8 million marks under the 1916 law and 1,617.2 million under Roedern's 1918 provisions. The tax on company profits was set at 60 per cent, but was reduced for profits of under a million marks, and could also be set against any losses registered in previous years. Increases in income were taxed on a scale beginning at 5 per cent for the first 10,000 marks and which rose in five steps to 50 per cent over 100,000 marks. The tax on property, although levied not on the increase in value but on the sum itself, was presented as a tax on accumulated income which had been capitalized. It was applied at a rate of one-thousandth on the first 200,000 marks, and also rose in five gradations, to five-thousandths on more than 1 million marks. Most of the indirect taxes fell on drinks, both alcoholic and non-alcoholic. Luxuries carried a purchase tax of 10 per cent. The biggest change was to the turnover tax, which at 5 per cent on all dealings not only produced 823.4 million marks in 1919 but also forced a foreshortening in the number of transactions and so discouraged speculation.[85]

Roedern's 1918 budget showed how little the fundamental lineaments of German thinking had shifted throughout the war. His indirect taxes were meant to yield an additional 1,564 million marks in 1918; they actually produced 486 million.[86] Germany's failure to milk fresh areas of liquidity was therefore more than a simple matter of fiscal lag. Peacetime yields were still being expected of taxes on consumption despite the

[85] Roesler, *Finanzpolitik*, 109–18, 189–94, 196; Lotz, *Deutsche Staatsfinanzwirtschaft*, 62–79; Knauss, *Kriegsfinanzierung*, 100–7.
[86] Roesler, *Finanzpolitik*, 120–1.

facts that national income was diminishing and that the state had appropriated the powers of production.

By the same token, Germany fudged the issue of direct taxation in new areas. War profits, after all, might be deemed sufficiently exceptional to be outside the ambit of the peacetime restrictions on direct taxation by the Reich. But Germany failed to establish a coherent model for the management of its war industry. The question of excess profits prompted the Reichstag to establish a committee on war supplies in June 1916, but it did not meet for the first time until December and it ended its proceedings, after fourteen meetings, in February 1918.[87] In July 1917 Wilhelm Groener, as head of the newly created war office, proposed controls on profits and wages and urged a sharpening of the war profits tax. Shortly thereafter he fell victim to the machinations not only of heavy industry but also of OHL itself.[88]

Industry successfully resisted government management. Only one company in Germany became subject to direct state control: on 6 March 1918 the Daimler motor works were placed under the oversight of the army. Daimler's shares, which had stood at 317 at the end of 1913, rose to 630 by 1916 and 1,350 in 1917: in 1916 and 1917 dividends of 35 per cent and 30 per cent were distributed. In the financial year 1916/17 the firm wrote off 100 per cent of the book value of its plant. Such accounting practices and their consequent profits did not prevent Daimler's management from asking the War Ministry for a 50 per cent increase in the prices of automobiles and spare parts for aero-engines at the beginning of 1917, and threatening to suspend night shifts and overtime if its demands were not met in February 1918.[89]

The difficulty in assessing the impact of the war profits tax is knowing how far a firm like Daimler was typical. Industries that were not benefiting from army orders were likely to experience decline; dividends as a whole, if related to the movement of prices, fell.[90] But many firms kept both their dividends and their balances low in order to avoid tax demands from the government and increases in pay for their workers.

---

[87] Wette, *Militärgeschichtliches Mitteilungen*, 36 (1984), 34–5.

[88] Feldman, *Army, industry and labor*, 385–404; Feldman, *Great disorder*, 68–70.

[89] Wette, *Militärgeschichtliches Mitteilungen*, 36 (1984), 44; Bellon, *Mercedes*, 89–90, 102–12; Burchardt, *Zeitschrift für Unternehmensgeschichte*, XXXII (1987), 98, 103.

[90] Mommsen, *Journal of Modern History*, XLV (1975), 535.

Their profits were hidden in increased capital and reserves. The sixteen most important steel and mining firms in Germany—admittedly businesses likely to benefit from the war—entered net profits of 285 million marks over its first three years. The dividends of iron-processing firms rose on average 175 per cent when allowance is made for inflation, and those of the chemical industry 200 per cent. The most successful heavy industries showed an eightfold increase in profits even against 1912/13, itself a peak year, and Rheinmetall a tenfold increase.[91]

But Rheinmetall's major rival, and Germany's principal armaments firm, Krupp, displays the danger of snap judgements. Shortly after the war's outbreak Gustav Krupp von Bohlen und Halbach declared to the firm's directors that he did not intend the company's profits to be any greater than was normal in peace. The firm's accounts suggest that this was not the empty rhetoric it was long assumed to be. In the immediately pre-war years average net profits had been 20 per cent of turnover; during the war they ran at 8.4 per cent, much lower than those of other major companies. Furthermore, Krupp's dividends, which had averaged 12 per cent in the three years up to and including 1915/16, fell to 10 per cent in 1916/17, and no dividend was paid in 1917/18. The key to the question as to whether Krupp made vast profits from the war but hid them lies in its depreciation policy. During the course of the war it wrote off 85 per cent of its plant. But factory space increased 170 per cent, and housing was provided for the workforce, which tripled. So, writing off assets was not simply an accounting device. Munitions production constituted about 80 per cent of its business, and drastic depreciation was its only protection against the end of the war. Even so, its reserves were not sufficient to prevent the firm confronting crisis in 1919/20.[92]

Krupp's ability to carry through such accounting policies was enhanced by the fact that, after the efforts of 1915/16, the fiscal grip of the state on war industry relaxed. Helfferich, enamoured of the workings of the free market, used his shift to the Ministry of the Interior to make sure that the apparent rigour of his 1916 budget was not sustained. He was to be counted among Groener's opponents in 1917.[93] When Hindenburg took

[91] Wette, *Militärgeschichtliches Mitteilungen*, 36 (1984), 42–3; see also Feldman, *Great disorder*, 79.

[92] Burchardt, *Zeitschrift für Unternehmensgeschichte*, XXXII (1987), 71–123.

[93] Chickering, *Imperial Germany's Great War*, 182; Groener, *Lebenserinnerungen*, 368.

over at OHL in August 1916 he set a programme of increased munitions production which effectively elevated output over price control. The conservative instincts of Bethmann Hollweg's government, reflected in economic liberalism, had been a partial restraint on costs; they were elbowed to one side by radical militarism. Because firms were left to bear their own investment costs in order to create sufficient plant for war needs, the state was required to be generous in the matters of depreciation and capitalization. Munitions manufacturers, like Krupp, aimed to write off their equipment costs in one or two years. But indulgence became laxity, and even collusion. Businesses could evade taxes, a once-and-for-all loss, by subscribing to war loans, a temporary sacrifice compensated for by the government. The obstructiveness of war industry in revealing the details of its accounts was borne with unreasonable patience by the War Ministry. Firms got into the habit of not operating to fixed prices, but of setting the final cost after delivery. The raw materials section of the War Ministry made allowances to employers for wage increases.[94] Thus the state, as the principal consumer, became the main bearer of the burden of the war profits tax. Germany had embraced the principle of price control, albeit unevenly in 1914; as its effectiveness waned after 1916, so the real returns on the war profits tax fell. Without price control, taxation—and certainly taxation levied at a lower rate in 1917 and 1918 than in 1916—was stoking inflation, not retarding it.[95]

The failure of the Reich to tax real incomes directly was made more severe by a shift in the financial policies of local governments. During the war they multiplied their spending four times (as opposed to five times for the Reich). They covered 35 per cent of it through borrowing, despite possessing the power to impose direct taxation, and, moreover, they moved from long-term debt to short-term. The federal states between 1914 and 1923 raised 6.1 billion marks through taxation, but required 3.5 billion of it to service their debts.[96] Thus, it was not only the company but also the individual for whom the impact of taxation was loosened in the war, rather than tightened. The legacy of Germany's failure to tax directly was not, therefore, the amount by which it failed to cover its war costs but

[94] Feldman, *Army, industry and labor*, 387–9.

[95] Roesler, *Finanzpolitik*, 99–102, 129–30, 163–6.

[96] Ferguson, *Paper and iron*, 116; Witt, 'Tax policies, tax assessment and inflation: towards a sociology of public finances in the German inflation, 1914–23', in Witt (ed.), *Wealth and taxation*, 141–3.

the degree to which it bequeathed the post-war government with the problems of monetary overhang.

The post-war focus on Germany has, however, served to obscure the even more dire position of Austria-Hungary's revenues. In Austria itself, the reluctance to introduce new taxes was not the consequence of a lack of pre-war powers or of a pre-war infrastructure. In 1913 total net revenue was 3,122.9 million crowns. Direct taxes on property and income produced 431.5 million crowns, customs 199.9 million, excise duties 418.1 million, charges on stamps and railways 265.5 million, state monopolies 433.1 million, state-run businesses (including the roads) 1,208.1 million, and income from administration 166.7 million. By the end of the war current prices had risen fifteenfold, but ordinary revenue in 1917/18 had only increased by a quarter in current prices, to 4,194 million crowns. Furthermore, Austria stubbornly maintained the fiction that the war was working no change in the value of money. If the crown was held at its pre-war value, the net revenue for 1917/18 fell to 417.7 million crowns. By the same token, government spending also fell. If war costs for 1914/15 stood at 100, the ratio in peace prices was 77 for 1915/16, 46 for 1916/17, and 36 for 1917/18. The proportions for the armed services were even more alarming: 100; 74; 41; and 27. Austria was spending less in real terms on the war at the end than it was at the beginning.[97]

The suspension of parliamentary activity in Austria until 1917 proved both a blessing and burden. On the positive side, government by decree removed the problems of parliamentary obstructionism and delay. On the negative, any new taxation lacked the imprimatur of popular approval and thus threatened to exacerbate internal tensions. The effect was to encourage the government to build on existing patterns of tax, but to fail to tap new sources. The first additional taxes of the war, not introduced until September 1915, were increases to existing levies—an addition to the duty on beer, and to the charges for inheritances, gifts, and social welfare. But these were not prompted by the war: they had been long debated in parliament and could now be imposed because of the latter's absence. They were therefore irrelevant to Austria's new circumstances. The yields on beer and spirits fell in line with the fall in consumption: indeed, because 77 million crowns of beer duty had to be

[97] Winkler, *Einkommensverschiebungen in Österreich*, 68–75.

passed over to the provinces, this particular account moved into deficit by the end of the war. The September 1915 increases netted a paltry 23 million crowns of additional income.

The decline in consumption, therefore, rendered indirect taxation an inadequate tool with which to tackle the government's target of covering the interest charges on war debt. But the principle of building on the existing system persisted. In September 1916, citing the precedent of the Italian war of 1859, the government introduced special war surcharges on existing direct taxes. Overtly, these struck at the wealthy and relieved the less affluent: the threshold for liability to personal income tax was raised from 1,600 crowns to 3,000 crowns. With indirect duties failing to tax lower incomes because of falling consumption, this was not a route to social harmony but to monetary inflation. Moreover, the new rates appeared fiercer than they were. The surcharges were expressed as percentages on the existing levels of taxation, not on the principal to be taxed. The surcharge on incomes between 3,000 crowns and 20,000 crowns was only 15 per cent. But the scale after that rose with apparent steepness to 100 per cent on incomes over 140,000 crowns, 120 per cent on incomes over 200,000 crowns, and 200 per cent over 1 million crowns. However, all these percentages were the supplements applied to existing (low) rates of tax, not to the income itself. Thus, the net additional yield remained relatively small. The tax on interest payments was expressed as a 300 per-cent surcharge; in practice this meant an increase in the basic rate from 2 per cent to 8 per cent, which was— furthermore—to be levied only when the money was withdrawn. The surcharge on the duty on share dividends was 20 per cent, raising the rate from 10 per cent to 12 per cent—with a complicated additional scale graduated according to the level of profit on the invested capital. The tax on business profits suffered a 100 per cent surcharge when the tax yield exceeded 60 crowns, and 60 per cent when it was below that. The only group for whom the real burdens increased were landowners, whose effective rate of tax had fallen by half between 1898 and 1914. The 80 per cent surcharge imposed on ground tax bit more deeply because the basic rate was 19.3 per cent, and the new effective rate became 34.7 per cent.[98] But the empire's agricultural

    [98] Müller, *Finanzielle Mobilmachung*, 157–8, 161–2, 164–9; Josef Wysocki, 'Die Österreichische Finanzpolitik', in Wandruszka and Urbanitsch (eds.), *Habsburgermonarchie*, i. 101–3; Wegs, 'Austrian economic mobilization', 27–8.

heartland, Hungary, was left unaffected for fear of antagonizing Magyar farmers: throughout the war there was virtually no change in Hungary's fiscal policies.[99] In 1917/18 Austria's yield on direct taxation had risen to 676.8 million crowns, but that was expressed in current values: in peace crowns it had fallen to 67.4 million.

The difficulties of genuine innovation, directed at new areas of liquidity, were amply illustrated by the travails of Austria's efforts to milk war profits. A royal decree of April 1916 aimed to tax the increased profits of all companies (not just companies benefiting from war industries) generated in the war years 1914, 1915, and 1916. When parliament reconvened in 1917, its deputies argued that the provisions of April 1916 were insufficiently rigorous. They wanted severer rates to be incorporated in a new scale which subsumed individuals as well as companies. However, the Upper House construed the proposals of the Lower as a socialist-inspired attack on productivity and capital formation. Conscious that a simple rejection of the deputies' proposals would give time for profits to be dissipated before legislation was in place to tax them, the Upper House proposed a short-term solution—which was promptly rejected by the Lower House in case it transmogrified into a long-term arrangement. The final result was compromise. For public companies, the basis of comparison was the average of the highest and lowest profits in the years 1909 to 1914; the first 10,000 crowns of war-related profit was not liable for tax, and thereafter a levy on a scale of 10 to 35 per cent was applied. For private firms and individual businessmen 1913 was the point of comparison, the first 3,000 crowns were not liable, and the rate was 5 per cent on the next 10,000 crowns, 10 per cent on the next 10,000, 15 per cent on the next 20,000, and 20 per cent on the next 20,000. But the law only applied to 1916 and 1917, and the whole debate was therefore rerun in 1918. On this occasion the scale for private firms was widened, so that profits over 300,000 crowns were taxed at 60 per cent—a ceiling set by the Upper House. The Lower House wanted the same principles applied to public companies, but the Upper House insisted that account should be taken of the profitability on capital investment, and the scale was set at two-thirds that of private firms in order to allow the creation of reserves. The effect of all this parliamentary rancour was inefficiency. Many profits

[99] Popovics, *Geldwesen*, 171–2.

earned in 1914 and 1915 escaped entirely; the yield for 1916/17, budgeted at 169 million crowns, proved to be 90 million; an anticipated return of 300 million crowns for 1917/18 came in close to target, but this was only 29.9 million peace crowns. Austria's hope was that it would make up the leeway—to the tune of 2,000 million crowns—after the war was over.[100]

Parliament's inability to embrace innovation was clearly recognized in Austria's first proper war budget, introduced in September 1917 and designed to cover the year July 1917 to June 1918. It revealed that normal receipts had risen (in current crowns) from 3,080 million in 1913 to 4,062.6 million in 1917, and that the surcharges and war profits tax added a further 720 million crowns. But normal expenditure had outstripped the additional yield, jumping by 2,220 million crowns to 5,681 million. Furthermore, the interest charges on the war debt—which Austria had previously hoped to cover through the surcharges of 1916—were running at 1,795 million crowns. Despite this clear evidence that Austria was no longer even covering its peacetime costs, the budget did no more than reiterate the policy of surcharges on existing sources of revenue. A suggestion that a property tax be introduced was crushed with the observation that the idea was 'not yet topical'.[101] So palpable was the budget's failure that new taxes had to be introduced long before the planned date of June 1918. These measures—adopted in January 1918— continued the notion of wartime supplements to existing direct taxes. The main novelties—a coal tax modelled on that of Germany, and a railway tax—had the effect of driving up production costs, and therefore committed the error of indirectly taxing the state itself. By these means the January 1918 interim budget added 820 million crowns to the existing total for war-related taxation of 720 million. But such figures were doubly insignificant—meaningless in the context of a total state expenditure for 1917/18 of 22,169 million crowns, and expressed in a currency that to all intents and purposes was fast becoming valueless.[102]

When Bulgaria entered the war in 1915 its Finance Ministry had succumbed to pressure from both left and right and accepted the

---

[100] Müller, *Finanzielle Mobilmachung*, 158–9, 169–74.
[101] März, *Austrian banking*, 192–3.
[102] Müller, *Finanzielle Mobilmachung*, 159–60, 163–4; Winkler, *Einkommensverschiebungen*, 71–3.

principle of progressive direct taxation. But the government's enthusiasm
for the idea was distinctly limited, not least because the bulk of foreign
loans it had contracted in 1904, 1907, and 1909 were secured on the
receipts from indirect taxation and from customs and excise. Between
1889 and 1911 Bulgaria's yield from direct taxation remained roughly
constant, totalling 38.2 million gold leva in 1889, peaking at 49.1 million
in 1905, and falling back to 41.6 million in 1911. By contrast, indirect
taxation grew from 9.3 million leva to 83.6 million over the same period.
The government used its entry into the war to argue that any change in
the balance should be postponed until the return of normal conditions.
Although a war profits tax was proposed in December 1916, it was
not adopted until May 1919. Direct taxation produced 24 per cent of
Bulgaria's revenue in 1914, and 21 per cent in 1918.

A significant pressure against radical change was Bulgaria's reliance on
agriculture, and the effect on it of war. The mobilization of the army
drained the land not only of men but also of draught animals and
vehicles. In 1912 17 per cent of the land was fallow; in 1917 29 per cent.
Grain production fell from 2,876,000 tons in 1911 to 1,065,000 in 1918.
About half of Bulgaria's direct taxation was derived from land tax. It
netted 17.33 million leva in 1911, but under the impact of the First Balkan
War slumped to 4.54 million in 1913.

By 1917 its yield had recovered to 13.96 million leva, and in 1918 to
19.26 million. The growth was principally due to depreciation. But it also
highlighted a shift to so-called industrial crops, and particularly tobacco.
Bulgaria's production of tobacco multiplied 3.5 times between 1912 and
1918. In meeting the cravings of the soldiers of the Central Powers,
Bulgaria ensured that its balance of trade moved from deficit in 1914 to
surplus in 1915, 1916, and 1917. By the latter year tobacco accounted for
70 per cent of Bulgaria's exports, as opposed to 9.9 per cent in 1909. Thus,
the government could offset its reluctance to move on the issue of direct
taxation by focusing on customs and excise, as well as its own monopolies, including patents for the production and sale of tobacco.

Total tax income, which stood at 120 million leva in 1914, fell to
97 million in 1916, but recovered to 151 million in 1917 and 278.7 million
in 1918. In real terms, however, the tax yield was a third that of 1914, and
thus made no contribution to the costs of the war. Nor did it soak up the
increased money supply, which saw the note circulation rise from

226.5 million leva to 2,298.6 million. Peasant debt was reduced, and bank deposits rose.[103]

If any of the belligerents had a weak administrative structure accompanied by a limited fiscal base, it was Turkey. When the tax on cattle was quadrupled, Kurdish breeders simply moved beyond the reach of the Turkish army.[104] On the other hand, the abrogation of the capitulations did create the opportunity, previously denied the Sublime Porte, to levy customs and excise. However, the tariff structure, designed on a provisional basis before 1914, charged imports according to weight, not value. During the war the latter rose while the former fell, but the Turks were reluctant to change for fear of trade suffering even more than was already the case. More successful were domestic taxes on non-essential items of consumption imposed in 1916/17. These included sugar, petrol, matches, coffee, tea, and playing-cards. The duty on alcoholic drinks was revised in 1918.

Arguably, the empire's most effective direct tax was the power to requisition goods in kind. A war tax for those of military age but exempted from service was a failure. The idea of war profits tax was canvassed by Djavid, the finance minister, in a budget speech on 3 March 1917. But he then affirmed his defence of the rights of private property and reassured his listeners by emphasizing his belief that in war as in peace personal profits added to the nation's wealth. His budget for 1917/18 assumed that outgoings of £T52 million would be offset by receipts of up to £T23 million, but it also reckoned on peace within six months. At that point the tax system would be revised to raise the state's income to £T35 or £T36 million. In November 1917, when it was clear that the war would not end as he anticipated, income tax was introduced, but it was not effective during the war itself.

Revenue therefore declined during the war, but the scale is hard to estimate. In 1913/14 Turkey's receipts were £T29,201,865. In October 1914 monthly spending if Turkey entered the war was projected to be £T500,000, but by February 1915 it had risen to £T1 million. In 1915/16 receipts fell to £T22,325,793, and although they rose by almost £T3 million in the following year the currency was rapidly depreciating and the cost

---

[103] Danaïllow, *Les Effets de la guerre en Bulgarie*, 61–4, 512–30; Crampton, *Bulgaria*, 479–87; Lampe, *Bulgarian economy*, 33–4.
[104] Ahmad, *Kurdistan*, 136.

of the war up to March 1917 averaged out at £T5 million a month. At that
stage Djavid reckoned actual monthly war spending to be £T7 million.[105]
After the war Karl Helfferich averred that Britain had covered only
about 12.5 per cent of its war expenditure from taxation. While conceding
that Germany had not done so well, he nonetheless argued that at least a
small part of its war spending had been met through tax. Recent calculations suggest that Helfferich claimed too little for both powers: Britain
covered 18.2 per cent of its war expenditure from taxation, and Germany
13.9 per cent.[106] But his central point remains valid. None of the belligerents was capable of meeting the major part of its war costs from
taxation. Helfferich's case contains less special pleading than might at
first appear. More united the belligerents in their fiscal policies than
divided them. All could have taxed with far greater severity than they
did. All could have made those rates of tax that they did in fact adopt
more realistic if they had accompanied them with truly effective prices-
and-incomes policies.

But it is this latter point that constitutes the basis for the criticism of
Helfferich. The former minister of finance was still seeking an explanation of war finance that related outgoings to income. What he had still
not comprehended was the relationship between taxation and the money
supply. During the war inflation had positive effects: it meant that some
of the war's costs were met by those whose incomes could not stay abreast
of rises in prices. It therefore functioned as a form of indirect, discreet,
and immediately productive taxation. If those on falling real incomes
ultimately ceased to buy goods, they released productive capacity for
other forms of (ideally) war-related production. Simultaneously, those
who profited from inflation simply became liable for higher rates of tax.
Josiah Stamp, reflecting Britain's relaxed view on inflation, concluded
that 'the illusion of prosperity, and the incentive to production created by
inflation have their real value in war-time, provided that they are not
carried out of hand'.[107]

It was this final caveat which Helfferich failed to grasp. All the
belligerents proceeded cautiously in relation to taxation for fear of

[105] Emin, *Turkey in the world war*, 157–9; Dschawid, *Türkische Kriegsfinanzwirtschaft*, 9–11,
30–1, 34–5.
[106] Helfferich, *Money*, 227; Ferguson, *Pity of war*, 323.
[107] Farr, 'McKenna', 241–2.

undermining the principle of consent on which its collection (especially when tax authorities were understaffed) rested. But taxation managed inflation by drawing in the surplus cash of consumers, and so moderating prices. Helfferich's anxiety concerning the fragility of the *Burgfrieden* seems to have blinded him to this relationship.

Inflation also eroded the real value of the national debt. Given Helfferich's preference for loans, herein is a further reason for his blindness to the wider functions of taxation. By reducing the value of investments, inflation had taxing effects. But again, the value of inflation as a mechanism for wartime finance depended on its relationship to taxation. Investors had to be persuaded to invest in government bonds. Fiscal rectitude, even if more an appearance than a substitute, helped sustain confidence at home and credit abroad. The former was an important prerequisite for domestic borrowing; the latter was part of the armoury for seeking foreign loans.

6

DOMESTIC
BORROWING

The principal functions of taxation in the First World War were the suppression of inflation and the maintenance of creditworthiness. Taxation did not cover the daily expenses of fighting—or at least not to any significant degree. At best (in the United States and Britain), taxation paid for less than a quarter of the war's ongoing costs; at worst (in France, Austria-Hungary, and Russia) for none of them. The war was therefore predominantly funded by borrowing—and this is a generalization applicable to all belligerents.

In August 1914 borrowing reinforced two aspects of the popular response to the outbreak of the war. The first was the sense that the war had healed social divisions, and so united the nation; the second was the belief that the war would be short. Unlike taxation, which was compulsory, loans were voluntary. They therefore enabled the warring peoples to cement their enthusiasm into positive action without at the same time courting the odium and awakening the divisions generated by proposals for new taxes. Furthermore, those most likely to contribute were the wealthy; levels of popular consumption remained unaffected. Thus, liquid capital could be mobilized with far more rapidity and far less pain than through taxation.

However, as it became clear that the war was not going to be short, the initial attractions of borrowing turned to disadvantages. On the one hand, loans put the burden of war finance on a minority of the population, who might feel aggrieved that others were not making a comparable contribution. On the other, the more loan stock an individual acquired, the more he was enabled to increase his wealth at the expense of the masses. The interest and principal would be paid off through taxation levied on the entire population. Moreover, the attractions of the investment were diverting capital from productive uses to unproductive. The long-term cost would be a reduction in national wealth which would afflict the population as a whole rather than the owner of the original capital. Thus, a continuation of borrowing on the principles applied at the beginning of the war made less and less sense as the war continued. Social division would replace social unity.

But it was no solution to this conundrum to switch from borrowing to taxation. Fiscally, it would be insufficiently productive; socially, the same problems would resurface, albeit in different form. Once they had begun borrowing, the nations had little choice but to continue. The buoyancy of war loan stock became an indication of confidence in ultimate victory; to change horses might set prices tumbling and so erode a state's credit-worthiness. To maintain the latter governments had to show that they could raise fresh loans, with the result that borrowing promoted more borrowing. The task of the government was to find a sensible balance in the management of debt. War loans had to be issued in denominations sufficiently low to draw in the small investor as well as the big; they had to offer a rate of interest sufficiently high to ensure success, but not so high as to suggest financial desperation or to saddle the taxation system with an insupportable burden of interest payment; finally, they had to be the means by which short-term borrowing and floating debt were converted into long-term obligations.

Most governmental debt was taken up not by private investors but by financial institutions. Short-term treasury bills were the dominant and immediate means by which governments procured the cash to pay for the war. The treasury bills were discounted by the banks. Having acquired the status of securities, the bills could then become the basis for new note issue. Thus, at the cost of expanding the money supply governments could extend their credit indefinitely. By spending the money so generated on war production, the state put the cash back into circulation. War loans were therefore a means of soaking up surplus money, and of shifting the government's short-term borrowing at the bank into long-term debt with the people. But the circle was not thereby broken, because war loan stock could itself be bought by the banks or be treated as security by them. So it too became the basis for an increase in the money supply. Therefore, domestic currency was freed from the restraint of a set percentage of gold cover. But the goods and services procurable with the purchasing power that the money represented were diverted from private individuals to the state. A. C. Pigou argued that bank credits therefore constituted a concealed form of taxation, albeit an inefficient one.[1] The most immediate and evident form of state credit was the quantity of unearned currency in circulation—'a form of interest-free forced loan'.[2]

The banks, therefore, became the essential intermediaries in the onward transmission and multiplication of government debt. Throughout the belligerent countries the banks saw an increase in deposits and in credits. In France the deposits of the Banque de France and the six leading commercial banks rose from 7,058 million francs on 30 June 1914 to 10,882 million by the end of 1918; their credit expanded 242.58 per cent, from 17,289 million francs to 41,937 million.[3] In Austria the deposits of the major Viennese banks rose from 163,628,000 crowns at the end of 1913, to 324,700,000 at the end of 1918, and of credits from 3,252,061,000 to 11,498,642,000.[4] In Italy, the deposits of the four Italian banks increased 344 per cent between 1914 and 1918.[5] In Germany the holdings of the seven major Berlin banks rose from 7,661 million marks to 21,979 million over the same period, and their credit from 4,508 million marks to 17,126 million.[6] The deposits of the Russian state bank grew from 184.7 million roubles in July 1914 to 2,454.7 million in September 1917, of savings banks from 2,073 million roubles to 6,739.8 million between the same dates, and of private banks from 3,393.3 million roubles in August 1914 to 9,153.3 million in July 1917.[7] In Britain the deposits and current accounts of the joint stock banks of England and Wales (excluding the Bank of England) grew from £809.4 million on 31 December 1914 to £1,583.4 million on 31 December 1918, and of all banks from £1,032.9 million to £1,988.3 million.[8] Although this expansion was expressed in depreciating

[1] Pigou, *Political economy of war*, 107–8.   [2] Knauss, *Kriegsfinanzierung*, 69.
[3] Fisk, *French public finance*, 40.   [4] März, *Austrian banking*, 223, 224.
[5] Teillard, *Emprunts de guerre*, 222.   [6] Roesler, *Finanzpolitik*, 220.
[7] Michelson *et al.*, *Russian public finance*, 402–5; Claus, *Kriegswirtschaft Russlands*, 17. Claus (p. 38) says savings banks' deposits grew from 1,704 million roubles to 4,915 million between July 1914 and October 1917; the figures in the text are from Michelson .
[8] Brown, *International gold standard*, 116; Morgan, *British financial policy*, 228.

currencies, the point was often lost on bankers gratified by the ease with which they had shuffled off the blows to private business and international commerce. The president of the Deutsche Bank, Arthur von Gwinner, was entirely positive in his annual report for 1917: 'the placement of deposits in the Treasury bills of the Reich, the federal states, and the large cities now offers the easiest opportunity to invest every available sum in a short-term and secure manner at acceptable interest rates which run at an average of $4\frac{1}{4}$ per cent to $4\frac{1}{2}$ per cent.' Not until the end of the following year would he recognize 'monetary depreciation' rather than real wealth as the source of the bank's increase in business.[9] Moreover, the key point remained: the banking systems of the belligerents proved capable of sufficient growth to keep pace with the demands of war finance.

Broadly speaking, the structural changes which underpinned this enlargement were in place before the war; the war accelerated their development rather than originated them. Most significant and most fortuitous was the establishment in the United States of the Federal Reserve System. Until 1914 the banks of America lacked any central organization, with the result that their reserves were scattered and immobile and their capacity for development severely restricted. Three months before the outbreak of war the Federal Reserve act divided the country into twelve districts, with a Federal Reserve bank for each district. All national banks were obliged to join the system, and others were encouraged to do so. The member banks subscribed capital to the regional Federal Reserve bank, and in return the reserves required to be held against deposits were reduced in varying percentages according to the size and status of the member bank. The interest rates of the Federal Reserve banks fell by up to 2 per cent between 1914 and 1916. In practice, the decline in the reserve ratios was offset by the gold imports generated through the war: on 5 April 1917 the reserve ratio was still 89 per cent, and on 17 November 1916 the reserves of the member banks were $2,536 million, of which only $1,510 million was actually required. The United States therefore possessed a flexible system for credit expansion of considerable capacity.[10]

Although no other belligerent underwent reforms so crucial to its capability to finance war industry, all saw an alteration in banking

[9] Gall et al., Deutsche Bank, 134–5, 161–2.
[10] Gilbert, American financing, 47–51; Bogart, War costs, 135–7.

profiles. In Italy the issue banks' proportion of the total assets of all banks rose from 23.9 per cent in 1913 to 46.1 per cent in 1918, largely at the expense of the savings banks and popular banks. The four or five largest credit banks expanded their assets from 16.7 per cent of the whole in 1914 to 33.9 per cent in 1919. And the government and the Bank of Italy combined forces in 1914–15 to create a new commercial bank, the Banca Italiano di Sconto, to contest the field with two Milanese banks, the Banca Commerciale Italiana and the Credito Italiano.[11] In Germany the existing banking structure was reinforced by the *Darlehenskassen*, which moved from being upmarket pawnshops to full-blown credit institutions. In Britain the process of bank amalgamations, already evident before the war (the number of British banks halved between 1895 and 1914), continued during it. Twelve of the largest London banks formed the 'big five'. The gap between them and their medium-sized competitors widened: the former commanded 70 per cent of deposits by 1918, and were able to write down their capital to only 5 per cent of deposits (when 13 per cent had been normal in 1910).[12]

Two general and interlocking trends predominated. First, the central banks were increasingly required to fall into step with government policy. In Britain this was symbolized by the Treasury's defeat of the nominally independent Bank of England over the policy to be followed on gold reserves and interest rates in July 1917. Secondly, the central banks became bankers to the commercial banks. In Russia the balances of fifty banks (representing a total of 782 branches) with the Russian State Bank increased from 64 million roubles at the beginning of 1914 to 160 million two years later.[13] Thus, the commercial banks as well as the central banks were enlisted for government service.

The banks therefore grew, but by means of state credit and at the expense of private business. In Germany trade bills constituted 17 per cent of the Reichsbank's assets in 1914 but only 0.7 per cent in 1918: the bank's role in refinancing commerce had been all but extinguished. Meanwhile, the credit banks themselves acquired 'the character of deposit banks lending chiefly to public authorities'; by 1918 government treasury bills constituted the bulk of the Deutsche Bank's liquid

---

[11] Forsyth, *Crisis of Liberal Italy*, 143–7, 310, 317.
[12] Grady, *British war finance*, 213–26, 247–50.
[13] Claus, *Kriegswirtschaft Russlands*, 43.

engagements.[14] At the other end of the banking spectrum the deposits of the savings banks grew 50 per cent during the war, but almost entirely through their handling of war loan stock: in Bavaria the savings banks dealt with 66 per cent of all war loan transactions.[15] In Italy the commercial portfolio of the banks declined 25 per cent between 1914 and 1916, its gross increase in these years being attributable to the discount of treasury bonds.[16] In the joint stock banks of Britain the ratio of other securities to British government securities declined from 86.8 per cent in 1913 to 24.6 per cent in 1918. The entire increase in bank deposits between June 1917 and December 1918, a total of £467 million, representing 40 per cent of total deposits, was generated by the needs of war finance.[17] In France in December 1914 31.07 per cent of all advances from the banks were made to the government; four years later this figure stood at 63.7 per cent. The gross profits of the Banque de France itself, which had averaged 52 million francs a year up to 1913, had reached 344 million in 1919—almost entirely through state business.[18]

Long-dated government stock and its absorption in a pattern of long-term bank deposits—for all its discounting and the consequent expansion of the money supply—had one major anti-inflationary effect: it reduced liquidity. The latent inflation generated by wartime borrowing could therefore be kept in check; the fact that governments adopted deficit financing during the war did not in itself guarantee hyperinflation after the war.

Germany's declared policy at the war's outset—that of borrowing—was certainly in marked contrast to Britain's formal position. But, to reiterate a point, its gross effect in cash terms was less different. By the end of the war 90 per cent of the ordinary budget was devoted to interest payments on war debt; in other words, Germany—unlike some other belligerents—serviced its war debt out of ordinary revenue and still had a surplus. Taxation made at least some contribution to Germany's war costs: the customary calculation is 6 per cent.[19] But total tax revenue, if the states are included, was at least 16.7 per cent, and possibly 17.7 per cent,

---

[14] P. Barret Whale, quoted in Gall *et al.*, *Deutsche Bank*, 130–1.
[15] Caesar, *Zeitschrift für bayerische Sparkassengeschichte*, V (1991), 72, 85–91.
[16] Teillard, *Emprunts de guerre*, 225.
[17] Grady, *British war finance*, 261; Morgan, *British financial policy*, 246–7.
[18] Fisk, *French public finance*, 42; Charbonnet, *Politique financière*, 143.
[19] Knauss, *Kriegsfinanzierung*, 175.

of all wartime spending.[20] The significant difference is the fate of the 94 per cent of Reich war costs not funded through taxation. In 1918 only 60 per cent of the debt was fixed in long-term loan stock, and fully 34 per cent consisted of floating debt. This was high, although certainly in France and possibly in Italy it was higher. But by 1920 the floating debt of the last two had fallen, while Germany's had grown to over 50 per cent.[21] Germany's primary problem at the war's end was excessive liquidity.

What was a vice in 1918 had been a virtue in 1914. At the war's beginning Germany's financial policy was directed to the achievement of liquidity. Borrowing was one manifestation of this overarching principle; the rejection of a formal moratorium was another. The limited and short-lived hike in interest rates served the same end: the Reichsbank's rate rose from 5 per cent to 6 per cent, but fell back to 5 per cent on 23 December 1914, and stayed there for the rest of the war. Anticipating that mobilization would not only generate a shortage of cash but would also leave industry short of hands, so causing unemployment and rendering plant idle, Germany flushed its economy with cash in order to stimulate activity. It recognized the danger of inflation, but believed that the evidence would be found not in the growth of the money supply but in the movement of prices. Price controls appeared reasonably effective in 1914 because prices were restrained by short-term unemployment. But, as employment levels rose and war orders generated competition for increasingly scarce goods, Germany needed to throttle back on liquidity. It could have applied harsher taxation or increased interest rates in order to draw in deposits. It did neither.

Symptomatic of the failure to rethink financial policy in terms of a long war and full employment rather than a short war and unemployment was the development of the *Darlehenskassen*. The *Darlehenskassen* offered an interest rate of up to 6.5 per cent (as against the Reichsbank rate of 5 per cent), and only required deposits to be fixed for between three and six months. Thus, cash remained effectively on call. Although designed to help commerce and private business surmount the liquidity

---

[20] Balderston, *Economic History Review*, 2nd series, XLII (1989), 228. By contrast Witt, 'Tax policies, tax assessment and inflation: towards a sociology of public finances in the German inflation, 1914–23', in Witt (ed.), *Wealth and taxation*, 141, reckons 97.7% of all expenses authorized during the war were covered by loans.

[21] Forsyth, *Crisis of Liberal Italy*, 101; Forsyth's figures give Germany's floating debt as 31% in 1918.

crisis of mobilization, their attractions soon drew in a different range of creditors. By 1916 25 per cent of their loans were to states and communes; a further 28.2 per cent were to banks; only 12 per cent were to trading and transport interests, 3 per cent to industry, and 0.7 per cent to agriculture. In 1917 74.9 per cent of loans were to states and communes. By then, of 7,700 million marks held in securities, only 89 million represented goods in kind; the vast majority were paper. At the end of the war the total issue of *Darlehenskassenscheine*, 15,626 million marks, was ten times the original authorization of 1,500 million. But, because the *Darlehenskassen* relieved it of a major burden, particularly in the funding of local government, the Reichsbank had little interest in calling a halt to what was going on. Moreover, the *Darlehenskassenscheine*, although currency in practice, were still not legal issue, and thus helped disguise the real—as opposed to the theoretical—increase in total circulation.[22]

The *Reichskassenscheine* (treasury notes) were declared legal tender on mobilization, and the Reichsbank intensified its efforts to trade these notes for gold. On 22 March 1915 10-mark notes—both the Treasury's and the Reichsbank's own—were introduced, and the total note issue was raised by 120 million marks. Thus, three types of irredeemable notes were in circulation—*Reichsbanknoten*, *Reichskassenscheine*, and *Darlehenskassenscheine*. Currency creation had become effectively autonomous, because it no longer rested on a combination of credit, goods, and gold but on credit itself. By the end of the war a third of the *Reichskassenscheine* in circulation were covered by deposited *Darlehenskassenscheine*, and a third of the *Darlehenskassenscheine* were held by the Reichsbank as security against their own note issue. In July 1914 total German circulation was 6,970 million marks: 2,909 million in Reichsbank notes, 172 million in treasury notes, 157 million in private bank notes, and 3,732 million in coin. In December 1918 circulation totalled 33,106 million marks: 22,188 million in Reichsbank notes, 10,109 million in *Darlehenskassenscheine* (i.e. minus the *Darlehenskassenscheine* held by the Reichsbank), 356 million in treasury notes, 283 million in private bank notes, and only 170 million in coin (as against a wartime low of 69 million in April 1918).[23] The quantity of notes and coin in circulation in Germany

---

[22] Knauss, *Kriegsfinanzierung*, 56; Bogart, *War costs*, 116–17; Dix, *Wirtschaftskrieg*, 216–17; Roesler, *Finanzpolitik*, 212–14.

[23] Roesler, *Finanzpolitik*, 217–18.

increased from 110 marks per head in 1914 to 430 million in 1918.[24] Most of this was in notes. Note circulation in Germany rose 1,141 per cent between late 1913 and late 1918, whereas the lack of small coin prevented shopkeepers giving change by 1916–17, and the coins that were in circulation were made of nickel and iron rather than silver and gold.[25]

Germany issued nine war loans between September 1914 and September 1918, with the purpose of redeeming its treasury bills and so wiping out its floating debt. Up until the issue of the fifth loan, in September 1916, this policy appeared to work.

The absence of a moratorium and the high level of liquidity at the war's outset enabled Germany to issue its first loan with alacrity. Given the underdeveloped nature of Germany's money market and the existing glut of government debt with which it was encumbered, it was essential that Germany exploit the initial mood of war enthusiasm in order to put its borrowing policy on secure foundations. In these terms, the first loan was a success. A total of 4,460 million marks was subscribed, producing a surplus of 1,832 million over the existing debt. The second, in March 1915, raised 9,060 million, a surplus of 1,851 million; the third, in September 1915, 12,101 million, a surplus of 2,410 million; and the fourth 10,712 million, a surplus of 324 million. But although the sums subscribed continued to rise in the subsequent loans, up until the eighth (issued in March 1918 and netting 15,001 million marks), they failed to keep pace with the growth in floating debt. The fifth loan was 2,114 million marks short of its target, the sixth (in March 1917) 6,732 million, the seventh (in September 1917) 14,578 million, and the eighth 23,970 million. The total of the last loan, issued in September 1918, fell back to 10,443 million marks, and left a shortfall of 38,971 million.[26] Thus, the Reich's floating debt doubled in the second half of 1916 from 7,000 million marks to 13,000 million, doubled again to 28,000 million by the end of 1917, and almost doubled again to 50,000 million by November 1918. Furthermore, these figures understated the problem, because war loans were directed at mopping up the short-term debt of the Reich and ignored its increasing use by local government.[27]

[24] Bartholdy, War and German society, 58; Cooper, Behind the lines, 119, 177.

[25] Hardach, First World War, 171.   [26] Helfferich, Money, 228.

[27] Manfred Ziedler, 'Die deutsche Kriegsfinanzierung 1914 bis 1918 und ihre Folgen', in Michalka (ed.), Der Erste Weltkrieg, 427; Chickering, Imperial Germany's Great War, 177.

Even before the fifth issue in September 1916 disquieting cracks were emerging. From 1915 the increase in subscriptions was falling behind the growth in the money supply and in the rise in prices. Thus their real value was declining. Indeed, the war loans were themselves contributing to this process. They were accepted as security by the *Darlehenskassen*, which issued their notes in exchange; these notes could be used by subscribers to buy more war loan stock, and by the Reichsbank as collateral for its own note issue. It was the war loan that gave the *Darlehenskassen* a higher profile: 70 per cent of their lendings were for subscriptions to the first issue, although their role declined thereafter.[28] Other credit institutions played key roles in the success of the scheme, but in doing so monetized goods or rendered liquid cash that was fixed. The savings banks were responsible for 19.8 per cent of the first subscription. For the third loan, in September 1915, the banks proposed special terms to those who had subscribed to the first and second issues. They would advance 75 per cent of their nominal value, and four times that amount could be subscribed to the new issue provided this stock too was deposited as collateral: thus, an initial investment of 10,000 marks in the first loan could grow to 36,997 marks over the nine loans of the war with no further cash payment.[29] The war loans were therefore mopping up money which they were helping to create.

The ability of the scheme to make real inroads into Germany's monetary overhang depended not on the financial institutions but on the loans' attractiveness to individual investors of modest means. Success here could compensate for a lack of rigour in direct taxation.

Overtly, this side of the story was more successful. The first loan offered individuals an interest rate of 5 per cent (as against an existing rate of 4 per cent on government stocks), convertible in tranches after ten years. Institutional investors were channelled towards treasury bonds which matured in five years. Subscribers totalled 1,177,235 and the stock, issued at 97.5, reached par very quickly. Helfferich capitalized on this success, which he felt justified the generous terms of the issue, by stressing the notion of 'financial conscription': loans were the contribution which those safe at home could make to the war effort. Available in small

---

[28] Helfferich, *Weltkrieg*, 211; Roesler, *Finanzpolitik*, 56–7.
[29] Bogart, *War costs*, 190; Feldman, *Great disorder*, 35.

denominations, advertised in posters and the press, and sold through post offices and banks, they were bought by increasing numbers of private citizens. The second attracted 2,691,060 subscribers, the third 3,966,418, and the fourth 5,279,645.[30] But these aggregates, as Helfferich's socialist critics were quick to point out, disguised some disquieting features. Of the total subscribed, 57 per cent had been taken up by 227,000 individuals, as opposed to 4 per cent by 3.3 million.[31] What concerned the socialists was that a few people in Germany still had the larger share of wealth; what concerned the organizers of the war loans was that the majority were not subscribing more.

The fifth war loan, that of September 1916, provided clear confirmation that the war loans policy was no longer meeting the objectives Helfferich had assigned it. Not only did it produce a shortfall on the floating debt to be consolidated, it also saw a decline in the number of subscribers to 3,809,976. Those contributing less than 200 marks fell from 2,406,118 for the fourth issue to 1,794,084: only for sums above 50,100 marks were the numbers of individual subscribers increased. The few were giving more; the majority less. In part this was a reflection of the cost of living, but it also bore testimony to the relatively depressing military situation. This interpretation is borne out by the sixth loan, issued in March 1917. Individual subscribers reached their highest total of the war (7,063,347) and those investing less than 200 marks more than doubled. Its success reflected the greater liquidity created by Hindenburg's programme for increased munitions output.[32] But it also coincided with two promises of ultimate victory—revolution in Russia and the move to unrestricted U-boat war. The seventh loan (September 1917) witnessed another fall in the number of subscribers, to 5,530,285, and it required the March 1918 offensives on the western front to pull the eighth back up to 6,869,901. The ninth, issued in September 1918, could draw in only 2,742,446 investors, with the wealthy minority making a disproportionate contribution. By 3 October exchanges were refusing to buy war loans, and the market price in Bavaria had fallen to 70 per cent of par.[33]

[30] Helfferich, *Weltkrieg*, 217–19; Roesler, *Finanzpolitik*, 54–7, 206–7; also Lotz, *Staatsfinanz-wirtschaft*, 32–41.
[31] Williamson, *Helfferich*, 138.   [32] Knauss, *Kriegsfinanzierung*, 152.
[33] Hanssen, *Diary of a dying empire*, 310–11.

The volatility of popular support for the war loans after 1916 prompted the government to pursue the big investor with more ardour. The consequences were doubly damaging. First, those workers who were in employment, and especially in war-related industries, were left with money in their pockets. Secondly, industry and finance insisted that they needed their resources in sufficiently liquid form to be available at the war's end for demobilization, reconstruction, and the recapture of export markets. Short-term loans at 4.5 per cent were not sufficiently disadvantageous, given a rate of 5 per cent on longer-term stock, to encourage a shift from the former to the latter. In March 1917, anticipating the redemption of the treasury bonds of the initial war loan issues in 1918, the Reich tried to lure institutional investors to convert their short-term stock into longer-term capital growth. Treasury bills, still paying 4.5 per cent, were offered at 98 but would be redeemable at 110. Redemption was phased according to the date of the war loan which was to be converted, and would be completed in fifty years, in 1967. But the possibilities for exchange were too limited, and only 2,100 million marks were consolidated in this way.[34]

Therefore, in 1917–18 large credit balances were accumulating in bank accounts, earning rates of interest comparable with, or little below, war loan stock. In the first half of the war, three-quarters of the floating debt was held by the Reichsbank; this changed after 1916, and by 1918 well over 50 per cent was taken up by the money market. The balances of the seven major Berlin banks rose from 11,140 million marks in 1916 to 21,979 million in 1918, the bulk of the increase being attributable to treasury bills. From here it entered the secondary reserve against note issue. But over the same period, 1917–18, the velocity of circulation more than halved. Money was not being spent, it was being hoarded. In the short-term, therefore, Germany's liquidity did not create hyperinflation. But the preconditions were in place.[35]

The broad intentions of Austria-Hungary's policy were the same as those of its ally, to finance the war primarily through borrowing. However, Austria-Hungary was less wealthy. The creation of liquidity was not, as in Germany, simply a matter of realizing goods and assets; it also

[34] Roesler, *Finanzpolitik*, 132–3; Lotz, *Staatsfinanzwirtshaft*, 35–9.
[35] Roesler, *Finanzpolitik*, 220, 91–5; Balderston, *Economic History Review*, 2nd series, XLII (1989), 238–40 .

necessitated raiding the empire's pre-war capital. There was a limit to what could be monetized. By 1918 Austria-Hungary's war expenditure, alone of that of all the belligerents, was below its pre-war annual national income.[36] Furthermore, a corollary of relative poverty was an under-developed money market. The postal savings bank was designed in 1910 to lead consortiums of banks in the raising of national credits; it failed to raise a loan of 100 million crowns in 1912, and during the war it remained more subject to the banks' views than vice versa.[37] As elsewhere, the activities of commercial banks expanded under the stimulus of war, but they did so from a lower base point than in Germany, and accordingly the government's debt was less widely distributed. In Austria-Hungary, therefore, a greater burden fell on the central bank. In Germany the advances made to the government by the Reichsbank were comparable in frequency with loans raised from the public; in Austria-Hungary the Austro-Hungarian Bank contributed twice as often as the public.[38]

The suspension of the Bank act on 4 August proved to be the first step towards a laxity in accounting from which the government benefited and of which parliament (because it did not meet) could not disapprove. Weekly accounts ceased to be published. Not until December 1917 did the bank hold its first general meeting of the war—when the close relation-ship between bank and state was at last fully revealed. In February 1918 a further meeting adopted in one fell swoop all the accounts for the years 1914, 1915, 1916, and 1917. By then the bank had advanced 13,000 million crowns to Austria and 6,000 million to Hungary.[39] At the end of the war these figures stood at 25,060 million crowns and 9,909 million.

The relationship between the bank and the empire, called into being by the mobilization and prolonged by the moratorium (which denied other possible approaches to the money market), was put onto a regular footing on 15 July 1915. The bank advanced the two governments 1,500 million crowns, secured on treasury bills paying 1 per cent interest per annum. No pattern of repayment was fixed; this was to be discussed six months after the war's end. No limit to the number of loans was agreed; by October 1918 the two governments had taken out twenty-one such loans. Each advance was for the same amount, but the periods between

[36] Bogart, *War costs*, 106.   [37] Spitzmüller, *Memoirs*, 62–3, 161.
[38] März, *Austrian banking*, 208.   [39] Müller, *Finanzielle Mobilmachung*, 33–41.

loans became progressively shorter: whereas Austria did not exhaust its first tranche for three months, its final instalment ran out in two weeks. In exchange, the two governments agreed not to issue any state paper currency. Therefore the bank had total charge of the note issue. It vowed to do its best to limit this. But the security on which the circulation rested was the loans which the bank advanced to the government, and these were unlimited.

After the war Popovics maintained he had done no more than his patriotic duty. He also suggested that the alternative to the July 1915 agreement was a takeover by the army. But, on his own account, his underlying fear was the threatened assumption of note-issuing powers by the two governments. Conversely, he regarded his primary achievement as the involvement of the issuing banks in the system of war finance: it was now up to them to offer interest rates high enough to absorb the currency which would enter circulation.[40] What he forebore to mention were the increased profits accruing to the Austro-Hungarian Bank as a result of government business. In 1914 the bank's profits had been 57.9 million crowns; in 1916 they reached 136.9 million. Although these were gained at the state's expense, they were—through the war profits tax and the tax on banknotes—in part recouped. Furthermore, the interest rate was reduced to 0.5 per cent because the income of the two governments could not keep pace with the increase in their debt. But Popovics still hoped to use the profits to build a reserve in gold and foreign exchange in 1917 and 1918. Ultimately, however, the bank's solvency had become dependent on the solvency of the empire itself.[41]

The yield of each loan was divided so that Austria received 954 million crowns and Hungary 546 million. The split, therefore, followed the budgetary allocation of financial responsibility. But it did not mirror the rate of wartime spending. Hungary's demand for cash was much less pressing than that of Austria. In part this reflected a slightly more vigorous pursuit of the alternative forms of credit, but more significant was the difference in burden assumed by the two monarchies. Austria was more industrialized and involved in more areas of warlike activity; it was also much more generous in welfare payments. At the war's end Austria owed the bank 25,560 million crowns, Hungary 5,740 million.

---

[40] Popovics, *Geldwesen*, 70–9.   [41] Müller, *Finanzielle Mobilmachung*, 38–41.

Furthermore, Austria had exhausted its credit on 30 October 1918; Hungary still had 5,500 million crowns in hand. The loans were therefore raised in accordance with the constitutional needs of the empire, not according to its spending requirements. However, it would be unreasonable to leave this as further evidence of a rapacious and parasitical Hungary. The currency which the borrowing policy depreciated was an imperial one, but the main cause of the depreciation was Austria. Thus, 'the forced loan' which the note issue represented was levied disproportionately on Hungary.[42]

Banknote circulation in the dual monarchy increased 1,396 per cent during the war. The average monthly circulation was 2,405,350,660 crowns in July 1914, and 34,888,999,890 in December 1918.[43] Metallic cover slumped from 40 per cent to 2.7 per cent by the end of 1917. Almost half of the note increase occurred in 1918 itself. Popovics blamed the recall of the Austrian parliament on 30 May 1917. Until then the balance in the relationship between Austria and Hungary had been preserved; after it Austria's bank debt all but doubled (from 13,000 million to 25,000 million crowns), whereas Hungary's grew by a third (from 6,200 million to 9,900 million).[44] Parliament spent money on reconstruction and on family allowances which pushed cash back into private pockets. However, unlike in Germany, money was not hoarded. The commercial banks saw a large increase in their business, but no proportionate growth in private deposits. Clients moved away from savings banks as they preferred to keep their cash on call.[45] Popovics's strategy depended on the issuing banks fixing the inflated currency through attractive interest rates. So comprehensively did the policy fail that in March 1918 the governments effectively reneged on their agreement not to issue their own currency by introducing *Kassenscheine*, treasury bills designed to mop up the excessive banknotes.

Austria-Hungary found itself locked in a paradoxical spiral of excessive liquidity and insufficient cash. Banking had too weak a foothold to cope with the liquidity created by the mobilization and government spending.

---

[42] Gratz and Schüller, *Wirtschaftliche Zusammenbruch*, 171–6; Winkler, *Einkommensverschiebungen*, 272.

[43] Walvé de Bordes, *Austrian Crown*, 46–7.

[44] Popovics, *Geldwesen*, 154.

[45] Müller, *Finanzielle Mobilmachung*, 67–72.

Small firms found their debts rapidly written off, not least by depreciation; the banks were then bypassed in the bid to acquire raw materials
before prices rose. Consequently money was moved into goods as soon as
possible, and the competition to do so—given the shortage of goods—
forced up prices, therefore creating the need for yet more cash. Rising
prices meant that assets in kind could always be sold at a profit, and the
difference between the cost of borrowing and the growth in prices assured
the middlemen of a dividend. Thus, in Austria-Hungary the velocity of
circulation grew even during the war, and—unlike in Germany—hyper-
inflation was already entrenched in 1918.

The publicly issued war loans could not in these circumstances be used
to redeem the advances made by the Austro-Hungarian Bank. Rather,
they were spent directly on the procurement of war-related goods. Short-
term debt was not consolidated; instead, it was renewed and extended.[46]

Although the watchword of the dual monarchy became 'the war
finances the war',[47] Vienna was slower off the mark in issuing its first
loan than Berlin. The moratorium made it difficult for those with assets to
get access to them; domestic liquidity remained low until government
spending entered circulation; and the military victory required for a
successful flotation proved stubbornly slow in coming. Despite the continuing lack of the latter, the exhaustion of credit and the return of
liquidity led to the first war loan in November 1914. In Austria the stock
was offered at 97.5, paying interest of 5.5 per cent, and redeemable in 1920.
In Hungary the price was 96.5 and the interest rate 6 per cent. No upper
limit was set. Austria raised 2,153.5 million crowns and Hungary 1,184.98
million.

The banks agreed to lend against the collateral of the war loans at the
current discount rate to 75 per cent of their face value. On this basis the
loans were an attractive proposition. The continued closure of the stock
exchanges shut off other avenues for speculation, and borrowing from
the bank to lend to the state would show a profit. However, the effect was
to draw in capital rather than income. Industrial investment was therefore undermined. Efforts were made to encourage the small subscriber:
the lowest denomination was 100 crowns, and units of 25, 50, and
75 crowns were offered through post offices. But the principal element

[46] Bogart, *War costs*, 195.   [47] Müller, *Finanzielle Mobilmachung*, 10.

in the subscriptions were advances of between 10,000 and 50,000 crowns. The lenders were drawn disproportionately from Vienna, the Alps, Bohemia, and Moravia—and in Hungary from the Magyars. Thus, despite the apparent success of the first loan, it already lagged behind the increase in circulation; and its claim on patriotism showed that feeling to be as unevenly distributed as the empire's private wealth.

The first three Austrian loans were issued as treasury bills, the maturity extending to ten years on the second and fifteen on the third. However, the fourth loan, framed in April 1916, offered a choice between a forty-year bond at 93 or a seven-year bill at 95.5, both paying interest at 5.5 per cent. The aim was, of course, to reduce the short-term debt and dampen domestic liquidity. Small savers—those investing in 100-crown units— constituted 258,000 of the loan's subscribers, as against 55,000 for the first issue. But the institutions were reluctant to commit funds for so long a period. As Austrian finance minister, Spitzmüller despaired of the commercial banks: 'I had to consider myself lucky if I succeeded in the conversion of at least one of the earlier war loans.'[48] And in subsequent loans the banks became the dominant element. Having taken 40.6 per cent of the first loan, they subscribed to 58.5 per cent of the eighth and last. They did not retain the stock which they acquired but quickly rediscounted it. Thus, the war loans were achieving neither of their principal fiscal roles—they were not absorbing privately held cash, and they were not shifting floating debt into long-term borrowing.

Austria's eight loans netted a nominal 35,129.3 million crowns. Hungary floated thirteen government loans, seven at 6 per cent and the others at 5.5 or 5 per cent, and a further four through the banks: they raised 18,851.8 million crowns. The greater frequency and better rates of Hungary's issues helped explain its lesser dependence on the Austro-Hungarian Bank. The ratio of sums raised between the two monarchies was in line with their budgetary relationship—64.7 : 35.3. But Hungary floated its stock on the Austrian market, and therefore added 3,200 million crowns to the burden borne by Austria.[49] Of the Austrian loans, the seventh, which totalled 6,045.9 million crowns, was nominally the most successful. In terms of real purchasing power, however, only the

[48] Spitzmüller, *Memoirs*, 161.
[49] Gratz and Schüller, *Wirtschaftliche Zusammenbruch*, 176–7.

third raised more than the first; the seventh was worth 41 per cent of the first, and the eighth 24 per cent.[50]

The fragility of Austria-Hungary's economic and industrial development confronted it with irreconcilable demands in its credit operations. It might have soaked up more note issues if it had raised interest rates. But it was pathetically anxious not to divorce itself from the patterns adopted by the other banks of Europe. Only too aware of its own underdeveloped money market, it mortgaged its short-term position in the hope of retaining its post-war status. But, even if the Austro-Hungarian Bank had increased its discount rate, the effect might well have been either neutral or nugatory. The war needs of the state were so insistent as to overwhelm the deflationary effects of any interest rate, however high. And ultimately, higher rates would only have added to the burdens of war finance already borne by the dual monarchy.[51]

Of the Entente powers, Russia's position was that most akin to Austria-Hungary's. Its banking system and money market were underdeveloped. The profits to be gained by the quick turnover of goods in a depreciating currency encouraged the growth of middlemen and caused the banks to be bypassed. These factors accelerated circulation. But, unlike Austria-Hungary, hoarding then had a dampening effect. Peasants reverted to type and simply opted out of the cash economy; one estimate has calculated that perhaps half the total note circulation was hoarded.[52]

The corollary of hoarding in Russia was the failure of the publicly issued war loans to draw in privately held funds. Russia issued seven war loans between November 1914 and March 1917. Most had a fifty-year life (the seventh was to run for fifty-five years) but could be redeemed after ten years. The first was offered at 95 and paid 5 per cent. It totalled 466.6 million roubles. The third, issued in May 1915, brought the price up to 99, but in return paid 5.5 per cent interest over the first six years and 5 per cent thereafter. The fourth (November 1915), fifth (March 1916), and sixth (October 1916) combined both the inducement of a low price, 95, and the higher interest rate of 5.5 per cent. The seventh, the so-called Liberty Loan issued by the Provisional Government, brought the interest rate down to

[50] März, *Austrian banking*, 134–42, 189–91, 208, 236–7, 243; Popovics, *Geldwesen*, 59, 65–6, 81–2; Winkler, *Einkommensverschiebungen*, 78, 272.

[51] Popovics, *Geldwesen*, 163–5

[52] Hardach, *First World War*, 168.

5 per cent, but went on sale at 85. This provided a total annual yield to the investor of 5.88 per cent (as opposed to 5.318 for the first loan), and brought in the highest nominal subscription, 3,841.4 million roubles. The combined proceeds from the seven loans were 11,378,289,000 roubles against a theoretical target of 12,010,000,000.[53]

The lowest unit offered in the first loan was 50 roubles. As elsewhere, press and propaganda campaigns tried to lure the small investor. The subscription period was extended from seven days for the first loan to forty-six for the fifth. But private individuals were reluctant to respond. The seventh loan was offered in units of 20, 40, and 50 roubles. The Provisional Government harped on its claims to popular support, and the soldiers' and workers' soviet hinted at more direct methods. But by July 1917, after three months, only 2 per cent of the Petrograd population and 4 per cent of Moscow's had subscribed.[54]

The success of the loan issues, therefore, rested with the banks. They took about three-fifths of the first two issues, and about half overall. Their commission—3 per cent at first, and 2 per cent on later issues—was high, and substantially reduced the total yield. Many of their subscriptions were in the form of paper securities. By December 1915 the State Bank's advances on paper reached 877 million roubles, and by May 1917— after a lull in 1916—topped 1,000 million roubles. The State Bank itself thus kept its own holdings of paper relatively constant, while the government found itself rediscounting existing government debt rather than clawing back circulating cash.[55] Indeed, the effect of the banks' involvement was to increase circulation, not reduce it. The savings banks drew in money that its owners intended to hoard, and which would therefore have been withdrawn from circulation. But by subscribing to war loans they put this money back into the hands of the government, who then spent it and so restored it to circulation.[56]

The actual note issue effectively doubled in each year of the war. From 1,633.3 million roubles at the end of July 1914, it rose to 2,946.5 million at the beginning of 1915, 5,617 million at the beginning of 1916, and 9,097.3 million at the beginning of 1917. By November 1917 and the Bolshevik

---

[53] Michelson et al., *Russian public finance*, 249–56; Bogart, *War costs*, 176–80.
[54] Michelson et al., *Russian public finance*, 274–5; Claus, *Kriegswirtschaft Russlands*, 4–6.
[55] Claus, *Kriegswirtschaft Russlands*, 6–7, 43.
[56] Michelson et al., *Russian public finance*, 265–9.

revolution 18,917 million roubles were in circulation. The impact of mobilization and then of the Provisional Government's policies can best be illustrated by the average monthly issue, which hit 310.4 million roubles after the outbreak of war in 1914, but fell in 1915 and 1916, only to rise after March 1917 first to 1,083 million and then—by October—to 1,516 million. The state printing works could not keep pace, and the involvement of private firms eased the path to counterfeit production.[57]

The State Bank's note issue was secured on the collateral of 5 per cent treasury bills. The initial authorization for 400 million roubles in treasury bills had risen to 6,000 million by the end of 1915, 12,000 million by October 1916, and 25,000 million by October 1917. The actual amounts outstanding never reached these ceilings. The vast majority were taken by the State Bank: it held 82.4 per cent of the total in July 1915. Efforts were made to distribute the short-term debt more widely. The bills became increasingly negotiable, and advances on them of 95 per cent of par at 5.5 per cent were authorized. The Provisional Government made payments in treasury bills for contracts, rising to 50 per cent of the total over 200,000 roubles. But although the State Bank's holdings reduced to 65.3 per cent of all treasury bills in June 1916, they climbed back to 73.7 per cent in September 1917. Efforts to convert this floating debt into long-term loans were no more successful. The interest rate on the treasury bills was sufficiently high to drive out treasury bonds by 1915— the 4 per cent 'series', interest-bearing notes with a life of four years which circulated like currency, raised only 850 million roubles.[58] By October 1917 48 per cent of Russia's debt was in short-term treasury bills.[59]

Russia's borrowing, therefore, rested just as much as Austria-Hungary's on an interlocking relationship between the government and the central bank. Of 38,649 million roubles of war expenditure, 16,426.5 million were funded through treasury bills, the majority of them lodged with the State Bank; of a further 11,408.2 million raised through domestic loans, over half was generated through the banks.[60] But the short-term treasury bills held by the State Bank as collateral did not keep pace with

---

[57] Ibid. 379–80; Claus, *Kriegswirtschaft Russlands*, 14–16, 18–19.

[58] Michelson *et al.*, *Russian public finance*, 280–6, 373–4, 381; Claus, *Kriegswirtschaft Russlands*, 7–9.

[59] Ferguson, *Pity of war*, 326.

[60] Michelson *et al.*, *Russian public finance*, 324.

the note issue held by the Treasury in exchange.[61] Thus, the government's debt was not even notionally covered by the credit-creating devices of the day. The issue of paper notes, over and above government borrowing, covered 31.1 per cent of war expenditure.[62]

Italy's story ought to have been similar—and in some respects was. The poverty of the population and the low level of national wealth both ensured that propaganda drives to urge small investors to subscribe to war loans would not prove particularly lucrative. Industry was urged to use its wartime profits to write off its own debts, not to buy government stocks. Thus, as in Russia, the state looked to the banks. But the inflationary implications were kept in check by relatively low levels of liquidity and by the consolidation of a higher proportion of the total borrowing in long-term debt.

Italy's first war loan was floated before it entered the war, in January 1915. Its arms spending prompted an issue of 1,000 million lire in twenty-five-year obligations, offered at 97 and paying 4.5 per cent in interest. Only 881 million was subscribed—a reflection, it was argued, of public support for Italy's neutrality. But in any case, the terms of the loan were not particularly attractive and the financial community proposed to wait until the government came back to the market with a better offer. A banking consortium, headed by the Bank of Italy, which had underwritten half the issue had therefore to produce the shortfall, 119 million lire. By late May 1915 the price of the stock had fallen to 95.32.

The concessions to experience in the second war loan, issued in July 1915, were minimal. The only change in the terms was the reduction in price from 97 to 95, and for subscribers to the original loan to 93. Once again the banks had to come to the rescue—underwriting 200 million lire and making loans of up to 95 per cent of the amount subscribed. A total of 1,145.8 million lire was eventually raised, but by the end of September 1915 the price was 93.92 and falling.

The terms of the third loan, in January 1916, were more attractive: a price of 97.5 at an interest rate of 5 per cent produced a real return of 5.13 per cent per annum. The target figure of 1,500 million lire was exceeded. Pre-war treasury bonds were accepted for up to half the total; most of the

[61] Claus, *Kriegswirtschaft Russlands*, 16.
[62] Michelson *et al.*, *Russian public finance*, 220.

first and second war loans were converted. A total of 3,018.1 million lire was raised, 891.4 million of it in securities. But again the price fell: in October 1916 it stood at 93.7.

The fourth war loan, that of January 1917, was a perpetual rent, and the government stated it would not be converted for fifteen years. Issued at 90 and paying 5 per cent interest, it raised 3,798.5 million lire, a third of which represented conversions of earlier stocks. Initially the price rose, but by June it had settled below 90. The final wartime issue, in January 1918, was offered in the aftermath of Italy's defeat at Caporetto. The banks thought 2,000 million lire a realistic ceiling, but Francesco Nitti, the finance minister, was determined to engineer a propaganda and political triumph out of the loan drive, and set a target of 6,000 million. By dint of extending the subscription period to March, and of offering life insurance policies against subscriptions, he succeeded. Two-thirds of the total was raised in cash, and one-third in securities.[63]

As elsewhere, the banks' support of the war loan issues provided the basis for the expansion of credit rather than for the absorption of cash. Industry was encouraged to take on loan stock; from October 1915 contractors could be paid in treasury securities; and from January 1918 firms could treat their loan subscriptions as capital exempted from war profits tax.[64] But having acquired the stock, companies rapidly disposed of it. Hence the fall in prices, which hit—and in due course deterred—the small investor. The government's securities were therefore taken on by the banks as collateral, so expanding their commercial portfolios. In December 1918 approximately 2,800 million of 10,845 million lire in treasury paper securities were held by the four largest commercial banks.[65]

But what was significant in the Italian case was that this process took root relatively late in the war. The first three war loans caused an expansion of credit as investors borrowed to subscribe to the issues, but contraction followed as banks called in their debts and as the stock price fell. Not until 1917, as the institutional share in the high targets increased, did the expansion of credit fail to fall after the issue of the loan.

Furthermore, the proportion of short-term debt to long-term also remained relatively low until late in the war. In 1914 5.59 per cent of the national debt was floating; in 1915 14.85 per cent; in 1916 15.6 per cent; in

---

[63] Forsyth, *Crisis of Liberal Italy*, 105–11, 117–21, 306.
[64] Teillard, *Emprunts de guerre*, 277–8.   [65] Forsyth, *Crisis of Liberal Italy*, 115–16.

1917 22.07 per cent; and in 1918 27.06 per cent.[66] The major increase in floating debt did not occur until the summer of 1916. Between July 1916 and November 1917 almost 1,000 million lire were advanced—in secret— by the Bank of Italy to the government on the security of low-interest treasury bills. In the twelve months after July 1916 short- and medium-term securities accounted for 58 per cent of all government securities (as against 20 per cent in the preceding year). But much of this was fixed in three or five year bonds, and much also was consolidated in the fifth war loan in 1918.[67]

Both Antonio Salandra, Italy's prime minister between March 1914 and June 1916, and the Bank of Italy pursued a policy of tight monetary control. The August 1914 crisis in the Italian case arose from the panic on the stock exchanges; falling prices for industrial shares hit the mixed banks that had financed industry, and undermined the value of the collateral held by the credit institutions. Salandra allowed only a small increase in note circulation, preferring to back the Bank of Italy's wish for a moratorium. The Bank remained liable for tax on additional note issue. Furthermore, it feared that any government guarantees on the lines followed by London would enable the commercial banks to pass on their bad debts to the state. Thus Italy risked recession in 1914—which it evaded through the war-led boom—rather than inflation.[68]

Italy's total note circulation rose 504 per cent in the First World War.[69] Between 1914 and 1919 the issue of the banks rose 618.75 per cent, and the issue of state notes 355.08 per cent.[70] The restraint of the government is evident in its handling of state notes, whose maximum, fixed at 500 million lire in December 1910, rose in steady but small steps to 2,200 million in November 1918. The main injection of cash came in the wake of Caporetto: the note issue expanded 23 per cent in 1914, 31 per cent in 1915, and 27 per cent in 1916, but 59 per cent in 1917 and 38 per cent in 1918. The total, which stood at 3,530 million lire on 31 December 1913, had by the end of 1916 doubled in three years, but by the end of 1918—after a further two years—had doubled again, amounting to 15,900 million lire.[71]

---

[66] Fisk, *French public finance*, 139; Forsyth, *Crisis of Liberal Italy*, 101, gives 5.9% in 1914 and 34% in 1918.
[67] Forsyth, *Crisis of Liberal Italy*, 111–16; Teillard, *Emprunts de guerre*, 168–73.
[68] Forsyth, *Crisis of Liberal Italy*, 125–30.   [69] Hardach, *First World War*, 171.
[70] Teillard, *Emprunts de guerre*, 338.   [71] Forsyth, *Crisis of Liberal Italy*, 134, 309.

France funded 83.5 per cent of its wartime expenditure through loans.[72] In 1919 its debt charges were 7,900 million francs a year, the equivalent of 120 per cent of its income from taxation.[73] By 1920 its internal debt expressed as a ratio of its national product was 1.64, as opposed to 1.26 for Britain and 0.27 for the United States. And yet its public debt grew more slowly in the war than did that of either of its western allies. This was a reflection of how high were the existing borrowings of the French government in 1914.[74] France's public capital was doubly immobilized at the outbreak of war—first by this debt and secondly by the moratorium.

The vital role played by the Banque de France in ensuring liquidity during the mobilization persisted for the rest of the war. On 4 May 1915 Ribot signed a new convention, setting a ceiling of 9,000 million francs (in place of 6,000 million) on the bank's advances to the government. In February 1917 the maximum was fixed at 12,000 million, in October at 15,000 million, in August 1918 at 21,000 million, and in June at 24,000 million. The Banque d'Algérie had advanced 75 million francs by December 1915, and contributed a further 45 million between then and May 1917, 80 million between May 1917 and January 1918, and 580 million over the last ten months of the war.[75] The principle of state financial probity, enunciated by Ribot, was affirmed by regular repayments of the debt from the yields of publicly issued war loans: by the end of 1918 7,400 million francs of Banque de France advances had been redeemed in this way, and 8,850 million in all. But 4,650 million francs were still outstanding. The practice was absurd, as the repayments in turn required the government to come back for regular increases in credit. A mechanism devised to surmount a short-term crisis became a funding method for conducting long-term war.[76] These advances constituted 10 to 15 per cent of total receipts from all sources between 1914 and 1919.[77]

The bank's loans took the form of an increase in note circulation. The maximum note issue, fixed at 12,000 million francs on 5 August 1914, settled at 40,000 million on 17 July 1919. Circulation rose progressively

[72] Jèze and Truchy, *War finance*, 193.   [73] Duroselle, *La Grande Guerre des français*, 154.
[74] Eichengreen, *Golden fetters*, 78–9.   [75] Charbonnet, *Politique financière*, 110–11, 145.
[76] Jèze and Truchy, *War finance*, 233–7; Martin, *Les Finances publiques de la France*, 132–5, 140.
[77] Fisk, *French public finance*, 14.

and evenly from 10,042 million francs at the end of 1914, to 13,216 million at the end of 1915, 16,580 million at the end of 1916, 22,336 million at the end of 1917, and 30,250 at the end of 1918.[78] The total increase over the war as a whole, 533 per cent, was comparatively modest.[79] Indeed, Keynes, in January 1915, felt that the Banque de France was being too conservative.[80] The emphasis on holding gold, almost for its own sake, meant the cover for notes was still 42.4 per cent in 1917. Thus, note circulation seemed to be set more by the needs of commerce and industry than by state policy. But the fact that it increased in line with the government's debt meant that for its critics the state was not as innocent as it claimed. In the first five months of 1918 circulation rose by 5,676 million francs, a rate of 247 million per week; one commentator averred that this was 'the only financial practice of a government whose chief blessed heaven that he had not been born an economist'.[81] By then too a major pressure for the increase in fiduciary circulation was the spending of the British and American armies, who purchased francs for pounds and dollars.

Treasury bills were—alongside the bank's advances—the other main method of French government borrowing in the early stages of the war. France used three main forms of floating debt. One, the advances of the *trésoriers-payeurs généraux*, was a revival of an earlier but dwindling practice. Two, national defence bonds and national defence obligations, were similar to the treasury bills used by other nations but were given more catchy titles to reflect the immediate needs of the state.

The advances of the *trésoriers-payeurs généraux* were effectively mortgages taken out by the government on taxation revenue that had yet to come in. By 1914 these loans, paying interest of 1.75 per cent, had fallen to 30 million francs. Ribot tried to revive them in December 1914, setting the interest rate at 2.25 per cent. But, although the return eventually rose to 3.5 per cent, only 285 million francs were raised in deposits.[82]

The most powerful competition to the advances of the *trésoriers-payeurs généraux* was national defence bonds. Before the war the ceiling

[78] Jèze and Truchy, *War finance*, 237–9.   [79] Hardach, *First World War*, 171.
[80] Johnson (ed.), *Collected writings of Keynes*, xvi. 48.
[81] Martin, *Les Finances publiques de la France*, 142; Duroselle, *La France et les français*, 211.
[82] Charbonnet, *Politique financière*, 150–4; Jèze and Truchy, *War finance*, 244–6.

on treasury bonds was fixed at 600 million francs, and the subscribers were banks and large companies. On 1 September 1914 the maximum was raised to 940 million francs, but only 350 million were in circulation. Ribot decided to rechristen them national defence bonds, and to invite public subscriptions. Paying 5 per cent free of tax, and sold in units of 100, 500, and 1,000 francs, for periods of three, nine, or twelve months, they proved immediately attractive. They functioned both as savings accounts for those looking for a hedge against wartime inflation and current accounts for those anxious to expand their businesses in wartime. They circumvented the constraints of the moratorium, they facilitated tax avoidance, and they did so against a background rhetoric of patriotic duty. They were fully subscribed by the end of November. A new maximum, of 1,400 million francs, was soon exceeded. National defence bonds raised 1,618.8 million francs in 1914, 7,985.8 million in 1915, 12,372 million in 1916, 12,630.7 million in 1917 and 16,429 million in 1918. The monthly increase in circulation—576 million francs in 1915, 785 million in 1916, 912 million in 1917, and 1,400 million in 1918—is probably a better indication of their enduring popularity. On 31 December 1918 22,000 million francs were in circulation.

National defence bonds were so easily convertible as almost to constitute currency; hence the importance of regular repayment if required so as to limit their inflationary effect. The Banque de France secured advances on the bonds of up to 80 per cent of their value. But, for all their importance in raising revenue the bonds were less successful in drawing in the deposits of small investors. Three-quarters of those subscribing in 1915 did so in blocks of 10,000 francs or more, and 34,692 subscribed for 100,000 francs each. For the rural smallholder, distant from a bank, the bonds' short-term convertibility was less useful: most in this category subscribed for one year, and many did not subscribe at all. Thus, the multiplication of types of unit available, not only upwards to 10,000-franc and 100,000-franc denominations but particularly downwards to 5- and 20-franc investments, was not as significant as might at first appear. In June 1918 the bonds were offered for periods as short as one month. By then the full 5 per cent was payable only on one-year investments; one-month bonds paid 3.5 per cent, three-month bonds 4 per cent, and six-month bonds 4.5 per cent. The disparity in interest rates was to some extent evened out by the price of issue, which for a three-month bond at 98.75 was closer to par than a one-year bond at 95.[83]

The success of the national defence bonds was both a blessing and a curse. The blessing consisted in France's success—at least compared with the other belligerents—in mobilizing the wealth of the public. Elsewhere almost all treasury bills and much of the war loan were taken up by financial institutions; in France most of the war loan and many of the treasury bills were held by private investors. The danger was the product of the very attractiveness of the national defence bonds: they were too nearly liquid. Little of the floating debt was fixed: between 1914 and 1919 76,000 million francs were raised in short-term debt and only 24,000 million in long-term. Furthermore, as the war ended Klotz loosened, rather than tightened, an already relaxed fiscal hold: 54,000 million francs of the short-term debt were issued between 1916 and 1919.[84] France's position seemed far more perilous than Germany's.[85]

What worried the government was less the spectre of inflation and more the fear that all its creditors would call in their debts at the same time. Ribot's intention was to consolidate far more of the debt represented in national defence bonds than actually proved to be the case.[86]

His first attempt, in January 1915, was to offer a series of ten-year national defence obligations at 96.5, paying 5 per cent interest free of tax. But the obligations failed to strike a chord with either the business community (who were reluctant to forfeit liquidity) or the public (whose enthusiasm was not encouraged by the obscure and complex methods of purchase). A second series was issued in February 1917. The five-year obligations were offered at par but paid a 2.5 per cent premium on maturity, and were thus designed to be held as investments until then.[87] They enjoyed no more success.

Initially Ribot was very reluctant to launch funded war loans. The evacuation of the government to Bordeaux, the desperate military

[83] Jèze and Truchy, *War finance*, 246–54; Charbonnet, *Politique financière*, 156–79; Ribot, *Letters to a friend*, 34–8; Martin, *Les Finances publiques de la France*, 149–55.

[84] Duroselle, *La Grande Guerre des français*, 160.

[85] Soutou, 'Comment a été financée la guerre', in La Gorce (ed.), *Première Guerre Mondiale*, 284; Eichengreen, *Golden fetters*, 79.

[86] Schmidt, *Ribot*, 121–2.

[87] Charbonnet, *Politique financière*, 191–203; Jèze and Truchy, *War finance*, 254–8; Knauss, *Kriegsfinanzierung*, 163.

situation, the closure of the bourse, and the effects of the moratorium—
all militated against a successful issue in 1914–15. Most immediate was the
effect of all these circumstances on the absorption of the 805 million franc
perpetual loan (*rente*) issued at 3.5 per cent on 7 July 1914. The loan,
intended to cover the equipment implications of the extension of military
service from two to three years, was nominally forty times oversubscribed. But it had been offered at a reduced price to institutions which
then planned to pass it on to private clients at a profit: the outbreak of the
war had checked this flow, requiring the institutions to pay the government but preventing the onward transmission to private investors. Thus,
the credit houses were immobilized. By the end of August 1914 the price of
the *rente* had already fallen from 91 to 82, and over half of the total had yet
to be paid. The government was obliged to rescue those who had specu-
lated on its stock if it was to free the market and guarantee its own credit.
On 11 September 1914 it admitted the principle of conversion at the issue
price provided the seller subscribed to future loans; it also used Banque de
France advances to buy up the stock. By February 1915 all but 30 million
francs of the target had been realized. The way was now open for the
launch of the first public war loan.[88]

Ribot's rescue package had effectively committed France to a policy on
war loans that followed the dictates of prestige and propaganda ahead of
those of fiscal prudence. To ensure success all four of France's war loans
were offered at rates well below par, with high levels of interest and free of
tax. The first and second loans (those of 1915 and 1916) were issued at 88;
the third (1917) was offered at 68.6 and the fourth (1918) at 70.8. Low
initial prices guarded against a fall in values and encouraged investment
for capital growth. However, the effect for the state was a decline in short-
term revenue and an increase in future debt. The necessary corollary of
such a policy ought to have been a low rate of interest. But France paid
5 per cent on the first two loans and 4 per cent on the last two.

This triumvirate of government forfeits was justified by the need to
consolidate the floating debt. The right to convert short-term stocks to
long-term issues was fundamental to the purpose of the scheme. But in
fact much pre-war debt, as well as all four war loans, were in the form of
perpetual *rentes*. And yet conversion from these as well as from national

[88] Charbonnet, *Politique financière*, 29–31, 35, 221–8; Ribot, *Letters to a friend*, 47–8; Johnson
(ed.), *Writings of Keynes*, xvi. 51; Jèze and Truchy, *War finance*, 259–62.

defence bonds was permitted in at least some of the war loan offers. Effectively, a fourth inducement was granted—the opportunity to transfer an existing long-term investment to yet more advantageous terms. For the state, the advantage in popularizing the *rentes* lay in the right of the government to choose when to repay its debt. Thus, it could stage its payments and so spread the burden; it could time redemption for when the price was low; and it could postpone it for so long that depreciation had eliminated the differential between the issue price and par.

The first war loan was launched in November 1915 and marked a definitive step to longer-term financial planning for the war. Individual subscribers totalled 3,133,389. Of 13,308 million francs raised, 6,285 million came in cash and 2,244 million in national defence bonds; the rest—national defence obligations, 3.5 per-cent 1914 *rentes*, and the pre-war 3 per cent *rentes*—represented existing long-term debt that was traded for more favourable terms. For the second loan, floated in October 1916, payments in instalments could be extended over six months, and pre-war 3 per-cent *rentes* were not convertible: it thus constituted a drive to draw in cash and national defence bonds. Of 10,082 million francs contributed, 5,425 million were subscribed in cash and 3,693 million in national defence bonds; 956 million came from national defence obligations; and just under 8 million from 3.5 per-cent *rentes*.

The profile of the third loan, opened on 26 November 1917, was remarkably similar—partly because Klotz set a target of 10 million francs, arguing that the length of the war now required regular, staged subscriptions rather than unlimited but less frequent drives for as much money as possible. Klotz put aside a small fund to enable the government to intervene in the market so as to keep up the price of the stock. The fourth loan, first offered on 20 October 1918, did not close until 24 November, and was dubbed the 'liberation loan'. Unlike the third, it was unlimited, and 7 million individuals subscribed 22,163 million francs—including conversions of 239 million francs of Russian government stocks.[89]

The relative success or failure of France's war loans policy can be measured in different ways. It never fully caught up with its late start: pundits in 1919 reckoned that France was two years behind on its loan

---

[89] Charbonnet, *Politique financière*, 254–320; Jèze and Truchy, *War finance*, 259–84; Ribot, *Letters to a friend*, 72–7.

issues. Their nominal yield—55,600 million francs—was reduced to 24,000 million net when allowance is made for the conversion of existing stocks.[90] Thus, they paid for a tenth of France's war expenditure, and their effective contribution was only a third that of national defence bonds. On the other hand, the issues never developed the institutional reliance on the banks characteristic of Austria-Hungary, Italy, and Russia. This is not to say that public subscription embraced large numbers of small investors. French sources are coy as to how many individuals subscribed to the second and third loans: the implication is that there were fewer than to the first. In the industrial area of Le Creusot subscriptions fell successively over the first three loans.[91] The average gross contribution per Frenchman in metropolitan France to all four loans was 1,405 francs; by contrast his compatriot in Algeria subscribed 1,633 francs.[92] The crux was the big private investor. Tax exemptions encouraged the very wealthy to advance more, and from 1917 the government accepted loan stock in payment for the war profits tax.[93]

France's management of its borrowing was, by the standards of pre-1914 financial orthodoxy, relatively cautious. It restricted its note issue as best it could; it fought to conserve its gold; its devices for domestic debt drew in privately owned deposits. By these criteria it should have been in a far stronger financial position after the war than Britain. Britain's total circulation in the war increased 1,154 per cent[94]—double France's and even slightly more than Germany's; it argued that gold was to be used, not hoarded; and it issued only three war loans, of which the first was directed at the banks and the last was offered as early as January 1917. Its annual average rate of borrowing as a proportion of its 1913 national income was, at 57.3 per cent, not significantly less than Germany's 62 per cent.[95] By the end of the financial year 1918/19 its total internal debt was £6,142 million, almost a tenfold increase on the national debt as it stood at the beginning of the financial year 1914/15.[96] Interest payments on the debt rose from 9.6 per cent of budgeted receipts in 1913/14 to 22.4 per cent

[90] Duroselle, *La France et les français*, 214–16.
[91] Becker, *The Great War and the French people*, 147.
[92] Meynier, *L'Algérie révelée*, 602.
[93] Jèze and Truchy, *War finance*, 278.   [94] Hardach, *First World War*, 171.
[95] Balderston, *Economic History Review*, 2nd series, XLII (1989), 229.
[96] Morgan, *British financial policy*, 114–15; Hirst and Allen, *British war budgets*, 14.

in 1920/1.[97] And yet Britain escaped the levels of inflation suffered by either France or Germany after the war.

It started the war with its debt at a historic low, and thereafter the sophistication of Britain's financial structure enabled it to withstand better the effects of wartime liquidity. Its patterns of borrowing—and indeed its sources of revenue as a whole—were much more diverse than those of other belligerents. It found it easier to change tack in its policies, and it was readier to do so. As the world's financial centre, London possessed a money market of greater sophistication and greater confidence. These qualities were important in enabling Britain to export its debt, to sell its stock overseas. Hence, much government debt did not enter the domestic banks' secondary reserves and so did not fuel the note issue; hence too, much of the interest paid by the government went to fill the pockets of overseas investors, so stoking inflation elsewhere rather than feeding monetary overhang at home.[98] But in addition, the confidence in Britain's credit which reinforced the marketability of its stock elsewhere, and especially of course in New York, was also an important element in enabling the absorption of government debt at home. The maintenance of the gold standard, however fictional in practice, may have had its most potent effects on the sterling–dollar exchange, but it was also a symbol of financial strength to investors in Britain.

The most obvious illustration of these points was the management of the increase in Britain's circulation. In June 1914, of a total circulation of £199 million, £161 million was in coin. By June 1918 £148 million was still in coin: an underpinning of hard currency was thus preserved. The significant change was, of course, the rise in note issue, from £38 million to £311 million over the same period. However, the impact of this expansion was diffused by the fact that it was accomplished in large part by the use of treasury notes. They were payable in gold, but because they had the imprimatur of the government their convertibility mattered less to the public than did that of banknotes. Initially the commercial banks made only limited use of them: authorized to accept the equivalent of 20 per cent of their deposit liabilities, a total of £225 million, they actually took only £13 million. Treasury notes entered the circulation, therefore, not in a

---

[97] Daunton, *English Historical Review*, CXI (1996), 883.

[98] This is the central argument of Balderston, *Economic History Review*, 2nd series, XLII (1989) 222–44.

flood but in a steady trickle. Government payments for contracts were their most obvious route. As the quantity increased so their issue was secured less by the gold reserve, which settled at £28.5 million in June 1915, and more by government securities. In August 1915 the ratio of gold to currency notes was 61 per cent; in August 1918 it was 16.9 per cent and, of £168.5 million in outstanding notes, £141.6 million were backed by government securities. Currency notes, therefore, freed both the government and the note circulation from the disciplines of the Bank of England. The government's credits were secured by loans, and it then transferred its credits back to its creditors so as to enable them to exchange the credits for the legal tender which the government also created. As long as no treasury notes were withdrawn, cash reserves increased in step with the government's borrowing.

The inflationary implications were immense. But two factors dampened their effects. The first was that, after the initial surge of liquidity on mobilization, the total circulation remained comparatively steady until 1917. The increase in the note circulation between 1915 and 1917 was offset by the withdrawal of £35 million in gold, and the total circulation rose by £56 million between June 1915 and June 1916, and by £42 million between June 1916 and June 1917. Not until after the summer of 1917 did the growth in the money supply again rise steeply. The pressures for cash included the desire to evade the excess profits duty, the need (as a result of inflation) for notes larger than £1 or 10 shillings, and the reluctance to use cheques after they became subject to stamp duty. Between June 1917 and June 1918 £98 million were added to the total circulation. The major increase, though large, was late.[99]

The second prop to domestic confidence in the note issue was its quarantining of the Bank of England. The beauty of treasury notes was that they ensured the liquidity required to fuel the war economy without impugning the status of the Bank of England's own currency or its gold reserves. Although the Bank act was suspended in 1914, the first major pressures on the Bank to increase its issue were not felt until 1917. By then the ultimate source of legal tender was no longer the Bank but the Treasury.

---

[99] Grady, *British war finance*, 14–36, 187, 194; Morgan, *British financial policy*, 216–26; Brown, *Gold standard*, 111–17.

This reversal in the balance of the relationship between the two would have been hard to predict in 1914. The principal agent in the creation of government credit on the outbreak of war was the Bank of England. Between August and November 1914 the government borrowed £35 million from the Bank. Known as 'ways and means advances', these funds represented the Bank's own borrowings from the commercial banks. When spent by the government, the money returned to the banks, so increasing their deposits and enabling them once again to lend to the Bank. The flow thus ran in parallel with that of treasury notes. The Bank's commanding position in this relationship was determined by its manipulation of its interest rate, which normally hovered two percentage points above the market rate. In 1915 the Bank rate was at times up to 3 per cent higher than that of the market. Internationally, the effect of the Bank's control was to give the London market a consistency and stability which it would not have enjoyed if the price for money had been determined by stockbrokers: this was the case in New York, and the rate there varied daily according to the dictates of the stock exchange. Domestically, the rate at which the Bank borrowed was ordinarily 0.5 per cent below that at which new treasury bills were issued. Thus, the Bank helped establish treasury bills, and hence government securities became much more attractive vehicles for investment than general deposits.[100]

The closure of so many stock exchanges in 1914 left many would-be investors searching for outlets for their funds. On 19 January 1915 the Treasury imposed an embargo on fresh capital issues that were not in the public interest. The effect was to reserve the London money market for government use. In 1916 the total value of capital issues in the United Kingdom was £585.6 million, as against £512.6 million in 1914, but of this total only £31.5 million (as opposed to £180.1 million in 1914) were not earmarked for government loans. The issues in 1917 were valued at £1,338.7 million, and all except for £40.9 million were government securities. The stock exchange was effectively regulated by the issue of treasury bills.[101]

By 4 November 1914 £82.5 million in six-month treasury bills had been sold at rates of between 3.5 and 3.75 per cent. Their issue was then suspended to allow the first war loan to be offered. The intention was

---

[100] Grady, *British war finance*, 66–8, 272–4; Sayers, *Bank of England*, i. 82–3.
[101] Grady, *British war finance*, 65; see also 59–66, 143–5, 276–9.

to repay the 'ways and means advances' and redeem the outstanding treasury bills. Priced at 95 and paying 3.5 per cent, the war loan's effective yield on maturity (between 1925 and 1928) would be 3.7 per cent. The Bank of England supported the issue by lending up to the full issue price at 1 per cent below the Bank rate. Not only did it lose on this deal (as the price fell to 90), but it also underwrote £113 million to enable the target figure of £350 million to be reached. The banks collectively subscribed £100 million as opposed to £91 million from the public. There were only 25,000 individual contributors. By pitching the minimum subscription at £100 (albeit payable in instalments over six months), and by keeping the interest rate low, the Treasury had deterred the public, and so failed to use the loan as an anti-inflationary device.[102]

With the launch of the first war loan completed the issue of treasury bills was resumed—initially with five-year exchequer bonds, and then with three-, six-, and nine-month bills, paying 2.75 per cent, 3.6 per cent, and 3.75 per cent respectively. Their aim was less to raise money than to stabilize the market rate of discount.[103]

In June 1915 McKenna launched the second war loan. Its aims were Keynes's—less the raising of new money and more the countering of domestic inflation by attracting small investors and the steadying of international exchange by pulling in American funds. Bonds of £5 and £25 and vouchers for 5 shillings were offered through post offices. McKenna employed Hedley Le Bas of the Caxton Advertising Agency, who had promoted army recruiting, to popularize its terms. 'We must give the investor something for nothing to make him lend his money to the country,' Le Bas observed. 'In other words, why not make patriotism profitable?'[104] Although the stock was issued at par, the interest rate was set at the much more attractive level of 4.5 per cent. The banks grumbled at the competition, but were softened by the Bank of England's readiness to lend to them so that they could in turn enable their customers to borrow in order to subscribe. The units were repayable in 1945, although they were redeemable at the government's option after ten years and could be converted for any later long-term loans at par. The principle of

[102] Knauss, *Kriegsfinanzierung*, 155–6; Johnson (ed.), *Collected writings of Keynes*, xvi. 95; Sayers, *Bank of England*, i. 79–81.

[103] Morgan, *British financial policy*, 108.

[104] Farr, 'McKenna', 119–20; see also 154–6 .

convertibility was also recognized for past issues, and accounted for £313 million (about a third of the government's outstanding stock) of the £900 million raised. McKenna had hoped for £1,000 million. Although the loan attracted over a million subscribers, over half of them bought units of £100 or more, and one-third of the new money was contributed by the banks.[105]

In 1916 government issues were dominated by medium-term stocks. Five-year exchequer bonds, paying 5 per cent, were issued in December 1915. In February 1916 war savings certificates, offered at 15s. 6d. but realizing £1 on maturity after five years, were aimed at the small investor. They were followed in June by war expenditure certificates, repayable in two years but convertible to war loans. In October a significant barrier was breached when exchequer bonds, convertible and paying interest free of tax, were offered at 6 per cent.

The 6 per-cent exchequer bond, designed to attract foreign funds, told a desperate story. Determined to reject exchange restrictions, the Bank had to counter the lure to investors of the New York market. In July it raised its rate to 6 per cent, far higher than that of any other belligerent. Three-month treasury bills, which paid 4.5 per cent in March 1916, were offered at 5.5 per cent in July; one-year bills earned 6 per cent between July and September. Outstanding treasury bills, to the tune of £800 million, clogged the money market in the late summer. The City was unhappy, as government rates were effectively depreciating existing stock. But the issue of a new war loan seemed inopportune as the battle of the Somme dragged on.[106]

Treasury bill rates fell in the autumn to accommodate the issue of exchequer bonds, and their sale was suspended altogether in January to allow the flotation of the third war loan. By now the American money market had eased, and the loan could be offered at a rate lower than 6 per cent. It was available in two forms—5 per cent stock issued at 95 and repayable in 1947, and 4 per cent stock issued at par, repayable in 1942, and free of income tax but not supertax. The former raised £2,075 million and the latter £52 million. The success of the 5 per-cent stock was

[105] Ibid. 108–9, 189–90; Knauss, *Kriegsfinanzierung*, 156–7; Johnson (ed.), *Collected writings of Keynes*, xvi. 103–5; Hirst and Allen, *British war budgets*, 57–64.

[106] Knauss, *Kriegsfinanzierung*, 157–8; Grady, *British war finance*, 143–4; Sayers, *Bank of England* i. 95–7.

interpreted as a reflection of confidence that taxation would fall after
the war. But it was also a product of conversion rights: almost all the
second war loan was exchanged for the third, and its price soared to 99.
The first war loan, which did not enjoy convertibility, fell to 84.75. The
arrangements for the third loan, therefore, included provision for a
sinking fund to buy war loan bonds when they fell below the issue
price. Just under half the total raised constituted new money.[107]

The third loan was the last of the war. Between 1914 and 1917 government policy was to consolidate floating and short-term debt through the
periodic issue of long-term stock. Thus, devices like treasury bills covered
the gaps between the major flotations. But after January 1917 short-term
and medium-term debt dominated. The effect was to bring interest rates
down and so make domestic borrowing cheaper. From April 1917, when
treasury bills were available on tap once more, their rate fell until in
February 1918 they paid only 3.5 per cent. The commercial deposit rate
declined even further to 3 per cent.

The first consequence of this policy was an inability to attract foreign
investment. In normal times the Bank would have responded to the
market and raised its rate. Its subordination to the requirements of the
state meant that it did not. But in November 1917 a differential rate was
established for foreign balances, which paid 4.5 per cent.[108]

The domestic consequence was a disincentive to the private investor.
By the end of 1917 the number of individuals holding government
securities had swollen from 345,000 in 1914 to 16 million. Of these, 10.5
million owned war savings certificates.[109] Lowering interest rates could
jeopardize this success, fostering liquidity and pushing up prices. That
the situation did not get out of hand was the result of extending the
policy of medium-term stocks begun in 1916. Five-year exchequer
bonds paying 5 per cent were made available again in April 1917, but
they only netted £82 million. In September they were withdrawn, and
replaced by national war bonds. Marketed in several different guises, but
embodying the principle of convertibility and interest rates of between
4 and 5 per cent, they raised £649 million in 1917–18 and £987 million in

---

[107] Morgan, *British financial policy*, 110–12, 192–4; Grady, *British war finance*, 131–3; Hirst and
Allen, *British war budgets*, 169; Knauss, *Kriegsfinanzierung*, 158–9.
[108] Morgan, *British financial policy*, 112–13, 179–80, 196.
[109] Knauss, *Kriegsfinanzierung*, 157–8; Bunselmeyer, *Cost of the war*, 137–8.

1918–19.[110] Thus, unlike the shorter-term debt of the other belligerents at the end of the war, much of Britain's was both more fixed and better adapted to absorb private purchasing power.

Nonetheless, the increase in medium-term bonds could not prevent a major surge in the floating debt. 'Ways and means advances', which had not been used in 1915 or for most of 1916, were resumed at the end of the latter year. By 31 March 1918 treasury bills totalling £973 million were outstanding. The debt was absorbed by the commercial banks. They contributed £400 million to the government's financing of the war between June 1914 and June 1917, but provided £470 million between June 1917 and December 1918. This represented the entire increase in the banks' deposits over the last eighteen months of the war; commercial advances fell from 49.6 per cent of their deposits at the beginning of the war to 32.5 per cent at its conclusion. The banks had become the creditors not of trade and industry but of the government.[111]

Britain, like the other belligerents, had a floating debt problem at the end of the war. But it was manageable and its reduction could be staged. Of its total domestic debt at the conclusion of the financial year 1918/19, £6,142 million, only £1,412 million was floating; £1,040 million was in medium-term debt due to mature in 1925. Furthermore, Britain had managed to distribute its debt over many sectors: by 1924 £765 million was held in extra-budgetary funds, £740 million in the banking system, £790 million by small savers, £1,775 million by larger individual investors, and £2,315 million in foreign and corporate holdings.[112]

Thus, through medium-term stock and through the spread of its creditors Britain contrived to mitigate the more inflationary aspects of its change in borrowing policy after 1917. Furthermore, its corollary, the low rate of interest, itself created a continuing confidence in British financial strength. Hindsight, conditioned by the knowledge that ultimately the international money market would shift from London to New York, from sterling to the dollar, might suggest that this was a false optimism. Remarkably, however, London's status as the world's creditor emerged from the war comparatively intact. In the month of the

---

[110] Knauss, *Kriegsfinanzierung*, 160; Morgan, *British financial policy*, 113–14.
[111] Morgan, *British financial policy*, 246–8, 296.
[112] Morgan, *British financial policy*, 114–15, 136.

armistice the London banks accepted $500 million worth of business compared to New York's $210 million.[113]

The crisis in British government borrowing had come in the autumn of 1916, when the interest rate peaked at 6 per cent. Domestically, short-term debt expanded to the detriment of long-term, while the Treasury faced a mounting burden of debt repayment. Internationally, Britain had a double dilemma. To maintain its hold on the money market, its rates had to remain competitive with New York. To draw in overseas funds it could, of course, let its rate rise, but to export its domestic debt it had to offer terms no more advantageous than those prevailing across the Atlantic. Its ability to surmount this crisis lay only partly in its own hands. The reduction in the cost of its own borrowing relied in turn on the maintenance of low interest rates in America. The sequence of exchange-rate crises and the complaints of harassed Treasury officials obscure the two fundamental financial advantages the United States conferred on Great Britain. It followed a policy of low interest rates, and it fostered the developing machinery of credit. Without the creation in New York of favourable conditions for the flotation of debt, the battle to preserve the sterling–dollar exchange would have been meaningless.

In April 1917 the banks of the United States were in an extraordinarily strong position, flush with gold, their structure reformed, and free of debt. But the American Treasury was still concerned that the Federal Reserve System was insufficiently flexible for the demands which it anticipated the United States's entry to the war would generate. On 21 June 1917 the legal reserve requirements of the member banks were reduced by 5 per cent. The effect was to create excess reserves which could then be used to expand deposits. Between June and December 1917 all deposits increased by 39.3 per cent and government deposits by 65.1 per cent. The member banks were required to pass their excess reserves over to the Federal Reserve district bank, so increasing the reserve ratio from 70.9 per cent to 78 per cent by August 1917. Between March 1917 and November the reserves of the district banks grew by 77 per cent, and by December 1919 by 125 per cent. On this basis the discounts of the Federal Reserve banks increased by a massive 2,548 per cent.[114]

---

[113] Bogart, *War costs*, 80–1.
[114] Gilbert, *American financing*, 177–88; also Petit, *Finances extérieures*, 439–43.

Expanded reserves also enabled an extension of the note issue. The crisis of August 1914 was bridged by the terms of the 1908 Emergency Currency act, fortuitously extended in 1914 for the purposes of covering the establishment of the Federal Reserve System. The act allowed up to $500 million to be added temporarily to the circulation on the security of shares and bonds. By mid-October 1914 $363.6 million were outstanding, but in November the Federal Reserve System became fully operational and the emergency currency was retired.[115]

The Federal Reserve act did not establish an absolute ceiling on American circulation; it confined itself to stipulating that a gold reserve of 40 per cent should be held against outstanding notes. The memory of the Civil War served to persuade Americans that the danger of inflation lay primarily in uncovered notes. Thus, their worry in the summer of 1917 was that for the first time since the war began their exports of gold exceeded their imports. Their response, to ban the export of gold and to concentrate holdings in the Federal Reserve System, meant that America ended the war with a gold reserve of $2,090 million against a Federal Reserve note issue of $2,802 million.[116] By then the Federal Reserve Bank held 74 per cent of the United States's monetary gold stock as opposed to 28 per cent at the end of 1916.[117] Even in relation to total circulation the gold cover looked more than adequate. In December 1916 $3,679 million were in circulation, in December 1917 $4,086 million, and in December 1918 $4,951 million. The ratio of Federal Reserve notes to the total circulation grew from .044 in June 1916 to .530 by December 1918.

But America's experience proved an object lesson in the dangers of simple or single explanations for inflation. Federal Reserve note issues rose 754 per cent between March 1917 and December 1919.[118] The money supply swelled by 60 per cent between 1913 and 1918, bank deposits increased by 94 per cent, but business only grew by 13 per cent. Thus, the mismatch between the availability of cash and the goods for purchase fed price increases.[119] America's industrial boom, fuelled by the Entente's orders for war goods, only exacerbated the problem. The pegging of exchange rates fixed American products at—by European wartime

[115] Noyes, *American finance*, 77–81.
[116] Helfferich, *Money*, 232; see also Petit, *Finances extérieures*, 440–3, 460–1.
[117] Chandler, *Strong*, 104.   [118] Gilbert, *American financing*, 188.
[119] Bogart, *War costs*, 356–7.

standards—artificially low prices. Thus, goods were taken out of domestic consumption while simultaneously overseas payments augmented domestic purchasing power.[120]

If inflation was the downside of American policy, the expansion of the stock market was the upside. Low interest rates contributed to liquidity but encouraged lending and investment. The Dow Jones index, which fell to 54.63 in January 1915 had recovered to 99.15 by December of the same year. From April 1915 New York was the only stock exchange which did not restrict the trade in foreign securities. As a consequence the growth in loans and non-governmental investments in 1916 was valued at $3,188 million.[121] Thus, the private financial sector was gearing up for wartime expansion before the American government itself generated any demands of it.

In April 1917 the United States's national debt was small and the burden of interest payments trivial. The scope for extension was considerable. But the success of McAdoo's borrowing policy was vitiated by the maintenance of low rates of interest. Already, between January and April 1917, government bonds suffered a slight fall, thus providing a clear indication that the popular success of war loans would depend on the attractiveness of their terms. McAdoo, however, was persuaded that patriotic sentiment, not financial self-interest, would woo the small subscriber. He insisted on selling government bonds at rates of interest less than those of the market. In doing so he helped keep down the price of money, to the benefit both of America's allies and of the industries of the United States. Expansion was never slowed because money was either unavailable or too costly. But the effect on government loans themselves was less positive. The price of the stock was depressed to below that at which it was issued and ultimately deterred the public. Consequently, America's war loans did not divert the growing purchasing power of its lower-income groups, and so failed to staunch inflation. Instead, the banks became increasingly important to government borrowing. The government's policy was that, by limiting credit to essential purposes and by encouraging the acquisition of long-term government securities, the war should be funded by 'the thrift of the people'. But in the three years up to June 1919 the commercial banks' credit

[120] Brown, *Gold standard*, 97; Gilbert, *American financing*, 43.
[121] Gilbert, *American financing*, 37, 42; Noyes, *American finance*, 101–8.

increased by $11,350 million, while their holdings of Treasury obligations and the loans on them rose by only half that. Thereafter the favourable conditions for credit were being exploited for non-essential purposes, and—as elsewhere—the expansion of the secondary reserve meant that war loans fuelled rather than quenched the money supply.[122]

McAdoo's general principle was that the war would be paid for by a mix of taxation and long-term war bonds. He met the government's current expenditure through short-term certificates of indebtedness. The Revenue act of 3 March 1917 authorized the issue of certificates of indebtedness to a ceiling of $300 million dollars; they paid 3 per cent interest. The legislation was linked to the receipt of taxation and therefore permitted a maximum maturity period of one year. But with the entry to the war the Treasury issued certificates of indebtedness which anticipated the four major war loans (or Liberty Loans, so called as they were to be used to wage war against autocracy). The first tax anticipation certificates were not offered until August 1918, and proved relatively unpopular—partly because their interest rate of 4 per cent was less than that then available through the loan anticipation certificates, and partly because the latter were more attractive to the banks. The Treasury prompted the banks to take up loan anticipation certificates so that subscriptions to the Liberty Loans proper would effectively be paid for before they were issued. It thus avoided large transfers of cash at any one time, and so prevented temporary restrictions on credit. From February 1918, anticipation certificates were marketed at fortnightly intervals; the banks were urged to subscribe 1 per cent of their gross earnings a week, and from April 5 per cent per month. The interest rate was fixed at 4 per cent in November 1917, and 4.5 per cent in February 1918. The banks responded by taking 83 per cent of the third and fourth Liberty Loan anticipation certificates. Non-bank subscribers, despite various taxation exemptions comparable with those available to holders of Liberty Loans, accounted for only 17 per cent. By 1 July 1919 48 series had been issued, totalling $21.9 million; 79.4 per cent of the Liberty Loan proceeds were used to refund Liberty Loan anticipation certificates.[123]

---

[122] Gilbert, *American financing*, 52–4, 117–19; Chandler, *Strong*, 109–18.
[123] Chandler, *Strong*, 145–61.

The first Liberty Loan was issued at par on 24 April 1917. The banks advised that a maximum of $1,000 million dollars could be placed at an interest rate of 4 per cent. McAdoo, persuaded by his own faith in popular patriotism, opted for $2,000 million at 3.5 per cent. The bonds matured in 1947, but the Treasury could redeem them after fifteen years. The smallest unit was $50, but special bonds of $10, which could be grouped into units of $100, were made available. Employers allowed employees advances on their salaries; firms fostered liquidity by declaring extra dividends; payment could be spread over five instalments. McAdoo's faith was rewarded with $3,035 million, subscribed by 4.5 million individuals. The bond-holding public in the United States expanded over ten times. Applications were therefore scaled down. Of the total subscribed, 42 per cent was in blocks of between $50 and $10,000; but of the $2,000 million of allocated units, 65 per cent was in this lower range. The effect was to restrain the benefits of the generous tax exemptions which the bonds offered. They were liable only for estate and inheritance duties, and thus a person paying income tax at the top rate of 67 per cent was being given the equivalent of 10.6 per cent in interest.[124]

McAdoo had been authorized to take out a loan of $5,000 million. He had therefore $3,000 million in hand. In August 1917 he requested authority to float the second Liberty Loan, which would incorporate the unused $3,000 million and add a further $4,500 million. His aim was to withdraw the privileges which the first loan had accorded the wealthy and to woo those on lower incomes. The new loan was therefore liable to supertax and to excess profits duty. In return the interest rate was raised to 4 per cent. The loan attracted 9.4 million subscribers, and raised $4,617.5 million. Only $568 million of the first loan was converted: for most of its holders tax exemptions were more valuable than an increase in interest rate.

By the time McAdoo applied to issue the third Liberty Loan, in April 1918, his policy was showing signs of strain. It had failed to win over the excess purchasing power of lower-income groups; its low rate of interest meant that the existing Liberty Loans traded below par; and only after the first loan had the government—albeit briefly—been free of debt. Local

[124] Ibid. 120–3; Bogart, *War costs*, 208–10; Petit, *Finances extérieures*, 444; Noyes, *American finance*, 183–7.

quotas were set as targets to popularize the new loan. McAdoo wanted to issue the stock at 4.25 per cent, in ten-year non-convertible bonds. The banks advised that non-convertibility should be compensated for by a rate of 4.5 per cent, not least because the government would not have to bear the higher rate on its earlier issues. The Treasury was authorized to buy up to 5 per cent of any of the issues in any one year in order to sustain the market price. To encourage investors to hold the bonds, they were made redeemable at par plus interest in payment of estate and inheritance taxes. No provision was made for purchase in instalments. The effect was, once again, to make the issue relatively more attractive to the wealthy. Of 18,376,815 subscribers who put up $4,176.5 million, 18,354,315 contributed $2,770.9 million in units ranging from $50 to $10,000. Thus, 99.8 per cent of subscribers received 66.5 per cent of the issue.

For the fourth Liberty Loan, in October 1918, the Treasury gave in to the market. All the Liberty Loans were trading below par, but the first had remained better priced than the others because of its tax exemptions. Therefore the fourth loan was exempt from surtax, excess profits duty, and war profits duties. For those who bought the fourth loan the exemption was extended to their holdings of the second and third issues. On this basis the interest rate could be held at 4.25 per cent, and the fifteen-to-twenty-year bonds made inconvertible. Over 22 million people subscribed $6,993 million for an issue of $6,000 million: most of these (85 per cent) wanted $50 and $100 bonds, but that accounted for only 9.8 per cent of the total sum.[125]

Including the Victory Loan (issued after the war had ended), only 20 per cent of the debt outstanding in June 1920 was held in units of $50 or $100, and some of these smaller denominations had been bought by companies as dividend payments for their shareholders. Thus, the bulk of American war loans were subscribed by the wealthy. Companies themselves had significant holdings: the United States Steel Corporation took almost $128 million of Liberty Loan stock.[126] But the failure of McAdoo's grandiose vision was only relative to its own ambition. Over a fifth of the population of the United States applied for the fourth loan. Moreover, McAdoo himself recognized that alternative devices were needed to

125 Gilbert, *American financing*, 124–42; Bogart, *War costs*, 210–24. Bogart's figures occasionally differ from Gilbert's, and in these cases Gilbert's have been followed.
126 Noyes, *American finance*, 189.

reduce the purchasing power of lower-income groups, and in January 1918 imported from Britain the idea of war savings certificates. Denominations of $5 were sold at $4.12, and gained 1 cent towards their final redemption value in each succeeding month. Thrift stamps, valued at 25 cents, could be collected towards the price of one war savings certificate. Monthly sales averaged $50 million, and in July 1918 they peaked at $211.4 million. In 1918 as a whole $962.6 million was raised through war savings certificates. But the scheme was too late in adoption and maturity too short-term for it to have a major deflationary effect.[127] McAdoo had been determined to restrict short-term debt, but in June 1919 it stood at 14 per cent, less than elsewhere but not significantly below that of Britain.[128] If McAdoo had really wanted to draw in the subscriptions of those on lower incomes, to attract spenders not savers, he would have had to forgo tax exemptions and to raise interest rates.

However, it was only the post-war preoccupation with inflation that cast the policy of low interest rates into doubt. During the war their effect was not entirely nugatory. Obviously the state, as the principal borrower in the market, benefited from the cheapness of money. This was a direct advantage. Indirectly, the success of the whole Liberty Loans scheme came to rest on low interest rates. The Liberty Bond act banned banks from using the bonds as security for note issues. Formally speaking, their task was to take up the certificates of indebtedness—the short-term stock, not the long-term. However, the act permitted all banks, including those which were not members of the Federal Reserve System, to accept deposits; it also released member banks from their reserve requirements in relation to deposits of government funds. The Federal Reserve banks increased their loans to commercial banks from less than $20 million in early 1917 to around $2,000 million in mid-1919. The commercial banks then offered preferential rates to clients seeking advances to buy Liberty Loans. The discounts of the members became increasingly secured by government stocks, and their own rediscounts were then secured on their holdings of these stocks. In January 1918 31.9 per cent of the banks' rediscounts were secured by government obligations; by the end of the year the figure was 70 per cent. The banks' holdings of government

[127] Gilbert, *American financing*, 163–70; Bogart, *War costs*, 228–30.
[128] Chandler, *Strong*, 112.

obligations rose 233 per cent, from $1,546 million in June 1917 to $5,147 million in June 1919. Thus, subscriptions to the loans rested on bank borrowings which themselves relied on low rates of interest.[129]

The consequent increase to the money supply was not more damaging because the United States's entry to the war was late, and its experience of war finance more restricted in time than that of the other belligerents. But of course low interest rates did not only serve America's own liquidity requirements in 1917–18. They were essential to the finances of its Entente partners. By April 1917 British, French, and Italian spending in the United States, funded principally through debt contracted in America in the first place, was so great that only America's active belligerence seemed capable of shoring up their international credit.

[129] Gilbert, *American financing*, 189–97; Brown, *Gold standard*, 122–3.

7

FOREIGN
BORROWING

Foreign borrowing fulfilled two main and interlocking objectives. First, it provided the funds with which to buy in imports. In peace, imports were—in ideal circumstances—paid for through exports, but in the war military demands on domestic industry eliminated any surpluses for overseas trade. Secondly, it could be used to manipulate exchange rates. The pressures of the war on a belligerent—a fall in exports, an increase in inflation, the possibility of defeat—tended to depreciate its currency against those of neutral powers. But by acquiring foreign funds for its own purposes, the belligerent could staunch depreciation. Thus the costs of foreign purchases could be controlled and, in the longer term, the path to post-war reintegration in international commerce eased.

However, Germany's need to achieve these two objectives was rendered ambiguous by the Entente's blockade. With the loss of 44 per cent of its merchant fleet and the curtailment of its exports, not only through the blockade but also by dint of domestic demand, invisible earnings slumped. The tendency of its wartime rhetoric was to make a virtue of necessity. 'Das Gelde im Lande',[1] the retention of wealth at home through the inability to import, became a clarion-call of propaganda; Helfferich lauded autarky as Germany moved towards a form of neo-mercantilism, stressing the economic reinvigoration that would be achieved through reliance on domestic resources and industrial ingenuity.[2]

---

[1] Dix, *Wirtschaftskrieg*, 243.
[2] Williamson, *Helfferich*, 132; Lotz, *Staatsfinanzwirtschaft*, 92; Knauss, *Kriegsfinanzierung*, 174.

At first policy followed the public posturing. Foreign creditors were denied access to German courts, and neutral funds thereby rebuffed.[3] But in practice Germany could not continue to be so xenophobic. Imports, albeit in smaller quantities, continued to arrive through the neutral states on its borders, and they had to be paid for. Its conquests, especially in France and Russia, forced it to acquire francs and roubles in order to administer the occupied territories. Warburgs called in short-term foreign assets to the tune of 241 million marks, particularly from the United States, via Amsterdam.[4] In 1915 the Russians suspected that roubles reached the Germans from Sweden.[5] In 1916 both francs and dollars were channelled through Switzerland. Thus remittances continued, not only between the Central Powers and their non-aligned neighbours, but even between the two opposing camps by way of neutral intermediaries.[6] Ethel Cooper, an Australian living in Leipzig, continued to receive payments in sterling into 1917, and did so at increasingly favourable rates of exchange.[7]

The exchange rate which mattered most was that between the mark and the currencies of those neutrals with whom Germany traded. By January 1916 the mark had lost a third of its pre-war value in the Hague, New York, and Stockholm. The Bundesrat therefore made efforts to eliminate speculation on the foreign exchanges and to curb the demand for foreign exchange from importers. It gave the Reichsbank the task of preparing a list of permitted imports, and it and the other main banks were formed into a consortium licensed to deal in foreign exchange. A year later all transactions in foreign exchange, not just trading agreements, were made subject to Reichsbank control. Steps were also taken to improve the inflow of exchange.[8] Both allies and neutrals importing from Germany were required to pay in their own currencies. German coal exports to Holland and Switzerland brought in a steady flow of Dutch florins and Swiss francs. In December 1917 Germany refined the system by

---

[3] Bartholdy, *War and German society*, 47–9.
[4] Bogart, *War costs*, 75; Frey, *Militärgeschichtliche Mitteilungen*, 53 (1994), 330–1; Ferguson, *Paper and iron*, 102.
[5] Michelson *et al.*, *Russian public finance*, 409–10.
[6] Petit, *Finances extérieures*, 603; Brown, *Gold standard*, 13–14.
[7] Cooper, *Behind the lines*, 32, 119, 184, 218.
[8] Knauss, *Kriegsfinanzierung*, 73–4; Lotz, *Staatsfinanzwirtschaft*, 86–7; Helfferich, *Money*, 259–62; Brown, *Gold standard*, 61–3.

issuing invoices in German marks but demanding payment in the appropriate foreign currency at the rate prevailing on the day of payment, thus contriving to generate a profit from its own depreciating currency. Its bid in 1918 to be paid for goods that had yet to be delivered was less successful.[9]

Efforts to gain control of Germany's foreign investments charted a similar path from voluntarism to compulsion. Germany held between 20,000 million and 28,000 million marks of foreign investments at the outbreak of the war. In 1915 the Reichsbank encouraged shareholders in possession of foreign bonds to sell them to the bank in exchange for marks. In this way it acquired $470 million on the New York stock exchange in 1915 and 1916.[10] But at the same time legislation in the enemy countries was confiscating German holdings; after America's entry and by the war's end 16,100 million marks were forfeited.[11] In August 1916 the Reichsbank calculated that, of 15,000 million marks of foreign holdings, only 2,148 million were 'seizable', and that of that 1,334 million marks were held by neutral powers (excluding the United States) or Germany's allies. As 700 million marks of this final figure represented investments in Austria-Hungary which were to all intents and purposes worthless, a bare 634 million marks remained that could be easily sold.[12] Efforts to encourage the transfer of privately held foreign securities and foreign currency to the Reichsbank were stepped up in August 1916, and in the new year it became mandatory to lend them to the state for the duration of the war.

In the circumstances the mark enjoyed an extraordinary stability on the international exchanges. Germany's efforts in January 1916 were rewarded with only a 4 per-cent variation in the position of the mark in Zurich between then and November. But the United States's entry into the war had the effect of aligning neutral markets with those of the Entente, and so isolating the Central Powers. By October 1917 the mark had fallen 50 per cent. It recovered after Soviet Russia's acceptance of humiliating peace terms at Brest-Litovsk, and it did not go into steep decline until the second

[9] Petit, *Finances extérieures*, 311.

[10] Frey, *Militärgeschichtliche Mitteilungen*, 53 (1994), 342–3; Frey, *International History Review*, XIX (1997), 547–8.

[11] Ferguson, *Paper and iron*, 102–3; also Ferguson, *Pity of war*, 253–4.

[12] Frey, *Militärgeschichtliche Mitteilungen*, 53 (1994), 346.

half of 1918.[13] Germany believed that the international position of the mark, in so far as it reflected inflation, did so because inflation was a product, not of domestic fiscal policy but of an adverse balance of payments. On this interpretation the recovery of Germany's ability to trade after the war would soon restore the mark to parity. The fact that this view was shared elsewhere had its effects in wartime too, since it prevented the mark from falling as far as other economic factors might have suggested was likely.[14]

At one level the comparative strength of the mark was a reflection of German weakness—an inability, thanks to the blockade, to import more. Because Germany imported less, it needed less foreign currency. Thus, the impediments to commerce also rendered less debilitating the consequences of Germany's comparative inability to place a greater proportion of its debt abroad.

The most important neutral money market until 1917, New York, remained all but closed. One problem was that of Germany's representation. A secret mission headed by Heinrich Albert of the Interior Ministry in August 1914 was both over-sanguine concerning Britain's observance of the declaration of London, and too dependent on the use of German treasury bills as payment for American goods. In spring 1915 the American moratorium on the purchase of belligerents' loan stock was breached by the Entente's representative, J. P. Morgan. Although in theory the path to the floating of a loan in the United States was now as open to Germany as it was to Britain, in practice Berlin had to deal with Morgan's dominance of the market. Only the comparatively unknown firm of Chandler and Co. would act for Germany: it took $10 million in treasury bills. By the end of 1915 the Reichsbank regarded the US bill market as effectively closed. The blockade, in addition to strangling German–American trade, also checked the movement of promissory bills and other commercial paper across the Atlantic. Three American institutions were prepared to handle German business: the National City Bank of New York, the Equitable Trust Company, and the Guaranty Trust Company; but in autumn 1916 the first of these capitulated to British threats to blacklist neutral banks which dealt with Germany. Germany's best hope seemed to

---

[13] Brown, *Gold standard*, 62–6; Knauss, *Kriegsfinanzierung*, 72; Roesler, *Finanzpolitik*, 139.
[14] Holtfrerich, *German inflation*, 163; G. H. Soutou, 'Comment a été financée la guerre', in La Gorce (ed.), *La Première Guerre Mondiale*, 291 .

be Kuhn Loeb, an associate of Warburgs. However, a plan to float a loan on behalf of the cities of Berlin, Hamburg, and Frankfurt in late 1916 was forestalled by Woodrow Wilson himself. Germany raised $27 million in the United States, just over 1 per cent of the total borrowed by the Entente over the same period.[15] The blockade meant that most of the proceeds were used to fund purchases from the border neutrals rather than the United States. The money that was spent in America was allocated to funding German propaganda, and so made no direct contribution to Germany's exchange problem or to its balance of trade.[16]

The problems of access to the New York money market and of the shipment of American goods made Holland, rather than the United States, the main focus of Germany's international borrowing by the end of 1915.[17] Germany centralized its purchases and so controlled prices through the establishment of the Zentral-Einkauf Gesellschaft. By November 1915 the ZEG had imported agricultural goods valued at 684.5 million marks since January, and reckoned it needed 25.3 million marks a month. A consortium of the Deutsche Bank, Diskonto-Gesellschaft, and Warburgs, formed in the summer of 1915 to fund the ZEG's buying, was no longer equal to the task. With the mark having depreciated 32 per cent against the guilder and with Germany importing goods to the tune of 100 million marks a month (as opposed to exports of 30–40 million), the German ambassador, Richard von Kühlmann, anticipated the collapse of German credit. By August Germany's Dutch imports had reached 100 million marks per month, and a credit of 100 million guilders negotiated by the Dresden Bank was not even sufficient to cover the ZEG's monthly purchases. The Dutch banks were of course flush with funds, but pressure from London hampered the negotiation of credits. On 16 December 1916 the German banks which had been authorized in January to deal in foreign currency came to an agreement with a consortium of Dutch

[15] Soutou, 'Comment a été financée la guerre', 282; Manfred Zeidler gives $35 million in 'Die deutsche Kriegsfinanzierung 1914 bis 1918 und ihre Folgen', in Michalka (ed.), *Der Erste Weltkrieg*, 424.
[16] Helfferich, *Weltkrieg*, 221; Knauss, *Kriegsfinanzierung*, 74; Nouailhat, *France et États-Unis*, 108; Petit, *Finances extérieures*, 409–10; B. Gilbert, *Lloyd George 1912–1916*, 371; Bernstorff, *Deutschland und Amerika*, 78–9, 97–9; Frey, *Militärgeschichtliche Mitteilungen*, 53 (1994), 330–8.
[17] The entire discussion of German-Dutch finances relies on Frey, *Militärgeschichtliche Mitteilungen*, 53 (1994), 340–53. The principal points are also made by Baer, 'Anglo-German antagonism and trade with Holland', 214, 220, 300–1.

banks based on the exchange of Dutch food for German coal and steel. The Dutch banks committed themselves to monthly credits of 6 million guilders for six months, at a 5 per-cent rate of interest. But it was still not enough: ZEG's total imports for 1916 were valued at 2,100 million gold marks, and after America's entry the exchange rate slumped to 2.68 marks to the guilder (pre-war parity having been 1.69). The Reichsbank shipped 50 million marks in gold at the end of June, but the principal effort was to try to get the Dutch banks to lend to German cities and communes: the local governments which co-operated with the Reich in this way were to get special treatment in the allocation of food supplies. But the terms on which settlement was reached obliged the cities to repay the marks which they borrowed from Dutch (and Swiss) firms in ten years' time in a currency of the lender's choice at pre-war parity.[18] The Dutch were becoming fearful of their dependence on Germany and were only too aware of the mark's vulnerability. Although gold and Belgian notes were used to help cover the trade gap over the summer of 1917, both devices were exhausted by September. Using its neighbours' reliance on German coal once again, Germany negotiated a new credit agreement in October 1917, handled for the sake of neutrality by the Diskonto-Gesellschaft; it provided 13.75 million guilders for six months. Despite further crises in German–Dutch relations in the following spring and summer, a fresh credit of 14 million guilders was negotiated on 24 August 1918. By the end of the war Germany owed Holland 1,600 million gold marks.

This constituted about half Germany's total debt to all neutrals. The leverage of Germany's coal enabled the contracting of debt in Switzerland (the Reichsbank had secured credits of 335 million gold marks by October 1917), and also in the two other border neutrals with which Germany sustained major trade—Sweden and Denmark (Reichsbank credits of 285 and 180 million gold marks respectively by October 1917). About 3,000 million marks had been raised through the sale of foreign securities and a further 1,000 million through the disposal of German shares; exports of gold totalled about 1,000 million marks.

Germany, therefore, paid for its imports primarily with notes; to that extent its foreign purchasing was deflationary. The consequences were

[18] Roesler, *Finanzpolitik*, 172; Feldman, *Great disorder*, 45; also Petit, *Finances extérieures*, 608.

inflationary in that virtually all Germany's debt was held domestically, and most of it in the Reichsbank. Thus, far more of Germany's debt was monetized than was the case in Britain. Germany's monetary base increased 56 per cent between 1913 and the end of 1917 and 76 per cent by the end of 1918; by contrast, Britain's grew 12 per cent by the end of 1917 and 32 per cent by the end of 1918.[19] Moreover, if war represents an unproductive use of capital, then Germany loaded the responsibility onto its own money market rather than onto those of others. Nonetheless, German bankers and shipowners were not over-anxious about the consequences of inflation for international reintegration as the war came to an end. Indeed, they saw the depreciation of the mark on the international exchanges as the fastest route to the recovery of Germany's export trade and the readjustment of its balance of payments. As Albert Ballin of Hapag put it in September 1917: 'The American who no longer gets for his dollar 4.21 marks worth of goods from us, but 6.20 marks worth, will rediscover his fondness for Germany.' Max Warburg was inclined to agree.[20] Therefore, the assumption in commercial circles was that the best policy after the war would be a quick return to pre-war parity.

A further source of consolation was the fact that, unlike the import-dependent Entente powers, Germany had avoided the need to export gold to support the exchange rate. Indeed, the Reichsbank's holdings of gold, pursuing the policy established by Havenstein before the war, swelled by 93 per cent during it.[21] Some of this gold was the fruit of conquest. The persistence into 1918 of the notion of the gold standard and of the faith in indemnities was confirmed by the Treaty of Brest-Litovsk, whose clauses included the requirement that the Russians surrender to the Germans 245,564 kilograms of fine gold valued at 200 million marks.[22] Much of it came from Germany's own population, the result of successive propaganda drives linking gold in the Reichsbank to an increased money supply. A great deal of it came from Austria-Hungary. Germany may not have borrowed abroad to any great extent, but its allies

---

[19] Balderston, *Economic History Review*, 2nd series, XLII (1989), 237; Feldman, *Great disorder*, 38.

[20] Ferguson, *Paper and iron*, 150.

[21] Brown, *Gold standard*, 94–5, 100; Roesler, *Finanzpolitik*, 171–2.

[22] Michelson *et al.*, *Russian public finance*, 452–5.

borrowed from Germany. Berlin did not lose the opportunity to confirm its economic suzerainty.

The pattern of Austro-German financial relations was set by the end of 1914. Austria-Hungary had a balance of payments problem before the war. Even in 1913 the empire had not managed to cover its own cereal needs, and in 1914 the harvest fell yet further; the pattern was to be repeated in every subsequent year, although the decline was less precipitate in 1917 and 1918. To feed it had to import, and to do that it needed foreign exchange. In November 1914 German banks, with the backing of the government, advanced 300 million marks on the security of Austrian and Hungarian treasury bills. Not all of this sum was released, because of constraints on the German capital market.[23] The notes paid 6 per cent up until 23 December 1914 and 5 per cent thereafter, and had a life of one year, although this was renewable. By July 1918 Austria had received credits of 2,124 million marks and Hungary 1,336 million; in the first six months of 1918 Germany was advancing the dual monarchy 75 million marks a month on condition that Austria-Hungary met the costs of German soldiers serving on its soil.

However, in addition to the needs of the two governments the Austro-Hungarian Bank required marks to service foreign trade. From the Bank Berlin demanded not paper securities but gold. Between December 1914 and December 1915 the Bank's holdings of gold fell from 1,055 million crowns to 684 million. By 31 October 1918 its stocks had dwindled to 268 million crowns.[24] In December 1918 Vienna's gold reserves were 79 per cent below those of December 1913, a collapse unparalleled in the finances of any other belligerent.[25] Only a decisive victory and a massive indemnity, it seemed, could restore the empire to the international gold standard. What rankled in Vienna was that the cause of this fall seemed to be not the war but the empire's ally.

Austria-Hungary's obvious route to salvation was to lessen its dependence on its gold-hungry partner and to increase its reliance on the gold-satiated neutrals. In January 1916 the leading banks undertook to negotiate loans with their peers in Switzerland, Holland, Denmark, and Sweden. But their success was limited. The banks themselves charged

---

[23] Rauchensteiner, *Tod des Doppeladlers*, 149.
[24] Popovics, *Geldwesen*, 120–5; März, *Austrian banking*, 137, 194.
[25] Brown, *Gold standard*, 100, 106; see also Spitzmüller, *Memoirs*, 115.

commission and they did not halt the haemorrhage of gold, being prepared to advance up to a third of their collateral in this form. Only the Dutch advanced significant sums, and even here talk of an Austro-Dutch trading company came to nought.

Intergovernmental arrangements secured in treasury bills promised to be much less costly. In November 1916 Austria and Hungary each concluded a loan with Holland, whereby the Dutch accepted two-year treasury bills paying 5 per cent to the value of 45,560,000 guilders and in exchange advanced 70 per cent of that sum in nine monthly instalments. In November 1917 a second agreement gave the dual monarchy a further 24 million guilders, and in three separate deals over 1917 Austria used its tobacco monopoly to get more Dutch advances. Denmark, between late 1917 and early 1918, advanced 20,569,150 Danish crowns to Austria and 8,815,350 to Hungary on the security of renewable, non-interest-bearing treasury bills. In late 1917 Sweden lent 4.2 million Swedish crowns to Austria and 3,755,707 to Hungary in exchange for a combination of exports and treasury bills. Switzerland proved the most reluctant, but Swiss francs were promised by a group of companies in late 1917 in exchange for deliveries of kerosene, benzine, and sugar.[26] As in Germany's case, the American market remained closed: contacts through Warburgs with Kuhn Loeb in New York came to nothing. Even where these deals were successful, they bore witness to Austria-Hungary's impoverishment: the nominal credits were vastly in excess of the cash advanced. Furthermore, although Austria-Hungary's dependence on Germany was eased, it was far from eliminated: of 717,234,000 crowns in foreign credits outstanding in February 1918, 510,790,000 were German.[27]

But the frustration was not all on one side of the relationship. What irked Germany was that the Austro-Hungarian Bank used the better-priced mark, rather than the rapidly depreciating crown, to finance its foreign purchases. Thus, Berlin's own efforts to sustain the mark were undermined by Vienna's tendency to spend the German currency it borrowed not in Germany but in the adjacent territories. Furthermore, Berlin felt, with good reason, that Vienna could make more strenuous

---

[26] Popovics, *Geldwesen*, 126–8, 140–2; März, *Austrian banking*, 196, 232–3.
[27] Popovics, *Geldwesen*, 133–4.

efforts to curb its flow of imports, and thus reduce its foreign-exchange dealings.

Germany's establishment of its own foreign exchange control mechanisms in January 1916 served to alleviate, at least temporarily, some of these tensions. Austria-Hungary collaborated with the German scheme. Central offices for foreign-exchange dealings were set up in Vienna and Budapest under the auspices of the Austro-Hungarian Bank. But the scheme was voluntary, demand exceeded supply, and the price of foreign exchange on the open market rose. In December 1916, under German pressure, the arrangements became mandatory: foreign dealings were confined to a list of approved firms, and foreign exchange gained through exports was to be handed over to the foreign-exchange office. In March 1917 all imports became subject to the approval of the two finance ministries. Finally, in June 1918 these various acts were consolidated, and ministerial and bank approval for imports had to be granted before negotiations began, not once they were in train.[28]

The depreciation of the crown on the international market suggested that all these measures were little and late. Like the mark, the crown stabilized in 1916, fell in 1917, recovered in early 1918, and plunged in September 1918. In July 1914 the crown traded against the dollar at 4.9535; by January 1916 it had reached 8.1440; in October 1917 it exchanged at 11.498, a rate which was not exceeded until eleven months later, when the crown stood at 12.010. In Zurich 100 crowns bought 105 Swiss francs at par, but 66.75 in June 1916, 44.02 in June 1917, and 43.01 in June 1918. During the war itself what mattered most of course was the crown–mark exchange. Depreciation here accelerated the exodus of gold and increased the cost of German imports. In January 1916 the crown stood 27 per cent over par; it reached 32.5 per cent by the end of 1917, recovered briefly with the hopes of victory at the beginning of 1918, and fell back to 47 per cent in December 1918.[29]

Nonetheless, what is surprising about this picture is not that it was bleak, but that it was not bleaker. The efforts to control imports in 1917–18 and the securing of credits in neutral nations over the same period helped slow the fall of the crown until it was overtaken by military collapse in the

---

[28] Ibid. 118–19, 136–47; Walvé de Bordes, *Austrian Crown*, 108–9; Lutz, *Fall of the German empire*, ii. 208–9.

[29] Walvé de Bordes, *Austrian Crown*, 114–15, 145, 146; Gratz and Schüller, *Wirtschaftliche Zusammenbruch*, 182; Popovics, *Geldwesen*, 115–16, 147, 151–3, table IX.

autumn of 1918. Moreover, the depreciation on the international exchanges bore no relationship to the increase in circulation in 1914–16 or to the rise in prices in 1916–18. Both the latter soared, undermining the value of the crown in a way that was not reflected on the international money markets during the war. The blockade, by controlling Austria-Hungary's balance of payments' deficit as it did that of Germany, hid the true decline in the crown until trade resumed at fuller levels on the conclusion of the war.

Germany's role as banker to its allies was even more pronounced in the case of Turkey. But, unlike Austria-Hungary, the Ottoman empire managed to resist exploitation by its powerful coadjutor. Arguably the ultimate destination of the gold provided by Vienna was not Berlin but Constantinople. Of 900 million marks in gold surrendered by Germany by June 1918, 844 million represented payments to the other Central Powers,[30] predominantly Turkey. Efforts by Berlin to get long-term concessions from Constantinople in return foundered repeatedly on the rock of immediate military necessity. The provision of ready cash seemed the only way to cut through Ottoman procrastination. Furthermore, Turkey's use of the aid it received was very different from that of the other belligerents: its economic backwardness curbed the implications of the balance of payments problem and Turkey's standing on the international exchanges was proportionately irrelevant. The Sublime Porte's foreign borrowing was applied predominantly to domestic purposes. Germany's task, therefore, was nothing less than to be the main financier of Turkey's war effort.

Turkey made this plain even before it entered the war. Enver's demand for a loan of £Turkish 5 million was set as a precondition of Turkey's fulfilment of the alliance obligations which it entered into on 2 August 1914. The Germans wisely made full payment conditional on active belligerence, and thus £T2 million was advanced in mid-October before the Turkish fleet attacked the Russian in the Black Sea, and the balance followed in six monthly instalments beginning on 1 December. The loan was secured in Turkish treasury bills, paying 6 per cent per annum, and redeemable a year after the end of the war.[31]

---

[30] Feldman, *Great disorder*, 44.
[31] Trumpener, *Germany and the Ottoman empire*, 48–9, 51, 271–2; Silberstein, *Troubled alliance*, 81–2, 93–4.

What alarmed Germany was that the export of its gold promised to continue for the duration of the war. The issue of paper money was in the hands of the Imperial Ottoman Bank, but the bank was effectively administered from Paris. The British and French managers of the bank in Constantinople were not removed from their posts until January 1915. Djavid, as finance minister, was reluctant to break the French link, a reflection of his pro-Entente sympathies as well as a recognition of the likely importance of France's investments to Turkey's post-war position. Ninety per cent of the £T40 million in circulation in 1914 was metallic, and the faith in notes was proportionately slender. Paper currency issued by any authority, and certainly paper money issued by any authority other than the Imperial Ottoman Bank, was unlikely to command confidence. Thus, it seemed that liquidity could only be maintained by further shipments of gold.

Djavid's solution was to propose that the Ottoman public debt be used as a bank of issue on a temporary basis. Helfferich favoured the idea but not its corollary—that, to gain public confidence, the notes be fully covered by German gold. The compromise was to make the notes re-deemable in gold six months after the conclusion of hostilities, but in wartime to keep the gold in Berlin, in the Deutsche Bank, for the account of the Ottoman public debt. On this basis 80 million marks were advanced in the spring of 1915.

For subsequent note issues the Turks agreed to accept the security of German treasury bills rather than gold. Furthermore, although the bills too were redeemable in gold, the period for repayment was progressively extended. For the second and third issues, in November 1915 and February 1916, payment was due a year after the end of the war. The fourth (August 1916) was not due to be fully redeemed until five years after the peace, and the fifth (February 1917) would not begin to be repaid until the redemption of the fourth issue was complete. On this basis Turkey added £T160 million to its note circulation. But the increased currency did not, as in the case of other belligerents, constitute a forced loan from its own public; it was instead a loan, worth almost 4,000 million marks, from Germany.[32]

[32] Trumpener, *Germany and the Ottoman empire*, 272–83; Emin, *Turkey in the World War*, 161–2; Bihl, *Kaukasus-Politik*, 54–5; Helfferich, *Weltkrieg*, 232; Williamson, *Helfferich*, 119; Gall et al., *Deutsche Bank*, 141.

Germany's financial obligations to its ally were not thereby resolved. The lack of public confidence in paper currency was not overcome. Before the war notes were issued in high-value denominations, £T100, £T50, and £T5, and were therefore rarely seen in market-place transactions. On 10 August 1914 the banks were relieved of the obligation to redeem notes for metal, and notes valued at £T1 and £T$\frac{1}{2}$ were issued. The result was that coin disappeared, not because it had been withdrawn from circulation but because it was hoarded. Notes were progressively less acceptable the further one moved from Constantinople. Their rejection contributed to paper's depreciation, as its availability exceeded its marketability. By 1916 paper money was exchanged even in Constantinople at 40 per cent below its face value, and in the provinces at 80 to 90 per cent. By 1917–18 £T1 in gold traded for £T6 in notes, and in Syria and Arabia for £T8 or £T10.[33] Lack of faith in paper currency was therefore a major cause of rising prices. Efforts to reform the currency had no appreciable impact. In April 1916 the currency was unified, but its primary aim was to prevent further deterioration in the value of Turkish paper money and common valuations of the same denominations did not follow.[34] On 1 January 1917 the National Credit Bank was founded, but as it had no powers of issue the dilemma created by the French management of the Imperial Ottoman Bank was not resolved.[35]

Lack of liquidity jeopardized military effectiveness. Between 1916 and 1918 the major Turkish war zones were in the southern parts of the empire, remote from the note-using metropolis. In Syria and Mesopotamia only gold was negotiable. Even in April 1916, when the Turkish 6th army was in the ascendant in Iraq, it found itself unable to buy food or horses for lack of gold.[36] In 1918 each Turkish army was given a float of £T1 million in paper. But the Arabs would only sell their goods for gold, and therefore preferred to trade with the British.[37] Thus, German support of the note circulation was not in itself sufficient to shore up Turkey's currency. Shipments of gold were required to enable the Ottoman armies to stay

[33] Pomiankowski, *Zusammenbruch*, 263, 319; Emin, *Turkey in the World War*, 144–7; Bihl, *Kaukasus-Politik*, 204; Dschawid, *Türkische Kriegsfinanzwirtschaft*, 9, 24, 29.

[34] Emin, *Turkey in the World War*, 166; Bihl, *Kaukasus-Politik*, 202; Stuermer, *Two war years*, 131–2.

[35] Bihl, *Kaukasus-Politik*, 202; Trumpener, *Germany and the Ottoman empire*, 282.

[36] Moukbil, *Campagne de l'Irak*, 184–6.

[37] Wallach, *Anatomie*, 262–3; Liman, *Five years in Turkey*, 236; Nogales, *Four years*, 284.

in the field. To all intents and purposes, Turkey reversed the normal pattern of foreign borrowing: it contracted debt in Germany to enable it to buy war goods within its own frontiers, and it imported, rather than exported, gold in order to try to stabilize the regional variations in the domestic exchange rate between metal and notes.

The most direct manifestation of the indissolubility of the link between German gold and Turkish military effectiveness was provided in May 1917. Berlin was scaling down its credit operations in the Ottoman empire, but its commitment to an offensive planned to recapture Baghdad required it to provide £T200,000 a month in gold, with a willingness eventually to allocate £T5 million.[38] If Germany wanted to ensure that Turkey conformed to its strategic priorities, it had little choice but to fund them directly. Thus, German gold and silver, valued at £T17.5 million, was pumped into pan-Islamic propaganda.[39] Since the notion of holy war furthered the principles of the Caliphate as well as the anti-British objectives of the Germans, Turko-German tensions were not thereby revealed. But when in 1915 the German foreign ministry offered an advance of 40 million marks to hasten the completion of the Baghdad railway, Djavid objected that the purposes were German and that a hasty and improvised construction would fulful the short-term needs of Berlin, not the long-term objectives of Constantinople. Terms were finally settled in January 1916, but only because Germany, not Turkey, provided the financial guarantees needed by the Bagdad-Eisenbahn-Gesellschaft.[40]

The Baghdad railway also highlighted how much Germany's financial aid was supplemented by the provision of equipment. Locomotives, machinery, and raw materials allocated to the railway by Germany were valued at 435 million marks. Total military supplies from Germany were estimated at 616 million marks.[41] The Foreign Ministry's final calculation of Germany's contribution, aggregating aid in kind as well as in cash, was £T235,056,344 or 4,700 million marks.[42]

Germany tried to get Austria-Hungary to take a share of the burden. The Turks preferred Skoda's artillery to Krupp's, and by April 1916, according to the calculations of the latter, its Austrian competitor had

[38] Wallach, *Anatomie*, 213.   [39] Larcher, *La Guerre turque*, 96.
[40] Trumpener, *Germany and the Ottoman empire*, 292–7.   [41] Wallach, *Anatomie*, 238.
[42] Trumpener, *Germany and the Ottoman empire*, 283; Bihl, *Kaukasus-Politik*, 5.

secured orders worth £T4.2 million. These were paid for by loans from
Austria-Hungary: an advance of 47 million crowns, agreed in May 1915,
had risen to 240 million by January 1917. Gwinner of the Deutsche Bank
was furious: 'German money is being used for Turkey via Austria and
competes or directly damages German interests.'[43] The transaction was
handled by the Orient Group, a consortium of Austro-Hungarian banks
which hoped to develop Austro-Turkish trade after the war. But Skoda's
primary obligation was to the Austrian army itself, and it never delivered
the full consignment of guns. Thus, the Orient Group did not fulfil its
aspirations, the Turks were left short of artillery, and the Germans
concluded that the proceeds of Berlin's loans to Turkey were being
spent in the dual monarchy and not in the Reich.[44]

Austro-German competition was also fuelled by the efforts of the two
allies to get Turkey to deliver raw materials to them and to agree post-war
economic concessions. Germany established a central purchasing agency
in Turkey in 1916, and Austria accepted that its ally should act on behalf of
both powers, with the produce being split in a ratio of 11 : 10 between
Germany and Austria-Hungary. Efforts focused on foodstuffs and metals.
However, once again Turkey got the better of the deal. By 1 October 1916,
the Germans reckoned that they had sent 600 million marks' worth of
goods to Turkey but had received only 50 million marks' worth in return.
Moreover, Turkey contrived a profit of 200 per cent on their exports and
insisted on payment in advance in cash. Even in 1918, when Ludendorff
and OHL used the leverage of German loans in a bid to get industrial and
raw material concessions, the Turks avoided any significant reciprocal
obligations to their allies.[45]

Turkey's strength in these negotiations derived ultimately from Germany's strategic dependence. However, in 1918 it also resulted, ironically
enough, from Germany's refusal to extend credit. Turkey was forced into
launching its first and only war loan. Thus, Constantinople diminished its
reliance on Berlin's funding. The terms of the loan were generous—
interest was payable in gold at 5 per cent—and it raised £T17,851,120. But

[43] Gall *et al.*, *Deutsche Bank*, 146.

[44] Pomiankowski, *Zusammenbruch*, 321; Bihl, *Kaukasus-Politik*, 120–1; März, *Austrian bank-ing*, 229–31.

[45] Wallach, *Anatomie*, 204–5; Bihl, *Kaukasus-Politik*, 122, 204; Trumpener, *Germany and the Ottoman empire*, 317–48; Emin, *Turkey in the World War*, 134–5 .

the target was £T37 million. In July Djavid was back, asking Germany for more money. By August so desperate was the position of the Central Powers that Ludendorff was robbed of the will to push for concessions in return, and £T45 million was advanced without conditions.[46]

The costs of the war to Turkey were, in fiscal terms, minimal. The public rejection of the note issue dampened its liquidity and curbed monetary overhang. In March 1917, when Djavid computed that his country's war debt would reach £T180 million by August, only £T15 million was domestic, and even that had been generated indirectly— through requisitions. At that stage of the war he still did not anticipate launching a war loan, and when one was eventually issued it was limited and late. Almost all of Turkey's war debt was external, and most of it was held by Germany. During the war Turkey was able to brush off domestic anxieties about its borrowing, claiming that it was guaranteed by the German government, whose ordinary budget (at least formally) had no deficit and whose international standing ensured that it would not default. Djavid reckoned Turkey would pay off its combined pre-war and wartime borrowings (calculated in March 1917 to be £T330 million) within twelve years of the war's end. In the event, the German debt was repudiated on Turkey's behalf by the Entente after the war. But Djavid's wartime declarations were not simply wishful thinking. If Turkey had had to pay Germany, the burden would not have been great. Turkey's foreign debt in 1914 was already large, £T161 million; it did not quite triple by 1918, when it totalled £T454.2 million.[47] Depreciation within Turkey—the domestic exchange rate—kept the real value of this debt remarkably low.

Very similar points emerge from an examination of Bulgaria's management of its financial relationship with Germany. It had funded the Balkan wars by three forms of credit. It borrowed from the national bank against increased note issue; it levied a compulsory domestic loan; and it raised funds from banks in France, Russia, and Austria-Hungary. Anxious in July 1914 to consolidate these floating and short-term debts, it secured 500 million gold leva at 5 per cent over a fifty-year period from a

---

[46] Trumpener, *Germany and the Ottoman empire*, 344–8; Emin, *Turkey and the World War*, 164–5; Larcher, *La Guerre turque*, 137–8.

[47] Larcher, *La Guerre turque*, 541. Macfie, *End of the Ottoman empire*, 150, and Ahmad, *Kurdistan*, 131, give slightly different but comparable figures. See also Dschawid, *Türkische Kriegsfinanzwirtschaft*, 12–14, 30.

consortium headed by the Diskonto-Gesellschaft. The deal was not without its domestic critics, both those averse to aligning Bulgaria with the Triple Alliance, and those angry at the rights over Bulgarian coal, railway construction, and post development which were conceded in exchange. The first tranche of 250 million leva was due on 30 September 1914, but when the war broke out Germany, as allowed under the terms of the agreement, made the funds conditional on Bulgaria's political alignment. An indication of Sofia's ability to manipulate Berlin was the fact that it secured 150 million leva in February 1915 not for belligerence but for its continuing neutrality. Moreover, Bulgarian obstructionism ensured that the benefits Germany derived from the mining concessions were minimal.

Therefore, Bulgaria did not enter the war in September 1915 to secure funds, but having done so ensured that its own disbursement on the war's conduct was matched—virtually in a 50 : 50 relationship—by Germany.[48] Germany agreed to provide its ally with a subsidy of 50 million leva a month at 5.5 per cent. The money was lodged in the Bulgarian national bank's account with Diskonto-Gesellschaft in exchange for Bulgarian treasury bills. Bulgaria's claim that its domestic economy thus derived no direct benefit was spurious. A law passed in 1912 allowed the national bank to treat foreign loans as metallic cover for its note issue. The bank's reserves of gold and silver rose only from 83.6 million leva in 1914 to 103.78 million in 1918 (as opposed to a tenfold increase in note circulation). By contrast, Germany's advances totalled 350 million gold leva. Thus, the German loans underpinned the growth in Bulgaria's money supply, which was in turn reflected in bank deposits. Those of the national bank rose from 42 million leva in 1914 to 85 million in 1917, those of the Bulgarian Agricultural Bank from 8.9 million leva to 14.1 million, and those of the Central Cooperative Bank from 8.4 million to 79.9 million. Flush with funds, the banks were able to support the creation of 155 new companies with a total initial capital of 156.7 million leva between 1913 and 1918; by contrast, in the first of these years only five new companies had been set up and their combined capital was a mere 4.5 million leva. Germany's frustration was compounded by the fact that Bulgaria's

---

[48] This is the calculation of Lampe, *Bulgarian economy*, 44; in general, see Danaïllow, *Les Effets de la guerre en Bulgarie*, 496, 530–45; Crampton, *Bulgaria*, 429–34.

tobacco exports kept the leva strong against the mark, thus enabling the Bulgarian banks to buy their allies' notes at low rates and sell them in Germany and Switzerland at a profit.[49]

Germany's toleration of this relationship did not—unlike that with Turkey—extend beyond December 1917. For the last year of the war Bulgaria had to fall back on domestic borrowing, primarily by discounting treasury bills with the national bank. Its debt in paper leva doubled from 319.99 million in 1917 to 688.88 in 1918, and at the year's end it had 822 million leva outstanding with the Bulgarska Narodna Banka. Inflation was no longer held in check, and prices doubled.

Nonetheless, although Bulgaria bore more of the real monetary costs of its war effort than did Turkey, it was far from facing them in their entirety. It never launched a domestic war loan, and its domestic debt, even in 1917, was a third that of its foreign borrowing. Moreover, the latter was written off by the peace settlement. Put crudely, the experience of both powers showed that the financial burden of fighting a world war for an underdeveloped power was less than that for a state possessed of industrial abundance. In this respect Turkey, and to a lesser extent Bulgaria, fulfilled at least some of the expectations of pre-war economists concerning the greater financial resilience of the more backward nations.

But the explanations for strength in the management of wartime finance are not monocausal. Forwardness was also an advantage; sophistication in the machinery of credit created flexibility. The Entente powers proved adept at externalizing their debt, and displayed in doing so a degree of mutual support which, however tinged with exploitative overtones, provided a clear instance of co-operation within the alliance. Admittedly this co-ordination was the consequence of one power's financial supremacy at any one time—Britain's in the early stages of the war, and the United States's in the latter. Moreover, pre-war national rivalries were not simply forgotten. France resented Britain's presumption of financial leadership, and was restrained largely by Ribot's Anglophilia and his determination not to compromise relations between the two powers.[50] Britain financed Belgium in the Congo because France was funding the Belgian army: 'we believe', wrote a member of Asquith's

[49] Crampton, *Bulgaria*, 487.
[50] Horn, *Guerres mondiales et conflits contemporains*, 180, (octobre 1995), 7–8, 27; Horn takes a harsher line than that adopted here. See also Horn, *Britain, France*.

cabinet in December 1914, 'that France would like to get the Belgians in her pocket—but we have not resisted a German protectorate over Belgium in order to have a French one.'[51] However, neither this jockeying for position nor the relative lack of collaboration between the military high commands of the allies until 1918 should obscure a much more broadly based and fundamental sharing of monetary and other resources from 1915 onwards.

The prime mover in effecting such a rapid progression towards financial fusion was not the wealth of Britain but the impoverishment of Russia. Russia's leverage over its allies in 1914–15 bore comparison with that of Turkey over Germany. Both Britain and France regarded their eastern ally as a source—by dint of its manpower—of latent military supremacy. Money was the oil to ease the machinery of the Russian 'steamroller'.

Neither Britain nor even France confronted major problems in their foreign borrowing until 1915 or possibly 1916. But much of Russia's pre-war industrialization was already predicated on investment by both London and, especially, Paris.[52] It filed its first request for British funds almost as soon as the war began, and in October 1914 the Treasury agreed to advance £20 million. Russia went on to borrow £568 million from Britain, almost £200 million a year for each year of its belligerence. Of £974.7 million in British loans to the Dominions and allies outstanding at the end of the financial year 1916–17, almost half, £400.6 million, was Russian debt.[53] France, which found itself shoring up the finances of Serbia, Belgium, and Montenegro as well, allocated at least a third, and by some calculations almost a half, of its foreign credits to Russia. At the war's end Russia owed Paris 3,530 million francs.[54]

Only a small proportion of this debt was contracted in order to purchase war materials directly from Russia's Entente partners. Its immediate purpose was to pay dividends on the shares and interest on the government loans already held abroad before the war. The few Russian stocks belonging to German and Austrian investors in 1914 migrated to neutral markets. Thus, there was no relief from the need to continue

[51] David (ed.), *Inside Asquith's cabinet*, 209.
[52] Trebilcock, *Industrialization of Continental Powers*, 244–7, 278–81.
[53] Morgan, *British financial policy*, 317.
[54] Petit, *Finances extérieures*, 164–6; Knauss, *Kriegsfinanzierung*, 93.

payment even on these.[55] Since 80 per cent of Russia's foreign cash balances were in France and consequently were caught by the French moratorium, they could be only gradually released. French government loans to Russia were therefore being used to reward the pre-war speculation of French private investors.[56] In August 1915 Bark told the Duma that of Russia's new, wartime debt 500 million francs and £10 million had been used to cover the cost of borrowing contracted before the war.[57]

Even without this prior call on Russian borrowing, little could have been spent within Britain and France. The war industries of both were fully taken up by their own nations' needs. The major source of Russian munitions was the United States. But Russia had no entrée to the American money market. A Jewish lobby in America, headed by one of the managers of Kuhn Loeb, and outraged by the anti-Semitism of the Tsarist government, blocked Russia's attempts to raise loans in New York before the war. Thus, although American policy sought improved relations with St Petersburg from July 1914, the infrastructure for the extension of American credit was not in place. Not until 1916 did a determination that America should dominate Russo-American trade lead the National City Bank to become active in the Russian loan market. In the first year of the war the Russians tried to borrow in the region of $1,000 million but came away with only $60 million. However, the barriers to American money did not constitute barriers to American goods.[58]

On 17 August 1914 Britain and France, as a result of a French initiative, established the Commission Internationale de Revitaillement. Its task was to co-ordinate and control allied purchasing, so as to keep down prices and to prevent inter-allied competition. Neither Britain nor France intended the Commission to become an agent of Anglo-French financial co-operation: they did not use it to obtain funds, and France placed orders outside it. But both did use it to manage the spending of their allies. In September Russia and Belgium joined the Commission, and in due course the other allies followed suit.[59] The effect was to give the weaker financial powers the credit status of Britain in international markets. Russia could

[55] Claus, *Kriegswirtschaft Russlands*, 9.
[56] Michelson *et al.*, *Russian public finance*, 288–90; Schmidt, *Ribot*, 124.
[57] Claus, *Kriegswirtshaft Russlands*, 11.
[58] Owen, *Historical Journal*, XIII (1970), 253–60; Parrini, *Heir to empire*, 59–60.
[59] Burk, *Britain, America and the sinews of war*, 44–5; Petit, *Finances extérieures*, 129, 181–3; Horn, *Guerres mondiales et conflits contemporains*, (octobre 1995), 9 .

therefore buy American produce under Anglo-French auspices, and pay for it with the debt that it contracted in London and Paris rather than in New York. American exports to Russia grew from a value of $32.2 million in 1913 to $640 million in 1916. The United States's funding of Russia was prodigious: by November 1917 $2,615 million had been advanced, $1,229 million between January 1916 and April 1917, and $902 million between the two revolutions. But of this, only $435 million constituted direct advances and only $840 million was secured in Russia's own name: $460 million was debt contracted in the name of France and $880 million in that of Britain. Thus, when Britain and France borrowed in the United States between 1914 and 1917, more often than not they did so on Russia's behalf. Over 70 per cent of American funds lent to the two west European powers in the period of American neutrality were destined for Russian use.[60]

By April 1917 58 per cent of all Entente borrowing, both that contracted between the belligerent powers themselves and that from the United States, had been generated by the needs of Russia.[61] Much of it was misapplied. Britain and France felt that their funds were being used not for the purposes of the war but to improve Russia's peacetime industrial infrastructure. Part of the problem was the difficulty of distinguishing what was civil from what was military in the conduct of war in the industrial age. Railway investment would benefit Russia after the war but was also vital during it: in 1916 and 1917 many of the goods shipped from the United States remained mired at Archangel for lack of transport.

Like that of other belligerents, the deficit in the balance of Russia's trade grew. But to blame the depreciation of the rouble on the balance of trade, as Bark did, was misleading.[62] The rouble fell 28.2 per cent against the dollar by August 1915, 41.8 per cent by January 1916, and 43.9 per cent by April 1917.[63] At their conference in February 1915 the finance ministers of Britain and France pledged to hold the rouble at par with the pound and the franc. As Russia paid for most of its imports with money borrowed from Britain and France, they—not Russia—bore the brunt of the rouble's depreciation. London, rather than Petrograd, was the

---

[60] Owen, *Historical Journal*, XIII (1970), 261–7; see also Michelson *et al.*, *Russian public finance*, 312–17.
[61] Harvey, *Collision of empires*, 289–90.
[62] Claus, *Kriegswirtschaft Russlands*, 26.
[63] Brown, *Gold standard*, 49.

main international market for roubles. The Russian government, therefore, used Barings to buy roubles in London so as to shore up their value.
In 1916, with the support of British Treasury funds, it set up an intervention account operated by Barings. However, these operations had little
effect in halting the rouble's downward slide.[64]

London felt that the heart of the problem lay in Petrograd. Part of its
solution was political: military victory and governmental reform would
generate greater international confidence. But there was also a monetary
aspect. The purchase of roubles on foreign markets had to be accompanied by effective blocks to the exodus of funds from Russia. Without them,
there would always be more roubles on the international market than the
market could absorb. No effective controls were ever put in place.

In November 1914, as part of an effort to prevent trade with the Central
Powers, a ban was imposed on the export of money or precious metals
worth more than 500 roubles. The order was doubly inadequate. First, no
limit was put on the number of transactions for sums of less than 500
roubles; thus, large amounts could be moved in successive small tranches.
Secondly, the prohibition only applied to the physical transfer of metals
and money, not to their consignment to overseas concerns.

However, the biggest weakness in the policy was that Bark did not
believe in it. He argued that some export of cash would facilitate Russia's
foreign purchasing, and that the notes would eventually return to domestic circulation. Thus, by the summer of 1915 the Ministry of Finance was
itself authorizing exemptions to permit the migration of Russian capital.
The trade was monitored by controls set up in July 1915, and centralized in
a single department in January 1916. But no further efforts were made to
restrict the movement of money until June 1916, and even the measures
then adopted did little more than regularize existing practice. Large
banks were allowed to consign sums to allied and neutral countries,
and private individuals could do so to Britain and France. The exemptions granted in 1915 were not ended until December 1916. The legislation
of the Provisional Government under this head also lacked substance.
Payments abroad were prohibited unless they enjoyed the approval of the
Ministry of Finance. But as the original allowance permitting exports of

<hr>

[64] Michelson *et al.*, *Russian public finance*, 431–3.

up to 500 roubles remained in place, those anxious to move large sums continued to transfer the permitted maximum every day.[65]

London's frustration at Russia's failure to control its foreign exchange was cumulative. Russia's resentment at the terms attached to Britain's first loan was immediate. The demand for gold worried a power whose perch on the gold standard was so precarious. It also bridled at the Treasury's efforts to determine how the proceeds of the loan should be spent. When the Russians asked for a second loan, of £100 million, in December 1914 the Treasury said that Russia's war needs suggested it only required £40 million, and that 40 per cent of any part of the loan spent outside Britain should be backed by gold. Britain justified its demand for gold by saying that it was acting on behalf of all the Entente powers in the neutral markets of the world.[66]

This, then, was the background to the tripartite allied conference on finance held in February 1915. At that meeting the French and Russians, albeit reluctantly, supported the British lead on the gold exchange standard.[67] The Russians, for their part, got about half of what they wanted but more than the British Treasury thought they needed—£25 million and 625 million francs.

The Russians were proved right. On Kitchener's suggestion the War Office set up a Russian purchasing committee in May 1915. Running in parallel with the Commission Internationale de Revitaillement, its job was to channel orders for munitions to the United States on Russia's behalf. But Russia persisted in buying outside both organizations. So great were Russian demands that a fresh loan was needed by June, and pressure on Britain to export gold to America followed in July. During the late summer orders were processed without the credit to fund them. On 30 September the British agreed to advance the Russians £25 million per month for the next twelve months. The money was secured by Russian treasury bills, but Petrograd was to be prepared to ship £40 million in gold within twelve months. The threat to the rouble caused by the export of gold was to be offset by a British credit of £200 million, on the basis of which new paper money could be issued. The agreement thus marked a further meshing of Entente finances. The Russians accepted that their

[65] Michelson *et al.*, *Russian public finance*, 407–24.
[66] Neilson, *Strategy and supply*, 54–7; Grigg, *Lloyd George*, 190–1.
[67] See above, 828–30.

gold could be advanced for the purposes of securing the credit of the whole Entente—not just of Russia—in the United States; they also acknowledged—in principle, if still not in practice—that they had no powers to purchase munitions abroad on a unilateral basis. Britain, for its part, had sacrificed long-term financial prudence for immediate victory.[68]

Bark, his negotiations in London complete, then crossed over to Paris at the beginning of October. His demands of the French were exorbitant, but he had most, if not all of them, met. He put Russia's needs at 1,500 million francs over the next twelve months. This total included provision for municipal loans, for the acquisition of foreign exchange for trade and industry, and for the maintenance of credits in Italy. In exchange he offered a hypothetical condition—the shipment of wheat and alcohol on the assumption that the Dardanelles would be reopened. Ribot refused to support Russia's Italian borrowing but he did accept the rest, for all its lack of direct application to the war effort. On 4 October 1915 Bark was given 125 million francs a month by France—a rate of payment endorsed in July 1916 and sustained until November 1917.[69]

The irony of Russia asking France to support its borrowing in Italy cannot have been lost on Ribot. Italy entered the war on the Entente's side on 24 May 1915. By the time of Bark's request the Entente had already had to come to terms with the indigence of its new ally. Indeed, both Britain and France had used the offer of loans from the outset in their wooing of Italy. Thus they accepted, at least implicitly, that if Italy waged war it would be at their expense. What was surprising was the low price Salandra, the Italian prime minister, put on Italy's entry on the Entente side. He demanded £50 million, a figure arrived at without discussion with the Ministry of Finance. Its small size reflected Salandra's conviction that the war would be short, and that Italy's primary objectives—not to be forfeited to requirements generated by financial necessity—were political and territorial. Nobody pretended that it was likely to be adequate.[70] By the end of the financial year 1918/19 Italy owed Britain £412.5 million.[71]

[68] Neilson, *Strategy and supply*, 100–7; Michelson *et al.*, *Russian public finance*, 305–9, 311; Neilson, *Britain and the last Tsar*, 353–4; Neilson, 'Managing the war: Britain, Russia and ad hoc government', in Dockrill and French (eds.), *Strategy and intelligence*, 108–9.

[69] Michelson *et al.*, *Russian public finance*, 296–9; Petit, *Finances extérieures*, 61.

[70] Forsyth, *Crisis of Liberal Italy*, 152–4.

[71] Morgan, *British financial policy*, 317.

Italy had had a healthy balance of payments in August 1914, but by April 1915, even before its entry to the war, its holdings of foreign exchange were running low. The war demands of the belligerent nations had meant that for the first time exports had exceeded imports. Nonetheless, the total volume of trade had declined, and the visible surplus was not sufficient to offset the loss of invisible earnings. Tourism, a major earner of foreign exchange for Italy, collapsed with the outbreak of war. More serious still was the decline in remittances from Italian emigrants. In 1913 these totalled 828 million lire; by 1915 they had fallen to 497 million lire, or 390 million in 1913 prices. Much of the fall was in US dollars, and was not balanced by any compensating increase in exports to America.[72] Italy tried to float treasury bonds on the American market in the autumn of 1915, but found themselves cutting across the negotiations of their more senior Entente partners, and had to be content with $25 million raised in October 1915.[73]

Italy's principal pre-war creditor was France. In 1911–12 the latter recovered about three-quarters of Italy's foreign debt repayment, and in 1914–15 France used this status in its bid to break down Italian neutrality. But the leverage vouchsafed France by its money market diminished as Italy increased its ability to contract debt at home: in 1909–10 only 11.8 per cent of Italy's debt was placed abroad, as opposed to nearly half in 1892–3. Furthermore, the balance of French loans was skewed to public funding rather than to private investment; here Germany was an increasingly important player. France therefore saw Italy's decision to join the Entente as an opportunity to re-establish its suzerainty over Italian finance. Its efforts focused on the Banca Commerciale Italiana, which in 1914 had eleven German directors to four French, although Frenchmen were responsible for six times more business than were Germans. By the end of 1915 France had two plans—one drawn up by a banker, Guiot, and driven by financial considerations, and the other developed by an industrialist, Devies, of Creusot. The Foreign Ministry went for Devies's scheme, principally because it could not agree on Guiot's. Its objective was to gain control of the Banca Commerciale Italiano, and then to establish a Franco-Italian industrial consortium as a basis for cornering the Italian

[72] Forsyth, *Crisis of Liberal Italy*, 12–13, 56–9, 150–1, 154, 321.
[73] Ibid. 163; Nouailhat, *France et État-Unis*, 278; Petit, *Finances extérieures*, 349, 357.

import market for France. But Germany's pre-war influence in Italian finance was a paper tiger; Italy, with seventeen directors, already dominated the board of the Banca Commerciale Italiano, and it had no intention of using its escape from Germany's thrall (if such it was) to resubordinate itself to France's. Italian industry boomed on the back of the war, and it did so in conjunction with a banking sector that was increasingly independent of foreign influences. France failed in its bid to re-establish pre-eminence in post-war Italian industry, and the focus of its efforts diverted it from a primary role in funding Italy's war effort. That responsibility passed to Britain.[74]

The terms agreed between Britain and Italy in Nice on 5 June 1915, a month after Italy's formal entry to the Entente, reflected the principles thrashed out by the three original partners in Paris in February. Italy, to its surprise, was required to transfer £10 million in gold to the Bank of England. In addition it deposited sterling treasury bills to the value of £50 million; the British then sold treasury bills for the same amount on the London market. The total credit of £60 million was made available at the rate of £2 million per week. The funding was therefore deemed sufficient for about seven months.

In fact it was in November 1915 that Italy's monthly credit was increased from £8 million to £10 million with effect from April 1916. As in their earlier negotiations, Britain insisted on a deposit of gold—a tenth of the total. Revealing of new pressures, however, were the restrictions on Italy's use of the money in the United States. Not more than £65 million could be spent in America, and Britain reserved the right to reduce Italy's dollar credits after March 1916 in the event of London being unable to procure sufficient loans in New York.[75]

The machinery of Entente finance that evolved in 1915 therefore rested on a fundamental premiss—that of British credit in international markets, and specifically in the largest neutral market, New York. Thus, while Britain and France extended loans to Russia and Italy, they in their turn had to seek advances from the United States. France's experience over the first year of the war suggested that this would not be straightforward.

---

[74] Raymond Poidevin, 'Les Relations économiques et financières', and Pierre Milza, 'Les Relations financières franco-italiennes pendant le premier conflit mondial', in Guillen (ed.), *La France et l'Italie*; also the comments by Leo Valiani on both essays, ibid. 348–9.

[75] Forsyth, *Crisis of Liberal Italy*, 162–3.

On 3 August 1914 the French government approached Rothschild's in Paris and J. P. Morgan in New York about the possibility of placing a loan for $100 million in the United States. Morgan's advised against. Both the fall of European trade and the sale of European stocks on the outbreak of war suggested that the American market was not primed to react positively. These commercial causes for hesitation were reinforced by political factors. William Jennings Bryan, the secretary of state, argued that loans to the belligerents were incompatible with American neutrality. He saw money as the most powerful contraband of all, since it directed all other commodities, and he feared that once Americans invested their wealth in the outcome of the war their loyalties would be divided, domestic disharmony would follow, and the United States itself might be propelled into hostilities.

In October the French government renewed its efforts in a much more modest form. It approached the head of the National City Bank, a Frenchman called Maurice Léon, with a view to placing £10 million in French treasury bonds. Léon consulted Bryan's subordinate, Robert Lansing. Lansing's response was predicated not on political principle but on financial self-interest. He argued that, if the United States blocked the belligerents' efforts to get credits, they would take their trade elsewhere and the American economy would remain depressed. He saw no incompatibility between neutrality and the private issue of bank loans to belligerents; America's objection was to the public flotation of government stocks. Thus, the National City Bank loan went ahead, and an important precedent was set.[76]

By the beginning of 1915 the contribution to American economic recovery of allied orders for munitions and other supplies was manifest. Between August and December 1914 French payments in America averaged 53.8 million francs a month; in February 1915 they rose to 76.9 million, in March to 135 million, and in April to 186 million.[77] British imports from America in 1915 were 68 per cent greater by volume and 75 per cent by value than they had been in 1913; they cost £237.8 million.[78]

[76] Nouailhat, *France et États-Unis*, 96–100; Renouvin, *Annales*, VI (1951), 289–94.
[77] Nouailhat, *France et Etats-Unis*, 109.
[78] Burk, *Britain, America and the sinews of war*, 62, 267.

To administer these orders, and to prevent confusion and competition between government departments, Britain appointed J. P. Morgan and Company as its sole agent in January 1915. Morgan's took a 2 per cent commission on the net price of all goods up to £10 million, and 1 per cent thereafter. To some the appointment seemed perverse: finance, not purchasing, was Morgan's forte. These doubts were allayed by the fact that it was indeed as financial agents that Morgan's fulfilled their most important services. Their attraction to Britain was their combination of Wall Street expertise and Anglophilia. As they emphasized discount business rather than the integration of industry and investment banking, their style and expertise accorded with British practices. Their profits derived from the flotation of loans, not from securing a niche for American exports. Thus, they were not exploiting Britain's short-term need in order to undermine Britain's long-term economic position. Others in America, particular Frank Vanderlip of the National City Bank, took a diametrically opposed line. But until 1918 it was the Morgan's approach which dominated American finance.[79]

With associated firms in London (Morgan Grenfell) and Paris (Morgan Harjes), Morgan's were well poised to represent the interests not just of Britain but of the Entente. Lloyd George pressed this point on Ribot in the aftermath of the February 1915 conference. As a result France agreed on 1 May to appoint Morgan's as its representative, but the relationship never became as close or as comprehensive. France appreciated full well how handsomely Morgan's was doing out of the Entente's needs. Between May 1915 and November 1918 Morgan's handled 2,445 French contracts, worth a total of $1,073.2 million, and paid out £18,000 million on behalf of the British. Octave Homberg was convinced that the cushion provided by their Entente contracts prevented Morgan's taking sufficient initiative on their clients' behalf. He accused them of favouring firms to which they were financially linked and of failing to increase their staff in line with the increase in business for fear of reducing their profits. In 1917 both governments reflected these criticisms by increasingly representing their own interests—France through Homberg himself.[80]

[79] Ibid. 20–2; Burk, 'A merchant bank at war', 158–9; id., 'The Treasury: from impotence to power', in Burk (ed.), War and the state, 89–90; Sayers, Bank of England, i. 86–8; Parrini, Heir to empire, 59–65.

[80] Nouailhat, France et États-Unis, 241–9; Nouailhat, Revue d'histoire moderne et contemporaine, XIV (1967), 366; Schmidt, Ribot, 125–6.

The basis of the French dislike of Morgan's was established in March 1915. Ribot sought to place $50 million in treasury bonds in America. Morgan's and the National City Bank were both keen to act, but proposed to buy the bonds in francs and sell them in dollars so as to elevate their own commissions. Ribot rejected their terms. The two banks, now joined by the First National Bank, came back, agreeing to take $25 million in French treasury bonds and to offer a further $25 million at option. Only $1.2 million of the second instalment was subscribed, despite the fact that France was paying a higher rate of interest (5.5 per cent) than that prevailing in the United State (4.5 per cent). French government credit was thereby impugned. Ribot's solution in June 1915 was to use French holdings of US railway stocks as security. Not only did Ribot raise $42 million in this way, but he also did so on very advantageous terms: he borrowed from the Banque de France at 1 per cent to buy shares selling at up to 4.56 per cent. In September he repeated the formula through Kuhn Loeb, and raised a further $2.5 million.[81]

Despite the eventual success of this operation, France never took a tight grip of foreign securities and thus failed to maximize their use in generating foreign credits. This caused particular annoyance in Britain. France's foreign investments in 1914 were as high as half those of Britain, but during the war it sold only 8 per cent of its entire foreign security portfolio. Part of the problem was that France's foreign investment was concentrated in the wrong places—countries like Russia where payments were slowed or blocked by moratoriums, and where military self-interest worked against their withdrawal. Not enough had been invested in the United States. But a further significant factor was France's reluctance to coerce the market. Thus, 30 per cent of privately held dollar securities still remained in individual ownership at the war's end.[82] Fear that restrictions on the market would forfeit France's international status circumscribed policy. Between 1915 and 1917 efforts focused on preventing the settlement in Paris—through the mediation of neutral banks—of shares held by the Central Powers. Even in 1917 French citizens holding neutral shares came under no more than moral pressure to pass them over to the government. The contrast with Britain was instructive. The Bank of

[81] Nouailhat, *France et États-Unis*, 110–13; Petit, *Finances extérieures*, 71, 339–42.
[82] Knauss, *Kriegsfinanzierung*, 82; Eichengreen, *Golden fetters*, 83.

England began buying dollar securities on the Treasury's instructions in July 1915. By the end of 1915 $233 million had been acquired in this way. The government then went public, offering either to buy securities at the current price or to borrow them at 0.5 per cent over their actual return. It thus approached the American money market as an owner, and could threaten to sell if New York did not lend. More significantly, stick followed carrot. In the April 1916 budget foreign securities became liable to punitive rates of income tax, and in January 1917 the Treasury was empowered to requisition all such securities.[83]

Nor was France any firmer in its management of foreign exchange. When Ribot suggested on 1 July 1915 that controls on foreign exchange might be appropriate, the Banque de France argued that the market was too sophisticated for controls to be possible: all that followed was a voluntary code. A whole succession of regulations, based on postal and commercial intelligence garnered by the general staff and by the organizations responsible for the blockade, took the form of advice and lacked legal penalties. After the entry of the United States the pressures on France were political as well as fiscal: France's western allies, fierce with themselves, expected France to fall into line. By not doing so, Paris was increasing the burden borne by New York and London. But the commission on exchanges, established by the Ministry of Finance in July 1917, built on the established regulations rather than began afresh. The banks were invited to restrict their sale of foreign exchange to legitimate operations, but their freedom of operation was circumscribed only by an appeal to their patriotism, not by the law.[84]

The combination of laxity in relation to foreign exchange and a severe imbalance in payments was soon evident in France's faltering exchange rate. In August 1914 the franc had gained 3.5 per cent on the dollar. However, by February 1915 the exchange was back to par, by April 1915 the dollar was trading at 8.5 per cent above the franc and by August at 15 per cent. The Swiss franc stood at 6.5 per cent above par in July 1915 and the Dutch florin at 9.69 per cent.[85]

---

[83] Morgan, *British financial policy*, 327–31; Stamp, *Taxation*, 101; Brown, *Gold standard*, 60–1; Farr, 'McKenna', 185.

[84] Petit, *Finances extérieures*, 66–7, 103–19.

[85] Jèze and Truchy, *War finance*, 289–90; Petit, *Finances extérieures*, 63.

The weakness of the franc generated friction within the alliance. French imports from Britain more than doubled in value in the second quarter of 1915, and, with the pound at a premium of 7.3 per cent over the franc at the end of June, a significant element of this expense was going on exchange. France protested that it was denied the access to the London money market promised it in February in Calais, but for the time being London itself remained unresponsive. Partly this was due to surprise; as recently as the new year France had seemed second only to Britain in its strength on international markets. But it was also due to McKenna's own priorities.[86]

The London–New York axis was more important to the pound than that between London and Paris. At the start of the war sterling too rose against the dollar, but by December 1914 it had fallen back to par, $4.86. In June 1915 it stood at $4.77. Morgan's reminded the Treasury of the surcharge thus being put on Britain's American purchases, but McKenna seemed relatively indifferent to exchange-rate problems. His fear was British indebtedness to the United States. His policies came under attack from two directions. Cunliffe resented the fact that the Bank of England was battling with the exchange rate single-handed, and in the cabinet both McKenna's predecessor at the Treasury, Lloyd George, and his successor, Bonar Law, were less fearful of American credits. The wavering market reflected the conflicting policies which emanated from London.

On 25 July Asquith told McKenna that contracts were not to be lost through lack of exchange.[87] In that month Morgan's arranged a loan of $50 million, four-fifths of which was guaranteed by American securities and one-tenth in gold from the Bank of England. But by August almost all this loan had gone and the exchange rate was still tumbling. On 14 August alone it fell from $4.73 to $4.64. Four days later the cabinet agreed to ship $100 million in gold to America, as well as to buy up British-held American shares.[88]

The decline of the British and French exchanges caused almost as much concern in New York as it did in London and Paris. McAdoo was well aware how contingent American prosperity was on Entente purchasing: he could not afford to let the value of the dollar price American goods out

[86] Horn, *International History Review*, XVII (1995), 62–3.

[87] Farr, 'McKenna', 158.

[88] Burk, *Britain, America and the sinews of war*, 62–4; Sayers, *Bank of England*, i. 89; Soutou, *L'Or et le sang*, 225–7.

of the market. The behaviour of the Federal Reserve Board reflected these commercial interests. Benjamin Strong was keen to use the war to promote the use of dollar acceptances for two reasons. First he saw no reason why trade between the United States and the rest of the world, particularly South America, should be funded by credits from London. Secondly, the alternative, for American exports to be paid for in gold, would render the United States vulnerable to the return of normal trading conditions, when the gold would emigrate once more. The Board adopted the principle of rediscounting commercial acceptances in April 1915, but made an exception for arms and munitions. In August, under pressure from McAdoo, the Board revised its policy, and banks were permitted to rediscount all commercial acceptances. Politically too—although the president remained reluctant publicly to commit himself—the mood changed. America's protest to Germany over the torpedoing of the *Lusitania* with the loss of American lives on 6 May prompted the strongly neutralist Bryan to resign. He was succeeded as secretary of state by Lansing, who had of course already shown himself sympathetic to the financial needs of the Entente. On 19 August 1915 a German U-boat sank the *Arabic*, and two more Americans were drowned. Not for the last time the German use of submarines came to the rescue of Britain's imperilled finances. When Britain enquired at the end of the month about the possibility of publicly launching a government loan in the United States, it was accorded muted approval. Wilson would not give any flotation his public benediction, but nor would he oppose it.[89]

McKenna's anxiety to enforce the primacy of British finances in the Entente remained. Thus, he proposed that a government loan launched in America should be in Britain's name only, although France and Russia should share the proceeds. Similarly, the cabinet decision of 22 August to ship gold rested on the presumption that both Britain's Entente partners would contribute to the pot. Ribot was not happy with either idea. At Boulogne on 21 August, the two finance ministers agreed that the loan would be joint, and that gold would not be sent immediately but that each power would hold $200 million in reserve in case it was needed. The speed with which the meeting was convened prevented Russia from being represented, but the two western allies shed few tears: they recognized

[89] Nouailhat, *France et États-Unis*, 272–85; Renouvin, *Annales*, VI (1951), 294–6; Chandler, *Strong*, 86–92.

that Russia's poor reputation in America could cause the failure of the loan.

However, the converse did not apply. Russia's exclusion did not guarantee the loan's success. Lord Reading, who was sent by the British government to negotiate the loan's terms, was told by McKenna that he would be happy with $100 million; his aim was to get America used to the idea of foreign loans.[90] In the event, the nominal capital of the issue was $500 million. It was sold at 98 and paid 5 per cent. But American investors were used to a rate of 5.5 or 6 per cent. Furthermore, they were not accustomed to a loan on this scale nor one which lacked collateral. Only $33 million was subscribed by individuals; on this evidence American sentiment remained strongly neutral—whatever the popular responses to the sinking of merchant ships or the financial self-interest generated by Entente purchasing. Indeed, without the latter the loan would have flopped completely. Six companies with major allied orders brought £100 million of the stock. Little interest was shown in the Midwest, where German agitation was strong. By the close, on 14 December 1915, $187 million was still unsold and had to be taken by the banks which had underwritten the issue. The banks' price was 96, the stock rapidly fell to 94 and, despite Morgan's intervention, it was trading even lower by the end of February 1916.[91]

Nonetheless, the loan achieved a number of important objectives. At the price of growing indebtedness in New York, it secured British exchange rates. By the beginning of 1916 the pound exceeded $4.77, and it never fell below $4.76 for the rest of the war. The loan thus provided a secure platform from which the British exchange committee could begin its operations in November 1915.[92] Furthermore, it linked the franc to the pound, thus stabilizing the former as well as the latter. The pegging of the exchange rate kept the dollar artificially weak, but in so doing sustained Entente orders and thus deepened America's own need to support sterling and its associated currencies.

The focus in the literature is on the sense of continuing crisis generated by the battle to secure American funds and to maintain the convertibility

---

[90] Farr, 'McKenna', 164.

[91] Petit, *Finances extérieures*, 73–5, 200–1, 347–8; Nouailhat, *France et États-Unis*, 287–91; Burk, *Britain, America and the sinews of war*, 67–76; Burk, *Historical Journal*, XXII (1979), 353–4.

[92] See above, p. 830.

of sterling in New York. But the irritability and frustration which bubbled up in London should not be allowed to obscure the specific advantages which accrued to Britain from the Anglo-American financial relationship. Nor should the attention to the deficit in Britain's Atlantic trade overshadow the broader picture of Britain's balance of payments. Shipping profits helped offset the loss of other earnings. In 1913 Britain's trading surplus (aggregating visible and invisible trade) was £181 million; during the war it still averaged £50 million; and only in 1918 did the account show a major deficit, £204 million.[93] Furthermore, Britain's economic leadership of the Entente helped compensate for the imbalance in its American trade. France spent almost as much in Britain during the war, 23,000 million francs, as it did in the United States (between 26,000 and 27,000 million francs). In 1913 French visible exports to Britain were worth 1,453.8 million francs, and its imports 1,115 million; by 1915 this modest French surplus had been turned into a deficit of 2,938.7 million francs, and in 1917 the deficit was 5,791.2 million francs.[94]

Britain therefore became the banker not only to Russia and Italy but also to France. Ribot opened an initial credit of £400,000 at the Bank of England at the outset of the war, and French treasury bills to the tune of £2 million were placed in London in October 1914. Negotiations for a loan of £10 million continued during the winter of 1914–15: Ribot felt the total was too low, but Cunliffe feared the short-lived strength of the franc and the possible depreciation of the pound. The fall of the franc and the February 1915 conference cleared the way for an Anglo-French deal in April. Ribot asked for, and got, £12 million to cover France's purchases in Britain for the next six months, and a further £50 million for acquisitions in North America: two-fifths of France's American costs in sterling were to be backed by gold sent to the Bank of England. In November 1915 Britain moderated its closure of the stock exchange to foreigners, allowing France to sell its first war loan stock, an operation which raised over £19 million. A continuation of the April 1915 agreement was negotiated in February 1916. Britain agreed to discount French treasury bills at the rate of £4 million per month from the end of June; it also advanced £6 million a month for three months from mid-April to cover French

---

[93] Peter Dewey, 'The new warfare and economic mobilization', in Turner (ed.), *Britain and the First World War*, 82–3.

[94] Petit, *Finances extérieures*, 44–6, 49–50, 696.

payments in New York. In exchange France shipped £1 million in gold to Britain for each of February, March, and April, so allowing Ribot to conclude the total credits were £11 million per month rather than £10 million, as the British reckoned.[95]

The two powers concluded their February 1916 discussions by saying they would meet again at the end of the year to concert their financial plans for 1917. But McKenna had promised that London would take measures to support the franc when the pound passed 25.50 francs. By the end of January it had risen to 28 francs. Paris's position in the United States had been secured until mid-April by the Anglo-French loan, but its deficit in Britain was increasing at the rate of 100 million francs per month. Cunliffe was prepared to make a sufficiently large advance to buoy the French exchange rate and to continue the migration of French gold to Britain: he suggested a credit of £120 million, to be divided between the Banque de France and the state, and to be secured one-third in gold and the balance in treasury bonds. Ribot regarded £120 million as insufficient: he wanted £160 million. McKenna, however, feared that a large British loan to France would hit the dollar–sterling exchange, and stipulated a maximum of £30 million over three months. On 14 April Ribot got £60 million, one-third covered by gold. The exchange rate, which had reached 29 francs to the pound, stabilized at 27 francs.

By May 1916 France had become dependent on British guarantees for its overseas purchases. Well over a third of Britain's advances to France in the war, £177.2 million of £445.75 million, were made in 1916. France's subordination was evident in the terms to which Ribot was bound in April. The agreement was to be suspended if the exchange rate became any more favourable to the franc, and the level of interest on the loan— when the 6 per cent payable on the treasury bonds was added to the loss of interest on the gold—aggregated at 9 per cent.[96]

While France was negotiating with Britain, its credit with the United States was ebbing away. By 8 July 1916 France owed Morgan's $726,686, and the payments on the Ministry of War's orders due in August totalled 264 million francs. The ministry's American purchases in 1916 were running at double the level of 1915. But Morgan's counselled delay in

[95] Horn, *International History Review*, XVII (1995), 68.
[96] Petit, *Finances extérieures*, 59, 77–9, 183–6, 196–7, 206–16; Jèze and Truchy, *War expenditure of France*, 299–301, 305–7.

the issue of a fresh loan. The 1915 Anglo-French loan stock remained depressed until April; the danger of a war between the United States and Mexico created the possibility that the American government itself would enter the loans market; and confidence in French military prowess as well as French financial strength was low.

France needed Britain's name to get credit in New York. In mid-July Ribot canvassed the notion of a second Anglo-French loan at a conference in London attended by all four Entente powers. But the remit of the conference was economic in its widest sense: it followed on a discussion of economic war aims in Paris in June, and its focus was as much material as financial. The need for munitions generated by the battles of Verdun and the Somme was as pressing a consideration as the method of paying for them. Lloyd George, driven as usual by the former rather than the latter, argued that America was more dependent on Entente orders than the Entente was on American money: he felt that presidential support for an Anglo-French loan would be forthcoming and therefore supported Ribot. However, McKenna reckoned America would not lend. His priorities were unchanged: to extract gold from Britain's allies, to curb Britain's indebtedness to the United States, and to float loans in Britain's name only.

Ribot left the conference under a misapprehension. He had shifted his own ground since December. He was now less determined in his subordination of war finance to the imperatives of strategy, and more appreciative of McKenna's general point, that the military effort might have to be scaled back so that it was more in step with financial capacity. France's overseas payments had totalled 282 million francs in January, and had risen to 500 million by June. But the fears he expressed domestically had been moderated by at least some of his allies. Asquith had intervened in April to overcome McKenna's doubts about the increased British loan to France. Now Lloyd George seemed similarly bullish. Ribot and McKenna agreed that the launch of any joint loan should be postponed until after the American presidential election in November. But their policies, although driven by similar interpretations of their own nations' individual needs, took divergent courses.[97]

---

[97] Horn, *International History Review*, XVII (1995), 69, and for what follows 73–4; see also Horn, *Guerres mondiales et conflits contemporains*, 180 (octobre 1995), 21–6.

Ribot pressed ahead with a scheme on which Homberg had been working since January. The evidence of 1915 showed that France would not be able to raise a loan on its own account without collateral. This upset Ribot: the name of the French government should be sufficient credit in itself. Homberg's solution was to form a banking syndicate, the American Foreign Securities Company, backed with $120 million in neutral shares. On this basis a loan for $100 million was issued on 19 July 1916, and was oversubscribed three days before it was due to close. The credit of the French government—or perhaps more properly Ribot's *amour propre*—remained inviolate.[98]

But Britain too needed credit in America. McKenna and Keynes felt that all that had saved the situation so far was the failure of American firms to deliver contracts to time and the lack of cargo space to ship those orders that had been completed.[99] But as American industry accustomed itself to allied war needs the first of these constraints on Britain's spending was eased. At the beginning of May 1916 the Treasury thought that the country could be bankrupt by the end of June, and McKenna warned Ribot that he might not be able to stick to the February 1916 agreement.[100] On 19 May the Treasury calculated that $434 million was required by the end of September, just to cover its existing commitments. At the end of August the British government, acting on the advice of Morgan's but against that of the Bank of England, floated a loan of $250 million. Britain, unlike France, acted in its own name, and furthermore provided as collateral North American and neutral securities worth $300 million.[101] The effect was to trigger a fall not only in the 1915 Anglo-French stock but also in the new French loan of July 1916. Ribot was furious. He had not been consulted. The principle which he had contested with Homberg had been subverted by the unilateral action of France's ally. A precedent had been set which France, partly through its reluctance to commandeer the neutral shares of its own citizens, could not follow. Henceforth an unguaranteed loan would be impossible, and in the short term the American Foreign Securities Company could not

[98] Nouailhat, *France et États-Unis*, 363–7; Nouailhat, *Revue d'histoire moderne et contemporaine*, XIV (1967), 356–74; Petit, *Finances extérieures*, 217–19, 378–83.
[99] Farr, 'McKenna', 245.
[100] Horn, *Guerres mondiales et conflits contemporains*, 180 (octobre 1995), 22.
[101] Burk, *Britain, America and the sinews of war*, 78–80.

return to a market glutted with British stocks. British credit, which Ribot had understood from the July conference was being held in reserve for joint use, had been expended. Moreover, the issue was not particularly successful: only $200 million was subscribed and its price fell.

McKenna and Ribot met at Calais on 24 August to rebuild the bridges of cross-Channel financial co-operation. McKenna denied that he had breached any earlier agreements but was probably more apologetic than he need have been. He said that the loan was a response to an immediate crisis on the exchanges. More to the point was the fact that Britain's action on the exchanges and in the export of gold was not entirely self-interested; it was designed to support the American purchases of all the Entente. He offered to increase French credits to £25 million per month for six months; £10 million of this was to be used by the Banque de France to support the franc. In return, Britain's allies were to disgorge a further £100 million in gold—half of which was to come from France, £40 million from Russia, and £10 million from Italy.[102] The real opposition to these proposals came not from Ribot but from Bark. Russia had not yet shipped £20 million of the £40 million in gold agreed on in September 1915. At the London conference in July Britain had accorded Russia credits of £25 million per month for the next six months, in addition to £63 million for immediate use in military orders and to a further £63 million in the autumn provided Russia held £40 million in gold ready for shipment. The Foreign Office feared that the Treasury was blackening Britain's image in Russia in its pursuit of gold, and McKenna moderated his demands. If the £20 million outstanding under the September 1915 agreement was remitted, Britain would only require a further £20 million; the first instalment was received in November 1916 and the second in February 1917.[103]

Neither Britain nor France could afford to be soft with their ally. McKenna had accepted at Calais that an Anglo-French committee on finance should be set up, and it held its only meeting between 3 and 10 October 1916. The two powers calculated that their spending in America over the six-month period October 1916 to April 1917 would

---

[102] Schmidt, *Ribot*, 134–5; Petit, *Finances extérieures*, 225–32, 384–6.

[103] Neilson, *Strategy and Supply*, 202–3, 237–8; Michelson *et al.*, *Russian public finance*, 307–9; Neilson, *Britain and the last Tsar*, 355–6; Neilson, 'Managing the war: Britain, Russia and ad hoc government', in Dockrill and French (eds.), *Strategy and intelligence*, 112 .

total $1,500 million. France expected its monthly deficit to run at between £8 million and £10 million despite the £25 million British credit. Two-fifths of Britain's daily spending on the war was disbursed in the United States, giving a monthly expenditure of $250 million.[104] In the five months ending on 30 September 1916, three-fifths of British spending in America had been covered by gold or by existing British investments in the United States and two-fifths by loans. The allied agreement to raise £100 million in gold could contribute $500 million towards the $1,500 million required, but prudence suggested that half this gold should be kept back. Thus, perhaps five-sixths of allied spending in the United States over the next half-year would have to be funded by loans—a total of $1,250 million. Borrowing on this scale would itself clog the market, as each issue would compete with the last. The principal problem was its pace: 'the question', Keynes wrote, 'is whether the money can be turned over in America and brought back to us in the form of loans as fast as we are spending it.'[105] Furthermore, nobody had any idea how the war could be financed beyond April 1917. McKenna, reflecting advice from Keynes, reckoned that by June 1917 the United States would be in a position to dictate terms.[106]

The only break in a dark and troubled sky was Morgan's view of the short-term state of the New York market. They reckoned it to be in a much more receptive mood. Britain therefore issued loans worth $300 million in October, half offered at 99.25 and maturing in 1919, and the other half at 98.5 and maturing in 1921: both paid 5.5 per cent. A credit for $50 million for French industry was organized by a group of American bankers in November 1916. At the end of September the city of Paris successfully floated a loan for $50 million, which it then transferred to the government; on 24 November Lyons, Marseilles, and Bordeaux followed suit.[107]

The French cities loan quickly raised $34.5 million, and then shuddered to a halt on 28 November 1916. On that day the press published a warning from the Federal Reserve Board to its member banks, advising against the purchase of foreign treasury bills. The announcement also carried an injunction to private investors to consider carefully the nature

[104] Burk, *Britain, America and the sinews of war*, 81–2; Petit, *Finances extérieures*, 236–9, 401.
[105] Johnson (ed.), *Collected writings of Keynes*, xvi. 207; see also 197–209.
[106] Soutou, *L'Or et le sang*, 367–8.
[107] Petit, *Finances extérieures*, 94–5, 400–10; Morgan, *British financial policy*, 325.

of their overseas investments, particularly in the case of unsecured loans. Allied shares fell, and $1,000 million was wiped off the stock market in a week. The ensuing run on the pound could only be staunched with the shipment of more gold. To save its exchange, Britain stopped its American orders and tried to curb those of its allies.

London's ire over the Board's declaration was directed more towards Morgan's than it was towards Washington. Morgan's had advised the British and French that an unsecured joint loan could be issued by both governments in January 1917. H. P. Davison, a partner in Morgan's, met the Federal Reserve Board on 19 November and told them that up to $1,000 million in treasury bills would be issued in the near future. Davison's manner, despite the fact that the Board had already halved the projected value of the French industry loan in the same month, was not conciliatory. He miscalculated the mood of the Board. Its membership was already divided as to future financial strategy. Benjamin Strong was most favourable to the Entente's position: he saw the creation of foreign credit as a hedge against the end of the war, when the gold that had poured into the United States during hostilities would move again. But Strong was ill. Possessed of the opposite view was Paul Warburg, a German by birth, who played on the fears generated by American dependence on allied orders. Inflation and a rising cost of living were only the obvious manifestations. In 1915–16, when allied purchases were predicated on shipments of gold, the war had boosted the reserve status of the banks and so brought forward the full effectiveness of the Federal Reserve act. But once unsecured medium-term loans began to oust gold the reverse process occurred. Moreover, these foreign obligations were denying short-term funds to domestic business and so distorting America's industrial growth. Thus there were long-term adverse implications in America's short-term prosperity. By extending credit, America was investing not only in the continuation of the war but also in the prospects of Entente victory: a sudden end to hostilities or—or even, and—the defeat of the Entente would cause an economic crash. On this interpretation America's best policy was to let allied orders wind down as the Entente's power to pay also declined. Thus, the adjustment could be gradual. These views convinced the Board's president, W. P. G. Harding.

The prime motor in the Board's declaration, therefore, was financial. But the force of its views was also political. In the recent presidential elections Morgan's had supported the Republicans, while the Democrat, Woodrow Wilson, campaigned on a neutralist ticket. Wilson was re-elected. By curbing Entente credits, he could pressurize the allies into peace negotiations. If this policy failed, then the probability was that America would be forced into the war on the Entente side. From an economic perspective its investment would give it little choice; from the political, German policy seemed to be eliminating any room for man-oeuvre. If America joined the war it would need its domestic loan market for its own military effort, flush with liquid funds and not already committed to medium-term foreign stocks.[108]

The Federal Reserve Board did not formally revise its statement of November 1916 until 8 March 1917. It then declared itself to have been misunderstood in November, said that it had no intention of impugning foreign credit or of limiting exports, and announced its permission for all forms of allied loans without any requirement for gold as cover. Thus, the immediate advice to the cabinet of Asquith and McKenna against pre-cipitate action was wise. The London exchange committee wanted a moratorium on payments to the United States, but this would have effectively ended the convertibility of sterling. A few days later both Asquith and McKenna were out of office, replaced by Lloyd George as prime minister and Bonar Law as chancellor. The new cabinet reflected the British frustration with Morgan's, and decided it needed direct Treasury representation with the Federal Reserve Board. Accordingly Sir Hardman Lever arrived in New York in February: Harding, already modifying the Board's position, responded to Lever's pressure.[109]

Until March, however, Britain had no choice but to muddle through the winter of 1916–17 as best it could. It shipped $300 million in gold; it let £358 million in uncovered debt accumulate with Morgan's; and it issued $250 million in stock in January 1917.[110]

It also reviewed its position with its allies. Unable to launch a major American loan for $100 million until late March, France could only raise

---

[108] Burk, *Britain, America and the sinews of war*, 83–90; Soutou, *L'Or et le sang*, 373–8; Renouvin, *Annales*, VI (1951), 297–303; Nouailhat, *France et États-Unis*, 373–8; J. M. Cooper, *Pacific Historical Review*, XLV (1976), 222–5; Petit, *Finances extérieures*, 411–22.

[109] Fiebig-von Hase and Sturm, *Militärgeschichtliche Mitteilungen*, 52 (1993), 32; Burk, *Britain, America and the sinews of war*, 89–93; Nouailhat, *France et États-Unis*, 416–18; Soutou, *L'Or et le sang*, 406–9.

[110] Morgan, *British financial policy*, 324–5; Soutou, *L'Or et le sang*, 388–90.

$15 million from Morgan's and $17 million through a credit with the National City Bank.[111] On 19 January 1917 the Bank of England revised the April 1916 agreement with the Banque de France, increasing its credit from £60 million to £72 million, but requiring the French bank to boost its deposit of gold from £20 million to £24 million. Further negotiations in March, designed to update the terms of the Calais accord of August 1916, were blocked by a French refusal to ship more gold. A compromise extended the existing arrangements for a further month.[112] Italy and Russia were easier to deal with, as all their American orders were effectively channelled via London, and by blocking them exchange could be saved.[113]

Nonetheless on 1 April 1917 Britain's cash in the United States was all but exhausted. In New York, against an overdraft of $358 million and a weekly spend of $75 million Britain had $490 million in securities and $87 million in gold. At home the Bank of England and the joint stock banks could command a reserve of £114 million in gold.[114] But just at the point when the exhaustion of Britain's finances was about to cut the Entente's Atlantic trade Germany declared unrestricted U-boat warfare, with the intention of achieving the same result. The effect was finally to precipitate the United States's entry into the war. Although Germany's U-boat campaign represented strategic miscalculation at a number of levels, this was the most significant in the long term. The submarine constituted the most serious threat of the war to Britain's maritime supremacy, but on one interpretation it saved Britain.[115]

The failure of German intelligence which produced this blunder cannot be attributed to lack of raw data. Britain's financial plight was evident to every American investor. Rather, what it displays is the narrow framework within which German strategy was shaped. Winning the war was seen to be a matter of operational solutions, whether by sea or by land, and the expanding power of OHL militated against a broader conception. Finance, seen by many before 1914 as the component which would end war soonest, had dropped out of German strategic

[111] Petit, *Finances extérieures*, 424–30; Nouailhat, *France et États-Unis*, 381–2.
[112] Petit, *Finances extérieures*, 241–3.
[113] Forsyth, *Crisis of Liberal Italy*, 169–70; Neilson, *Strategy and supply*, 213–14.
[114] Burk, *Britain, America and the sinews of war*, 95.
[115] Cooper, *Pacific Historical Review*, XLV (1976), 228.

calculations by 1917. Max Warburg, an opponent of U-boat warfare, declared in February 1916 that, 'If America is cut off from Germany, that means a 50 per cent reduction in Germany's financial strength for the war and an increase of 100 per cent for England's and France's'.[116] But Warburg was a representative of the very commercial interests which the industrial associations had already begun to marginalize before the war and which were now increasingly isolated thanks to it. The liquidity in industry generated by war-related profits made the big firms independent of the banks, and this found reflection in German economic thought more generally. Helfferich, minister of the interior and deputy chancellor since May 1916, opposed unrestricted U-boat warfare during the course of 1916, but declared his support in the Reichstag in January 1917. Even in his post-war reflections he could do no more than acknowledge in passing the financial boost American belligerence gave the Entente:[117] because he himself saw financial policy as the servant of Germany's war effort, not its master, or even its partner, he could not envisage its potentially decisive implications for the Entente's war effort.

Many Germans did, of course, feel that the United States, by dint of its supply of munitions and of the availability of its credits for war orders, was already a covert belligerent before April 1917. On this reading America's formal entry to the war did no more than make public and legal what was already practice. By contrast, there were moments in the ensuing eighteen months when some in Britain felt that the shift in American policy after April 1917 was not sufficiently dramatic or altruistic to represent a full acceptance of alliance obligations. Certainly, those in the Treasury who hoped that Britain, having financed the Entente and its overseas orders for three years, would now be able simply to pass that particular function over to the United States proved to be both optimistic and naive.

The American Treasury did not, as the British had done, take finance as a self-contained component of the war economy. McAdoo wanted to create an inter-allied economic committee, but his objective was to restrict and co-ordinate Entente purchasing in America, not to pursue a joint policy in relation to borrowing. By eliminating wastefulness in the

[116] Ferguson, *Paper and iron*, 134; also 108–9; see Gall *et al.*, *Deutsche Bank*, 155–8; Feldman, *Stinnes*, 501.

[117] Helfferich, *Weltkrieg*, 355; on his Reichstag speech, see Hanssen, *Diary*, 164–5.

orders of the European allies, he would of course reduce their need for credits. But he did not see the support of their rates of exchange as a component of this strategy. Nor did he see the undertaking of long-term financial support to the allies as desirable or sensible. Indeed, he argued the reverse: by restricting American support to short-term funds he would force the allies to confine their demands to immediate necessities.

Thus, America's entry helped develop the machinery for the acquisition and distribution of commodities. The joint committee on war purchases and finance was established in August 1917. But Britain's pre-existing leadership in the area of co-ordinated purchasing (particularly for wheat) and Woodrow Wilson's insistence that America was an 'associate' rather than an 'ally' of the Entente both militated against true American economic leadership. Even on the basis of co-ordinated and restricted orders, the Entente's demand for goods exceeded the United States's ability to deliver. The committee's remit therefore came to embrace purchases in neutral countries as well as in the United States. However, since America banned the export of gold in September, it could not aspire to the dominant position in Entente overseas finance enjoyed by Britain. America resisted British pressure to take over the Entente's debts in the United States and yet at the same time insisted that the allies should spend their American credits in America. Consequently America's entry helped soften adverse balances of payments. But it did not ease the pressure to husband gold reserves or to acquire foreign exchange. Nor did it enable the weaker Entente currencies to use dollars to bolster their own credit. Finance itself became subject to largely bilateral negotiations, and Britain, for all its huffing and puffing, found that its primacy in the field was never as comprehensively usurped as its parlous position suggested.[118]

Lever told the US Treasury on 9 April 1917 that Britain needed $1,500 million as soon as possible, with a third of that necessary just to cover the spending of the next thirty days. On 25 April McAdoo began to eke out a succession of short-term loans to America's new allies. Britain got $200 million, France and Italy $100 million each, and a further $100 million was pledged to Russia and $45 million to Belgium. The effect was to displease everybody. The advances were not only insufficient to meet the

---

[118] Soutou, *L'Or et le sang*, 479–80, 510–17.

Europeans' demands, but they also gave them no idea as to what they could expect on a regular monthly basis. On the other hand, they were sufficient to threaten America with a mounting short-term debt which could reach $7,000 million in six months.[119]

McAdoo's response in June was to try to cut the Entente's demands for credits. Britain, as the biggest American borrower and also the biggest Entente creditor, was the principal victim. It was running an overdraft of $400 million with Morgan's, was confronting earlier loans which were now falling due, and was continuing to provide more than twice as much financial support for its allies as the United States. On 20 June Lever demanded $50 million with immediate effect and a promise of funding for the next two months. When McAdoo only agreed to $15 million, Britain threatened to default in the United States. If this had happened the dollar–sterling exchange would have collapsed, and with it the whole structure of Entente finance. Confronted by a choice that was no choice, McAdoo conceded the full $50 million. But he still refused Britain satisfaction on its basic demands—that America should pay the debt with Morgan's, that American loans could be used to support the exchange, and that America should take over from Britain responsibility for Entente purchasing in the United States. McAdoo complained of a lack of information. The Americans were being asked to take on trust the British claim that it was carrying the burden for the Entente. This was the premiss on which Britain demanded that the pound be held at $4.76 and that it receive seven-tenths of the American funds available for foreign loans. If it were not true, British policy smacked of self-interest rather than of alliance altruism.[120]

Britain was in part paying the penalty for its reliance on Morgan's to speak for its interests in America—a dependence ingrained in 1915 and 1916. Its experience in those years had been with Wall Street, which was Republican in sympathy, rather than with the American government and its Democrat president. The declaration of the Federal Reserve Board in November 1916 had warned of the need to change tack. However, Lever's mission, for all its short-term success, did not establish the ideal basis for Anglo-American financial relations at the governmental level. McAdoo

---

[119] Petit, *Finances extérieures*, 436–7, 440–1.
[120] Burk, *Britain, America and the sinews of war*, 195–203.

did not get on with Lever; he did like Lord Northcliffe, who was appointed to co-ordinate all the British missions in America on 31 May 1917, but Northcliffe lacked financial expertise. Moreover, Northcliffe's presence crystallized a bifurcation in British representation in America: on the one hand were the wartime missions speaking for economic interests and concentrated in New York, and on the other was the embassy, focused on traditional diplomacy and based in Washington. On 5 September 1917 Lord Reading was appointed to succeed Northcliffe. Reading, though Lord Chief Justice, had worked in the City of London and in the wartime Treasury. In February 1918 he replaced Sir Cecil Spring Rice as ambassador, and thus the two arms of British policy were united under one head.[121]

Reading's frankness with McAdoo helped transmute the latter's reluctant and short-term concessions to British demands into a more pragmatic relationship. On 23 July 1917 the United States agreed to a pattern of monthly advances—$185 million for August and $400 million for September. On 16 August McAdoo accepted in practice, if not in principle, that the United States would sustain the sterling exchange rate at $4.76. The resolution of the Morgan's overdraft proved more protracted and tested the patience in particular of the British government's principal financial adviser, J. M. Keynes. Between February and September 1918 the American Treasury helped Britain meet its maturities and outstanding debts, but did so while subrogating Britain's collateral. Keynes's sense of humiliation found reflection in a draft memorandum of May 1918 which, although never sent in its entirety to Reading, reflected the fact that, for all the latter's success, McAdoo's policy was still guided by the same principles as it had been twelve months earlier. The conditions of the Americans' financial support were unpredictable; their understandings were committed not to paper but to 'vague oral assurances'.[122]

But Keynes's frustration conveniently neglected the fact that his own advice of 28 July 1917, that Britain abandon the gold standard, had not had to be followed through. In the final analysis, the United States did not use the war to force out sterling as the principal medium of international

---

[121] Ibid. 10, 65, 138–43, 163–6, 167–8, 175–7, 181, 185; Petit, *Finances extérieures*, pp. 439–40 .

[122] Johnson (ed.), *Collected writings of Keynes*, xvi. 287; for all above see Burk, *Britain, America and the sinews of war*, 202–20.

exchange; it was instead prepared to see the dollar shore up the pound, and thus sustain both as convertible currencies.[123] In March 1918 Bonar Law went so far as to suggest that America should finance the purchases of France and Italy in the United States, while Britain continued to carry this responsibility elsewhere in the world. France and Italy were to pay Britain in dollars obtained from the American government. Thus, Britain's own need for dollars would be limited, its pivotal position in the world's trade would be protected, and yet America would relieve it of final responsibility for the borrowings of its Entente partners.[124] Although this suggestion reeked of British self-interest and was understandably not accepted as it stood, much of its spirit was reflected in Entente practice in 1918. That this was so was largely due to the changed, and improved, tenor in Anglo-French financial relationships prompted by America's entry.

Bonar Law effectively outflanked the United States by reorganizing Anglo-French relations in advance of Anglo-American. On 29 May 1917 France accepted that its purchases in Britain would be limited to goods originating in Britain; thus, Britain's credit to France for June was fixed at £14 million. France was to forward francs to cover the expenses of the British Expeditionary Force and Britain would reimburse France in sterling. France accepted that it would pay Britain in dollars for all the expenses that it incurred on France's behalf outside the British empire, and that it would be responsible for its own dollar exchange and its own American payments.

However, America's reluctance to move to firm arrangements for lending to its allies drove back up France's need for sterling. At the end of June Britain suggested it advance £16 million a month for two months from July and France countered with a request for £18 million a month for three months. But America's attitude also increased Anglo-French solidarity. Because the franc rested on the pound, the French had a direct interest in measures designed to reinforce the pound against the dollar. On 7 August the French agreed to pass over to Britain $40 million for that month, and to pay in dollars for goods bought through the Entente purchasing machinery, including food acquired from within the British empire. McAdoo's frustration at Entente measures calculated to weaken

[123] Soutou, *L'Or et le sang*, 467–76; see also Parrini, *Heir to empire*, 10, 259.
[124] Johnson (ed.), *Collected writings of Keynes*, xvi. 281–3; Skidelsky, *Keynes*, i. 344, 348.

the dollar was countered by allied sophistry, to the effect that if the Allied Wheat Executive had not provided wheat from India bought with sterling it would have had to do so with wheat from America secured through American credits.

At the same time, however, Britain used America's pressure for the allies to co-ordinate and control their overseas purchasing to reinforce its own efforts in the same direction. France's regulation of its imports was still lax: about £4 million of its monthly imports in mid-1917 were generated by private commerce, and the French government knew the exact use of, at most, two-thirds of its British credits. On 1 March 1918 Law reckoned that Britain's loans to France had climbed back to £22 million a month. He tried to get all French orders, not just those of the government, channelled through the Commission Internationale de Revitaillement. Klotz resisted this, but in July 1918 the French government began at last to put its own house in order, grouping and monitoring the main categories of import, and their cost. Britain's credits to France tailed off as 1918 progressed: Law had been anxious to keep them below £20 million a month, and the final average for the year was only £10.5 million. On 13 August 1918 the exchange rate fell below 27 francs to the pound, the basis of the agreement of August 1916. France reckoned that the recovery of the franc should mark the return to a self-regulating market. But the Treasury went further and called on France to reimburse its bonds. France countered with a request for interest on the gold France had transferred to Britain. This formed the basis for a trade-off in October 1918.[125]

Like Britain, France created its own governmental missions to represent its interests in the United States, with André Tardieu as its high commissioner. Ribot put his country's needs at $218 million a month, of which $133 million would be spent in the United States and $85 million elsewhere in the world. McAdoo advanced $100 million for each of May and June 1917, plus $10 million for the population of the battle zones of northern France. Firmer arrangements would, he said, have to await the outcome of the first American loan issue in July. He suggested that the French could then expect $150 million a month until the end of 1917. The French were disgruntled on three counts. First, the British were doing

[125] Petit, *Finances extérieures*, 100–1, 248–326.

better out of the United States than they were. Secondly, they resented
America's demand that the money be spent on the purchase of American
goods, and that it be channelled through the banks of the Federal Reserve
System. Thirdly, the Americans wanted to know how the money was spent.
The French in Paris responded by demanding $160 million a month. The
French in Washington told their compatriots not to antagonize the
Americans, and that $130 million would be enough. In the event, so
successful were American efforts to control France's imports—or so profl-
igate had been France's policy hitherto—that the full monthly credit was
not actually spent. France disbursed $150 million in July and only $130 million in August. By the end of 1917 the United States had advanced France
$1,130 million since May, but the latter had spent only $1,082 million.

Nonetheless, Franco-American tensions multiplied. Only a third of
France's expenditure, $355 million, represented government purchases in
the United States. The proportion of private buying funded through
government loans, $250 million, was comparable with the pattern of
French purchasing in Britain. But most vexing for McAdoo was the fact
that $331 million of the total had been transferred to Britain. France, for
its part, was having to refinance loans contracted with American banks
early in the war, but was doing so without the public backing of the
American government, and in one case at an interest rate of 7.5 per cent.
In October 1917 France's interest and redemption payments totalled
$38.5 million. Thus both powers approached the negotiations at the
beginning of 1918 on a collision course. Although French spending in
January totalled $134 million, Klotz wanted $170 million for the month.
McAdoo, mindful that American troops were now spending dollars in
France, and anxious to confine France's credits to French payments
in America, envisaged $60 million as an appropriate credit for February.

McAdoo came off worst. On 12 March he suggested that the French
should hold a maximum reserve of $30 million, and that they should only
seek fresh credits when their cash in hand fell below this sum. On this basis
each advance remained higher than McAdoo wanted, between $100
million and $150 million, but the period for which it lasted was not
fixed and was related to the size of the unexpended balance. Nine days
after France accepted these terms, on 21 March, the Germans mounted the
first of a series of successful offensives. The loss both of territory and of
population reduced France's yield from loans and taxation. At the same

time the growth of the allied armies in France increased the note circulation. On this basis France secured a modification of the agreement of 12 March. Rather than reduce American credits to France as France's receipt of American army dollars rose, the Americans continued to give credits in dollars to France and used dollars to buy francs for their troops. The French intention was to continue to fund current purchases in America through American credits while creating a reserve of dollars in France for post-war use. In June 1918 Clemenceau, France's prime minister since the previous November, intervened, adding to France's demands a delivery of gold to cover the note increase generated by the expenditure of the American army. The Americans refused the gold but agreed to an extraordinary credit of $200 million in August. When this was added to ordinary credits of $895 million for the year, America's support for 1918 was only marginally less than that for May to December 1917. The dispute over the trade-off between French credits in America and the spending of American troops in France continued until 1919. But procrastination was now in France's interests. The franc recovered against the dollar from late August, and thus the relative cost of the redemption of maturing French loan stock diminished with each succeeding day.[126]

At times between 1917 and 1918 France felt itself squeezed between Britain and the United States. But given the reluctance with which it curbed its overseas purchasing, such sentiments reflected more the needs of self-justification than of legitimate grievance. McAdoo would no doubt have argued the reverse—that the United States was being squeezed between France and Britain.

In the case of Italy the United States was more successful in warding off British efforts to secure dollars in compensation for its credits. By 31 March 1919 Italy owed 10,676 million lire to Britain as opposed to 8,332 million to the United States.[127] But Anglo-Italian financial links were not as embedded by April 1917 as those between Britain and France, and the United States therefore found it easier to insert its own concerns into the relationship. Moreover, the picture was complicated by the fact that the growth of French and Italian trade during the war

[126] Petit, *Finances extérieures*, 446–56, 464, 472–98, 501–9, 515–29; Jèze and Truchy, *War finance*, 315–16; Kaspi, *Le Temps des Americains*, 51–7, 330–3.
[127] Teillard, *Emprunts de guerre*, 175–6.

(it roughly quadrupled in value) made the flow of funds four-sided rather than tripartite.[128]

Britain's call on the dollars lent by the United States to Italy was couched in terms similar to those developed in the French case. In 1917, to save on Mediterranean shipping, Britain ceased to provide coal for Italy, and the responsibility was taken up by France. But Britain continued to demand compensation as France replenished its own coal stocks by increasing its imports from Britain.[129] In the same fashion, Britain contended that if it exported steel to Italy it, in its turn, had to increase its steel imports from the United States. Ultimately Britain could, by using these arguments, make things sufficiently unpleasant to get its own way at least some of the time. Thus Italy, like France, paid Britain in dollars for wheat imported from India on the grounds that Britain had to import a similar quantity from the United States. On 27 July 1918 British credits to Italy were fixed at £8 million a month, of which £1.5 million was useable outside the British empire; the United States, by contrast, agreed to provide $10 million per month to be used by Italy in neutral markets, and to allow a proportion to be transferred to Britain so that it could purchase on Italy's behalf.[130]

The crucial check on the extent of British control was the fact that the lira never came to depend on the pound in the way that the franc did. In 1916 the lira was left to float freely; in 1917 it depreciated rapidly, and after Caporetto it crashed. Nitti immediately set about its stabilization. His objective in doing so was to facilitate a massive increase in Italy's foreign debt. He aspired not only to get the British and Americans to pay Italy's war costs, but also to enmesh them in a commitment to Italy's post-war recovery. The Americans responded to the crisis of Caporetto with an advance of $230 million.[131]

But Nitti's initial efforts to control Italy's foreign exchange were frustrated. The Finance Ministry lacked the manpower for the job and the Bank of Italy opposed the thinking behind the scheme. In January Nitti formed a national institution for exchange with the co-operation of the seven principal commercial banks. Only they were authorized to deal in foreign currency; all imports required a licence and all

[128] Petit, *Finances extérieures*, 623.   [129] Ibid. 629.
[130] Forsyth, *Crisis of Liberal Italy*, 173–4, 186–7.   [131] Ibid. 175–8.

foreign-exchange earnings had to be passed over to the national institution for exchange. The institution began operations in March, but it
lacked sufficient reserves, and contracts were therefore concluded in lire
at rates below those fixed by the institution. Thus the depreciation of the
lira was not halted.

Italy's proposal to deal with the problem was an inter-allied exchange
office. This might have commended itself to the American Treasury if the
latter's approach to allied financing had been similar to that of Britain.
But it was not. The United States wanted Italy to redeem its debts first,
and thus France—which, like Italy, stood to benefit from such an arrangement—withdrew its backing. Therefore, the pattern of bilateral
agreements continued.[132] The significant outcome was that the United
States supported the lira on the foreign exchanges through the establishment of a joint committee of the Italian national institution for exchange
and the Federal Reserve Board. In June 1918 the Americans undertook to
finance Italy's commercial deficit in the United States, and the Federal
Reserve Board advanced $100 million for the support of the lira. The
Americans correctly reckoned that with the end of the war emigrant
remittances to Italy would recover and that as demand for America's
holdings of lire increased the exchange rate would go up.

The effect of the agreement was to exclude Britain from the routing of
dollars to Italy. Britain's first response was to refuse to co-operate in
support of the lira. But as the gap between the value of the lira in New
York and the value in London widened, Britain found itself being confronted with exclusion from Italian trade. This threat to the City of
London's international position compelled the modification reflected in
the agreement of 27 July 1918.[133] On 4 August France too came to the
support of the lira. Compensation for existing debts was settled and
Italian advances for French troops in Italy regulated. France opened a
monthly credit of 25 million francs for Italian payments in France, secured
on Italian treasury bonds.[134] The lira recovered rapidly against the dollar
in July and August, and more steadily against the pound and the franc.

The United States's entry to the war may ultimately have ensured
the Entente's victory, particularly if in twentieth-century warfare such

---

[132] Petit, *Finances extérieures*, 147–9.   [133] Forsyth, *Crisis of Liberal Italy*, 178–87.
[134] Petit, *Finances extérieures*, 638–41.

outcomes rest on economic resources. But to the allies in 1917 and 1918 there were times when dollars seemed as hard to come by as they had been before 1917. America's decision to create a mass army, effectively from scratch, meant that its government wished to reserve a larger proportion of New York's money market for its own use. British, French and Italian loans had to compete with American.

Thus, the last eighteen months of the war accelerated and deepened the need to expand the network of borrowing to other nations. Neutrals acquired gold and dollars as they exported commodities to the belligerent states; their holdings exceeded their domestic needs and threatened inflation. The logical step for the belligerents was to borrow from this neutral wealth in order to pay off their debt in the United States. McAdoo, however, insisted that Britain use the dollar proceeds to fund its current purchasing in America, and so ease the burden on the US Treasury. Bonar Law agreed to this in April 1918, provided the United States would replace the funds so raised if Britain was required to repay its American debt.[135]

Two factors dictated the geographical spread of this borrowing. The first was the need to focus purchasing in states that were geographically contiguous in order to economize on shipping; this pressure was, of course, particularly acute after Germany's declaration of unrestricted U-boat warfare in 1917. The second was the necessity to acquire food, particularly meat and grain. The combined result was to concentrate the acquisition of credits in neutral Europe and in South America.

By 1915 France was already aware of its changing trading relationship with the neutral European powers. Its lack of shipping increased the need to import from Spain, Switzerland, and Scandinavia. But the effect was to upset the balance of trade and to depress the franc against other European currencies. By August 1915 the peseta had gained 11 per cent on the franc. In May 1916 France negotiated its first Spanish credit, for 200 million pesetas. The deal, which was secured on French holdings of Spanish shares, fell foul of Spanish nationalist efforts to repatriate foreign holdings and to prevent the export of capital. But its pattern was repeated elsewhere that summer. Between June and August banks in Switzerland, Sweden, Norway, Holland, and Denmark all opened credits for the

---

[135] Burk, *Historical Journal*, XXII (1979), 370–1 .

French government. In the Dutch case, the advance, for 12 million guilders to buy food, was secured against French shares with a margin of 30 per cent. But in the other instances the securities were principally French holdings of shares of the country in which the loan was contracted.[136]

The continuation of this policy, therefore, depended on France's ability to command the foreign shares held by its citizens. The rejection of compulsory sequestration curtailed its development. After April 1917 Britain and the United States increasingly restricted their credit to sums sufficient to meet France's expenses only in those two countries, but France's efforts to extend its borrowing among the neutrals were hamstrung for lack of sufficient appropriate guarantees. Norway accepted French treasury bonds deposited in the Banque de France, and Swiss credits were secured on French railway stock. But in Spain France had to sell French holdings of Spanish shares and of Spain's own overseas debt.[137] France's strength in international finance no longer rested on its pre-war position as an exporter of capital.

Instead, what gave France leverage in the money markets was its membership of the Entente. By 1917–18 the alliance constituted the most powerful economic bloc in the world's commodity markets. Central allied ordering, beginning with the Allied Wheat Executive in 1916, and continued with McAdoo's policies in 1917, created near-monopolies in the purchasing of major foodstuffs. The implementation of the blockade and the control of shipping (in itself another near-monopoly) conferred on the allies the power of coercion. Neutral producers of raw materials still needed markets, and access to those markets, for their goods. Thus neutral credits could be turned on through the tap of trade.

Franco-Spanish bilateral negotiations over finance foundered in 1917. The Spanish were sympathetic to the Germans and were opposed to exports; the French refused to requisition the Spanish shareholdings of their citizens. Since Spain did not need to import from France, France lacked the foothold to clinch a lasting agreement. But Spain did need coal from Britain and cotton and oil from the United States. Furthermore, its agricultural produce was more dependent on overseas markets than some chauvinists cared to admit. Therefore, it was on Spain's initiative

---

[136] Petit, *Finances extérieures*, 89–92, 539–47, 601–4.
[137] Petit, *Finances extérieures*, 102, 123–5.

that a central bureau for allied purchases in the peninsula was created in December 1917. Spain was still not keen to advance credits to France. But the United States suspended exports to Spain and put an embargo on Spanish ships until it did so. In March 1918, a Spanish banking consortium advanced 350 million pesetas, at a rate of 4.5 per cent per annum, and secured in French treasury bonds. France was required to spend a proportion of the money on Spanish wine and fruit, but it also got metals and pyrites.[138]

The United States gave France comparable support in its negotiations with Switzerland. The Swiss too had an export problem: demand for Swiss luxuries, and particularly chocolate, had fallen. But France could not afford to make its acquisition of Swiss credits conditional on increased French consumption of Swiss chocolate. The Swiss needed American wheat, and this was channelled through France. In December 1917, in exchange for easing the blockade and for a limited French purchase of Swiss luxury goods, the Swiss government permitted the Swiss banks to open credits for the French government of up to 150 million francs.[139]

The fact that America itself was buying goods in Spain and Switzerland also in due course helped to stabilize the franc. The United States had turned its face against the export of gold and also found its dollar advances committed to Entente needs. Imports from neutral powers were therefore most easily paid for in the currencies of its associates, and especially in francs. But the effect was to depreciate the franc yet further, and so increase the dollar credits required by Paris. At first America's solution was to buy pesetas and Swiss francs with dollars, but as the demand for pesetas increased it negotiated credits to buy pesetas from France and thus simultaneously supported the franc.[140]

The strength which America's entry gave the Entente in its negotiations for European credits was made most manifest in its handling of Sweden in May 1918. The Swedes agreed to channel their purchases of food, and particularly of wheat, via the Entente. In exchange, the Entente bought timber and minerals from Sweden, and the Swedes provided a credit of 50 million crowns to facilitate this. Thus, Germany was elbowed out of the Baltic trade, and finance was fused with economic warfare.[141]

[138] Ibid. 548–97.   [139] Ibid. 607–17.
[140] Ibid. 510–14.   [141] Ibid. 124–5.

Wheat was the centrepiece of this strategy. By monopolizing its purchase, the belligerents could control its price for themselves and secure neutral exchange through the surpluses they sold within Europe. Most of Europe's major suppliers—the United States, Canada, Australia, and India—lay automatically within the Entente's nexus. The principal exception—and, of course, an outstanding meat producer as well—was Argentina. In the first three months of 1917 France spent 860 million francs on Argentinian produce.

In July 1917 the Allied Wheat Executive proposed to buy the entire Argentinian harvest. On the face of it much conspired against Argentinian co-operation. The 1917 harvest was low and initially exports were banned. Argentina could best exploit its position as a food producer in an open market. But, like other South American countries before the war, Argentina had been heavily reliant on foreign capital. Hostilities had switched off the flow of overseas funds while boosting trade; the cost of servicing the foreign debt expressed as a percentage of the value of exports halved between 1913/14 and 1918/19. By the end of 1917 the consequent strength of the peso, although reducing the burden of foreign debt, threatened to be an embarrassment to Argentinian exports. What was therefore attractive about the allied desire was its potential to stabilize the exchange. But the United States blocked Britain and France from using either gold or dollars in the proposed purchase. The two European partners therefore wished to fund their acquisition through a credit of 200 million gold pesos raised in Argentina: the effect would be to settle the peso and facilitate exports. No doubt American inducements to facilitate Argentina's imports of coal, or allied threats to block them, also prompted Argentina's decision. In January 1918 Britain and France were accorded credits to buy 2.5 million tons of cereals at fixed prices.[142]

The need to shorten shipping routes focused these credit negotiations on the western hemisphere. The extension of foreign borrowing to the Pacific basin was confined to powers that were themselves belligerent. Japan opened credits for Russia, France, and Britain in 1917, primarily to pay for munitions for the first-named. After Russia's exit from the war,

[142] Petit, *Finances extérieures*, 306–7, 645–54; Albert, *South America*, 65–6, 143–8; Forsyth, *Crisis of Liberal Italy*, 170–1.

both France and Britain carried on with the combination of selling bonds and retiring existing loans. Japan raised a total of 860 million yen.[143]

For those historians who see London's money market and its pre-1914 domination of world finance as evidence of 'informal' empire, neither Argentina nor Japan was as independent of Britain's thrall as their political status nominally suggested. But the biggest burden on the pre-war exchequer was the defence of the 'formal' empire. After 1914 that relationship changed in military terms: imperial forces made significant contributions in all theatres of war. But Britain proved less successful in changing the arrangements for funding the empire's war effort. The Dominions did not become, in net terms, creditors of Britain itself. Outstanding loans to the empire as a whole rose from £39.5 million in 1914/15 to £194.5 million in 1917/18.[144] The debate in India was instructive. Formally speaking, India was precluded from paying for military operations carried on by Indian army troops beyond India's frontiers. Its patriotic contribution was to accept the same financial responsibility for its forces as it would have incurred if the troops had remained on the subcontinent, a total of £26.4 million.[145] Britain met the balance.

Given the demands of the war, the Treasury was anxious to restrict the use of British credits for the capital development of the empire during the course of the war itself. At a conference in March 1915 it stipulated that the Dominions should use the London money market to settle maturing obligations, to meet commitments under contracts placed before the war's outbreak, and to pay for expenditure necessarily incurred in respect of works already in progress. But it was unsuccessful. In Australia the individual states increased their total debt from £387.6 million to £417.3 million during the course of the war, without making any direct contribution to the war's costs. In 1917 London suggested Australia should shift its borrowing to New York, but the latter resisted on the grounds of imperial loyalty.[146]

[143] Petit, *Finances extérieures*, 92–3, 122–3; Morgan, *British financial policy*, 321; Michelson *et al.*, *Russian public finance*, 317–18; Claus, *Kriegswirtschaft Russlands*, 13; Dua, *Anglo-Japanese relations*, 181–2.

[144] Morgan, *British financial policy*, 317; also Bogart, *War costs*, 129–30, 184–5; Brown, *Modern India*, 188; A. J. Stockwell, 'The war and the British empire', in Turner (ed.), *Britain and the First World War*, 37.

[145] Lucas, *Empire at war*, v. 197–8.

[146] Scott, *Australia during the war*, 481–93.

Britain effectively funded a war-related boom in each of Canada, Australia, and New Zealand. Demands for commodities—wheat from Canada, meat and wool from the Antipodes—ensured that the current accounts of all three moved into surplus on the back of customs and excise receipts. Britain's subsidy extended to the provision of a guaranteed market at prices in excess of those prevailing within the United Kingdom or within the Dominions' domestic markets. Beginning in 1916/17, London bought the entire wool clip of Australia and New Zealand at a price 55 per cent higher than that pertaining before the war.[147] The shipping shortage ensured that Australia and New Zealand revenues fell after 1917, but not to the point where their public accounts went into deficit. New Zealand had accumulated £11.5 million by the war's end, but none of it was used to pay off the public debt, which had doubled from £92 million in 1914 to £201 million by March 1920. Instead, it was retained as a reserve fund and invested in British government securities.[148] Canada, whose greater proximity to Britain meant that its boom coincided with the shipping shortage, and therefore began later and lasted longer than those of Australia and New Zealand, retired $113 million of its eventual public debt of $1,200 million by March 1918.[149]

The change that the war did accelerate was the domestication of this debt. Australia borrowed £43.4 million from Britain but £188 million through seven domestic war loans; New Zealand raised £26 million from Britain but £54 million internally; and $700 million of Canada's debt of $1,200 million represented Canadian investment in Canadian war loans.[150] To that extent, therefore, the Dominions were funding their own military costs. The success of war loans, however, also shows the growing wealth of the Dominions' farmers and rentiers. Tax regimes were light, justified in the cases of Canada and Australia by the argument that the power of direct taxation lay with the individual provinces or states. Canada introduced a business profits tax in 1916, but reduced the liability of individuals for income tax, which was adopted in September 1917, in proportion. Australia was braver, embracing estate duty in 1914, income tax in 1915, and a war profits tax in 1917, with the result that by 1920 revenue had covered £71 million of the total £333.6 million which the war

---

[147] Andrews, *Anzac illusion*, 71–2; Lucas, *Empire at war*, iii. 241.
[148] Lucas, *Empire at war*, iii. 249–52.   [149] Ibid. ii. 59.
[150] Ibid. ii, 59; iii. 251–2; Scott, *Australia during the war*, 496, 500.

had cost. New Zealand increased taxes on land and income in 1915, and added an excess profits tax in 1916. It was abandoned in 1917, although higher incomes now became subject to tax rates of up to a third. By putting the weight less on tax than on war loans offered at very attractive rates of interest, the Dominions enabled those who had already profited from the war to do even better.[151]

Each of the Dominions made a significantly greater financial contribution to military expenditure than it had before 1914. But their own healthy balances of payments did not affect the imperial relationship as radically as they might have done: Britain still felt beholden to subsidize their efforts despite the self-sufficiency of their economies. India offered £100 million towards the cost of the war, £78 million of which was raised by the issue of a war loan within India and the balance by taking on the interest payments on an equivalent sum in British war loans. Such devices simply enabled Indian princes to widen their investment portfolios.[152] Canada alone used its position on the Atlantic trade route and its adjacency to the United States to change the imperial relationship from that of debtor to creditor. In 1918/19 its debt to Britain stood at £72.4 million, but Britain's to Canada at £135.4 million (£91.8 million of which was lent by the government, and the balance by bankers for the purchase of wheat and munitions).[153] This was a process commenced in November 1915: 'Canada the borrower', McKenna then declared, 'has become Canada the lender.'[154]

Entente yields from credit operations in neutral or non-North American markets were small. Of 43,585 million francs borrowed overseas by France between 1914 and 1919, 40,839 million were derived from Britain and America.[155] Britain's external debt at the end of the financial year 1918/19 stood at £1,364.8 million: of this £1,162.7 million was owed in the United States and Canada.[156] But neutral credits were symbols—first, of the diversification of the international money market which the war set

---

[151] Lucas, *Empire at war*, ii. 11–13, 14–16, 27–9, 39–41, 59–60; iii. 235–49; Scott, *Australia during the war*, 481, 495–6.
[152] Lucas, *Empire at war*, v. 198; Sanjay Bhattacharya, 'Anxious albatross: British India and the armistice', in Cecil and Liddle (eds.), *At the eleventh hour*, 189, 196.
[153] Morgan, *British financial policy*, 317, 320.
[154] Lucas, *Empire at war*, ii. 29.
[155] Jèze and Truchy, *War finance of France*, 286.
[156] Morgan, *British financial policy*, 320–1.

in train, and secondly—but paradoxically—of the increasing leverage which the Entente came to exercise within that market.

The fact that the United States did not opt to maximize its opportunities for full financial leadership in 1917–18 left the initiative with the allied purchasing agencies, themselves based in Europe and more the product of British shipping dominance and of the British-led blockade than of McAdoo's policies in 1917. Thus, the picture remained more variegated than a crude shift in the balance of power from London to New York. Moreover, through the alliance machinery London was able to continue to exercise more influence than the real strength of sterling suggested was probable.

Part of this resilience was itself a product of Britain's and France's success in exporting their debt. Britain funded about 25 per cent of the gross increase in its national debt through foreign borrowing, and France 19 per cent of its total war costs.[157] They thereby reduced domestic inflation in two ways. First, such debt did not enter their secondary reserves and so was not monetized. Secondly, they reduced the interest and maturity payments due on loans extracted from their own citizens. At the same time they pegged their exchange rates, and so made overseas purchases artificially cheap; this boosted the demand for imports, but once again exported and diffused excessive liquidity. These operations sustained their presence in the international market during the war, and so limited the consequences of its revitalization after the war. Germany was, therefore, doubly disadvantaged. During the war its debt was concentrated at home, with the attendant implications that followed from that. After the war the reopening of trade and the accessibility of foreign credit became key factors—in the view of some historians—in creating the excessive liquidity which spawned hyperinflation in the early 1920s.[158]

Foreign borrowing in wartime was by its nature short-term. In this it contrasted starkly with peacetime debt, which was intended to pay for capital investment and thus generate income for the borrower (as well as for the lender) over the long term. However, the choice in the war lay not between those two sorts of overseas credit, but between short-term and relatively unproductive foreign debt and the spending of domestic

[157] Balderston, *Economic History Review*, 2nd series, XLII (1989), 238; Soutou, 'Comment a été financée la guerre', in La Gorce (ed.), *Première Guerre Mondiale*, 284.
[158] Holtfrerich, *German inflation*, 75–7.

capital. All the Entente powers had in varying degrees to employ the latter as well as the former. The Central Powers had no choice. The Entente's readier access to foreign credits is crucial to explaining the proposition that the war cost twice as much to win as to lose, $147,000 million as against $61,500 million.[159] Those figures focus on direct fiscal input—taxation and borrowing; they leave disinvestment and potential investment foregone out of the account. Effectively denied access to overseas money markets, Germany and Austria-Hungary—having taxed their populations and having borrowed from them—could do no more than spend their accumulated assets. National wealth in Germany in 1913 totalled 350,000 million marks; 220,000 million was invested in buildings and land, which could not be realized; 50,000 million represented machinery and plant; 75,000 million was liquid. The latter having been spent, the residue of war expenditure was funded through disinvestment. This traded not only on the future, through a failure to reinvest, but also on the past, through the consumption of existing wealth. It was manifested in two ways, falling real incomes and declining output.[160]

The relative availability of foreign borrowing was not in itself decisive for the war's outcome. Overseas credits, although possessed of signal fiscal benefits, remained means to an end—the procurement of materials with which to wage the war. Ultimately, the war was paid for not through money or credit but through the goods and services which they could command. The long-term significance of disinvestment lay in the houses that were not built and the plant for peacetime production that was not renewed. The short-term significance lay in defeat on the battlefield, the result of the Central Powers' inability to match the Entente in a strategy determined by the application of superior resources.

The argument that finance played a role in the immediate outcome of the war commensurate with pre-war expectations has to proceed counterfactually. If the United States had not been propelled into the war by Germany's decision to adopt unrestricted U-boat warfare, would it have left Britain, and with Britain the whole of the Entente, to confront its effective bankruptcy? The American ambassador in London, Walter H. Page, cabled the president on 5 March 1917 to point out the

[159] Ferguson, *Pity of war*, 322.
[160] Roesler, *Finanzpolitik*, 151–8; see also Winkler, *Einkommensverschiebungen*, 14–15, 60, 69–70, 81–2, for similar points in relation to Austria-Hungary.

implications for the United States of not sustaining Franco-American and Anglo-American exchange.

The inevitable consequence will be that orders by all the Allied Governments will be reduced to the lowest possible amount and that trans-Atlantic trade will practically come to an end. The result of such a stoppage will be a panic in the United States. The world will therefore be divided into two hemispheres, one of them, our own, will have the gold and the commodities: the other, Great Britain and Europe, will need those commodities, but it will have no money with which to pay for them. Moreover, it will have practically no commodities of its own to exchange for them. The financial and commercial result will be almost as bad for the United States as for Europe.[161]

The financial collapse of the Entente would have triggered economic crisis in the United States. The corollary of continued American neutrality, therefore, might not have been a cessation of American credits and an end to American warlike supplies. American self-interest alone suggested that the reverse was more likely. Indeed, for all the long-term implications for sterling in such an outcome, it could be argued that in the short-term American neutrality might have proved as beneficial to the Entente as American belligerence. Its own military preparations would not have competed with the needs of the Entente in the American domestic money market and in the productive capacity of American industry, while at the same time the financial commitment to the Entente would have bound the United States to its survival and even victory, whatever America's formal position in relation to hostilities.

The fact that the Balfour mission emphasized Britain's financial peril in April 1917 as greater than the submarine threat[162] reflected Britain's sense of how America could best contribute to the war effort in the short term. The creation of a sizeable American army seemed two years distant; credits to procure munitions for the existing allied armies would have more immediate effect. But in venting such views Balfour revealed how powerful in British strategy pre-war fiscal orthodoxies remained. Indeed, they became stronger in 1917–18 as the Treasury, through its negotiations in the United States, reasserted its suzerainty not only over the spending departments of Britain but also over the extravagance of Britain's allies. McKenna's values may have been routed in a political sense with Lloyd

---

[161] Hendrick, *Page*, ii. 270.   [162] Ibid. ii. 268.

George's triumph in December 1916, but they remained enmeshed in the counsels of Keynes and others. Britain's gloom about its financial position in 1918 was less a realistic response to the current position than a continuing coda on the prevalence of pre-war views on the limits of war finance.

FURTHER READING

In what follows and where possible, references are to authors only; short titles are given to avoid ambiguity where necessary. Full details of title, place and date of publication are to be found in the bibliography.

Comparative, recent general treatments of war finance are few. Hardach is widely available and reliable. Soutou is the most intelligent writer on the subject but his principal interest is in war aims. He provides a brief survey of finance in La Gorce (ed), *La Première Guerre Mondiale*. Balderston's article is very good on Britain and Germany, especially in relation to overseas borrowing. Comparing the performance of the two powers is a leitmotif of Ferguson's *The pity of war*, and of his chapter, 'How (not) to pay for the war', in Chickering and Förster. Financial cooperation, as opposed to competition, can be better explored for the Entente than the Central Powers. Horn has made Anglo-French relations his own, Neilson deals with Anglo-Russian funding in *Strategy and supply*, and Burk is mistress of the Anglo-American relationship, both before and after 1917.

The world was on the gold standard in 1914, and international finance aspired to remain so. Eichengreen is the most recent scholar in the field, although William Brown still repays reading. The impact of the July crisis on money markets and stock exchanges is covered by Cecco and Seabourne, and for Britain by Peters and for France by Becker, *1914*.

The subsequent stages of war finance have not attracted many recent scholars. They commanded more attention in the 1920s, when their link to reparations and also to interpretations of the pressures underpinning hyper-inflation made them both topical and highly politicised. Knauss is an early attempt to be synoptic and systematic, but is in German. Bogart wrote in English, albeit with a more overt purpose. After 1929 the financing of the war became even less of a self-contained issue and until very recently almost everything written on finance treated the war as little more than the precursor of the great slump. However, it was in this period that the Carnegie series on the economic and social history of the war came on stream. Divided into national series, not all volumes—

and particularly not all those written about finance—were translated into English. If they were, they were often abridged. In general they are less good on money than on industry and demography. Moreover, they were written from a classical and liberal perspective, that peace was the norm and that state intervention was exceptional. Despite these observations, they remain fundamental—not least because many of the authors had themselves been responsible for policy.

In the cases of both France and Russia, the Carnegie volumes have not been replaced. Much the fullest book in the series, Petit on France's overseas borrowing, was never translated; those of Jèze and Truchy on French domestic finance were abridged and rolled into one for an English readership. The same fate befell Michelson, Apostol and Bernatzky for Russia. In their case Claus provides additional detail. Italy, unusually, has been the subject of an excellent recent study by Forsyth. The funding of all three allies became dependent on the credit of Britain. Hirst, who with Allen wrote the Carnegie volume on budgets, was editor of the orthodox, free-trading journal, the *Economist*, and it shows. Stamp dealt with his bailiwick, taxation, but has been replaced by Daunton. E. Victor Morgan is the fullest treatment of Britain's war finance, but is now over fifty years old. As surprising is the current state of scholarship on the United States. Charles Gilbert rules the roost with a methodical and workmanlike treatment. More sophisticated and more recent, Koistinen is principally concerned with industrial mobilization.

In the case of Germany, the combination of reparations and inflation has worked to produce a body of literature far richer than that of any other belligerent. Kroboth, Witt and Zilch set the pre-war scene, and in the process also say pertinent things about the debate on the war's origins. Lotz's slim Carnegie volume has been replaced by Roesler. Holtfrerich builds up to the crash of 1929, as does the outstanding work in English, Feldman's *The Great Disorder*. Germany's financial support of its allies deserves more sustained treatment than it has received. The grants to the Ottoman empire are best followed through general works on the alliance, like Trumpener and Bihl. Emin gives Turkey's finance a cursory and not very satisfactory glance. Bulgaria can be pieced together from Crampton, Danaïllow and Lampe. März makes the key points about Austria-Hungary, and does so in English. For a book published as close to the events as 1918, Stefan von Müller's is perspicacious. The

Carnegie volume by Grebler and Winkler is full of important and inter-
esting observations, although, as the double authorship reveals, the
English version is abridged from two volumes in German. The contributions to the series on Austrian war finance by Gratz and Schüller and by
Popovics were never translated.

Popovics was governor of the Austro-Hungarian Bank. Other princi-
pal players who have left their versions of events—or at least their views
on money and its management—include two finance ministers for
France, Ribot and Klotz, and one each, Helfferich and Spitzmüller, for
Germany and Austria-Hungary. More seductive and more illuminating is
Keynes, whose wartime papers have been edited by Elizabeth Johnson.

BIBLIOGRAPHY

Adams, R. J. Q., *Arms and the wizard: Lloyd George and the Ministry of Munitions* (London, 1978).

Addison, Christopher, *Four and a half years: a personal diary from June 1914 to January 1919*, 2 vols. (London, 1934).

Afflerbach, Holger, *Falkenhayn. Politisches Denken und Handeln im Kaiserreich* (Munich, 1994).

Ageron, Charles-Robert, *Les Algériens musulmans et la France (1871–1919)*, 2 vols. (Paris, 1968).

Ahmad, Kamal Madhar, *Kurdistan during the First World War* (London, 1994).

Albert, Bill, with Paul Henderson, *South America and the First World War* (Cambridge, 1988).

Ally, Russell, 'War and gold—the Bank of England, the London gold market and South Africa's gold, 1914–1919', *Journal of Southern African Studies*, XVII (1991), 221–38.

Andrews, E. M., *The Anzac illusion: Anglo-Australian relations during World War I* (Cambridge, 1993).

Armeson, Robert B., *Total warfare and compulsory labor: a study of the military-industrial complex in Germany during World War I* (The Hague, 1964).

Assmann, Kurt, *Deutsche Seestrategie in zwei Weltkriegen* (Heidelberg, 1957).

Baer, Alexander, 'The Anglo-German antagonism and trade with Holland, with special reference to foodstuffs, during the First World War', Cambridge University Ph.D. thesis, 1997.

Balderston, T., 'War finance and inflation in Britain and Germany, 1914–1918', *Economic History Review*, 2nd series, XLII (1989), 222–44.

Balfour, Michael, *The Kaiser and his times* (London, 1964).

Bartholdy, Albrecht Mendelssohn, *The war and German society: the testament of a liberal* (New Haven, 1937).

Baudrillart, Alfred, *Les Carnets du Cardinal Baudrillart (1914–1918)*, ed. Paul Christophe (Paris, 1994).

Becker, Jean-Jacques, *1914: comment les français sont entrés dans la guerre* (Paris, 1977).

——— 'Union sacrée et idéologie bourgeoise', *Revue historique*, CCLXIV, (1980), 65–74.

——— *The Great War and the French people* (Leamington Spa, 1985; first published 1983).

Becker, Jean-Jacques, 'L'Union sacrée: l'exception qui confirme la régle', *Vingtième siècle revue d'histoire*, 5 (1985), 111–20.

—— *La France en guerre 1914–1918: la grande mutation* (Brussels, 1988).

—— and Stéphane Audoin-Rouzeau, *Les Sociétés européennes et la guerre de 1914–1918* (Paris, 1990).

Bell, A. C., *A history of the blockade of Germany and of the countries associated with her in the Great War, Austria-Hungary, Bulgaria, and Turkey* (London, 1937; actually published 1961).

Bellon, Bernard P., *Mercedes in peace and war: German automobile workers, 1903–1945* (New York, 1990).

Berend, I. T., and Gy. Ránki, *The development of the manufacturing industry in Hungary (1900–1944)* (Budapest, 1960).

Berghahn, V. R., *Germany and the approach of war 1914* (London, 1973).

—— *Modern Germany: society, economy and politics in the twentieth century*, 2nd edn. (Cambridge, 1987).

—— and Martin Kitchen (eds.), *Germany in the age of total war* (London, 1981).

Bergson, Henri, *The meaning of the war: life and matter in conflict* (London, 1915).

Berliner Geschichtswerkstatt (ed.), *August 1914: ein Volk zieht in den Krieg* (Berlin, 1989).

Bernard, Philippe, and Henri Dubief, *The decline of the Third Republic 1914–1938* (Cambridge, 1985; first published 1975–6).

Bernstorff, Johann-Heinrich, *Deutschland und Amerika. Erinnerungen aus dem fünfjährigen Kriege* (Berlin, 1920).

Bihl, *Die Kaukasus-Politik der Mittelmächte. Teil 1. Ihre Basis in der Orient-Politik und ihre Aktionen 1914–1917* (Vienna, 1975).

Birkett, M. S., 'The iron and steel trades during the war', *Journal of the Royal Statistical Society*, LXXXIII (1920), 351–400.

Bitsch, Marie-Thérèse, *La Belgique entre La France et l'Allemagne 1905–1914* (Paris, 1994).

Blake, Robert, *The unknown prime minister: the life and times of Andrew Bonar Law 1858–1923* (London, 1955).

Bloch, I. S., *Modern weapons and modern war* (London, 1900).

Bloch, Jean de [i.e. I. S.], *La guerre*, 6 vols. (Paris, 1898).

Boemeke, Manfred F., Roger Chickering, and Stig Förster (eds.), *Anticipating total war: the German and American experiences 1871–1914* (Cambridge, 1999).

Bogart, Ernest Ludlow, *War costs and their financing: a study of the financing of the war and the after-war problems of debt and taxation* (New York, 1921).

Böhme, Helmut, and Fritz Kallenberg (eds.), *Deutschland und der erste Weltkrieg* (Darmstadt, 1987).

Bosworth, Richard, *Italy and the approach of the First World War* (London, 1983).

Bourne, J. M., *Britain and the Great War 1914–1918* (London, 1989).

Bourne, K., and D. C. Watt (eds.), *Studies in international history* (London, 1967).

Brécard, Général, *En Belgique auprès du Roi Albert: souvenirs de 1914* (Paris, 1934).

Bridge, F. R., *From Sadowa to Sarajevo: the foreign policy of Austria-Hungary 1866–1914* (London, 1972).

—— and Roger Bullen, *The great powers and the European states system 1815–1914* (London, 1980).

Brock, Michael, and Eleanor Brock (eds.), *H. H. Asquith: letters to Venetia Stanley* (Oxford, 1985; first published 1982).

Brown, Ian Malcolm, *British logistics on the western front 1914–1919* (Westport, Conn, 1998).

Brown, Judith, *Gandhi's rise to power: Indian politics 1915–1922* (Cambridge, 1972).

—— *Modern India: the origins of an Asian democracy* (Delhi, 1985).

Brown, William Adams, jr., *The international gold standard reinterpreted*, 2 vols. (New York, 1940).

Bunselmeyer, Robert E., *The cost of the war 1914–1919: British economic war aims and the origins of reparation* (Hamden, Conn., 1975).

Burchardt, Lothar, *Friedenswirtschaft und Kriegsvorsorge. Deutschlands wirtschaftliche Rüstungsbestrebungen vor 1914* (Boppard am Rhein, 1968).

—— 'Walther Rathenau und die Anfänge der deutschen Rohstoffbewirtschaftung im Ersten Weltkrieg', *Tradition*, XV (1970), 169–96.

—— 'Zwischen Kriegsgewinnen und Kriegskosten: Krupp im Ersten Weltkrieg', *Zeitschrift für Unternehmensgeschichte*, XXXII (1987), 71–123.

Burk, Kathleen, 'The diplomacy of finance: British financial missions to the United States 1914–1918', *Historical Journal*, XXII (1979), 351–72.

—— 'J. M. Keynes and the exchange rate crisis of July 1917', *Economic History Review*, 2nd series, XXXII (1979), 405–16.

—— *Britain, America and the sinews of war, 1914–1918* (Boston, 1985).

—— 'A merchant bank at war: the house of Morgan, 1914–18', in P. L. Cottrell and D. E. Moggridge (eds.), *Money and power: essays in honour of L. S. Presnell* (Basingstoke, 1988).

—— (ed.), *War and the state: the transformation of British government, 1914–1919* (London, 1982).

Bussy, Carvel de (ed.), *Count Stephen Tisza, prime minister of Hungary: letters (1914–1916)* (New York, 1991).

Caesar, Rolf, 'Die Finanzierung des Ersten Weltkrieges und de Rolle der Sparkassen', *Zeitschrift für bayerische Sparkassengeschichte*, V (1991), 57–127.

Cain, P. J., and A. G. Hopkins, *British imperialism: crisis and deconstruction 1914–90* (London, 1993).

Calkins, Kenneth R., *Hugo Haase: democrat and revolutionary* (Durham, NC, 1979).

Carnegie, David, *The history of munitions supply in Canada 1914–1918* (London, 1925).

Cassar, George H., *Kitchener: architect of victory* (London, 1977).

—— *The tragedy of Sir John French* (Newark, 1985).

—— *Asquith as war leader* (London, 1994).

Cecco, Marcello de, *The international gold standard: money and empire*, 2nd edn. (London, 1984).

Cecil, Hugh, and Peter Liddle (eds.), *Facing Armageddon: the First World War experienced* (London, 1996).

—— and —— (eds.), *At the eleventh hour: reflections, hopes and anxieties at the closing of the Great War, 1918* (Barnsley, 1998).

Chandler, Lester V., *Benjamin Strong, central banker* (Washington DC, 1958).

Charbonnet, Germain, *La Politique financière de la France pendant la guerre (août 1914–novembre 1920)* (Bordeaux, 1922).

Chickering, Roger, *Imperial Germany and the Great War 1914–1918* (Cambridge, 1998).

Chickering, Roger, and Stig Förster (eds), *Great War, Total War: Combat and Mobilization in the Western front 1914–1918* (Washington, 2000).

Claus, Rudolf, *Die Kriegswirtschaft Russlands bis zur bolschewistischen Revolution* (Bonn, 1922).

Coetzee, Frans, and Marilyn Shevin-Coetzee (eds.), *Authority, identity and the social history of the Great War* (Providence, 1995).

Contamine, Henri, *La Révanche 1871–1914* (Paris, 1957).

Cooper, Caroline Ethel, *Behind the lines: one woman's war 1914–18*, ed. Decie Denholm (London, 1982).

Cooper, John Milton, 'The command of gold reversed: American loans to Britain, 1915–1917', *Pacific Historical Review*, XLV (1976), 209–30.

Cornwall, Mark (ed.), *The last years of Austria-Hungary: essays in political and military history 1908–1918* (Exeter, 1990).

Craig, Gordon, *The politics of the Prussian army 1640–1945* (London, 1955).

—— *Germany 1866–1945* (Oxford, 1981; first published 1978).

Crampton, Richard J., *Bulgaria 1875–1918: a history* (Boulder, Col., 1983).

Crouzet, François, 'Recherches sur la production d'armements en France (1815–1913)', *Revue historique*, CCLI (1974), 45–84.

Crow, Duncan, *A man of push and go: the life of George Macaulay Booth* (London, 1965).

Cruttwell, C. R. M. F., *A history of the Great War 1914–1918*, 2nd edn. (Oxford, 1936).

—— *The role of British strategy in the Great War* (Cambridge, 1936).

Cutlack, F. M. (ed.), *War letters of General Monash* (Sydney, 1935).

Dallin, Alexander *et al.*, *Russian diplomacy and eastern Europe 1914–1917* (New York, 1963).

Danaïllow, Georges, *Les Effets de la guerre en Bulgarie* (Paris, 1932).

Daniel, Ute, *The war from within: German working-class women in the First World War* (Oxford, 1997; first published 1989).

Daunton, Martin, *Just taxes: the politics of taxation in Britain, 1914–1979* (Cambridge, 2002).

——'How to pay for the war: state, society and taxation in Britain, 1917–24', *English History Review*, CXI (1996), 882–919.

David, Edward (ed.), *Inside Asquith's cabinet: from the diaries of Charles Hobhouse* (London, 1977).

Davis, Belinda J., *Home fire's burning: food politics, and everyday life in World War I Berlin* (Chapel Hill, 2000).

Davis, Lance E., and Robert A. Huttenback, *Mammon and the pursuit of empire: the political economy of British imperialism 1860–1912* (Cambridge, 1986).

De Groot, Gerard J., *Blighty: British society in the era of the Great War* (London, 1996).

Deist, Wilhelm (ed.), *The German military in the age of total war* (Leamington Spa, 1985).

Delbrück, Clemens von, *Die wirtschaftliche Mobilmachung in Deutschland 1914* (Munich, 1924).

Delbrück, Hans, *Krieg und Politik 1914–1916* (Berlin, 1918).

Dereymez, Jean-William, 'Les Usines de guerre (1914–1918) et le cas de la Saône-et-Loire', *Cahiers d'histoire*, II (1981), 151–81.

Dewar, George A. B., *The great munitions feat 1914–1918* (London, 1921).

Dignan, Don, *The Indian revolutionary problem in British diplomacy 1914–1919* (New Delhi, 1983).

Dix, Arthur, *Wirtschaftskrieg und Kriegswirtschaft: zur Geschichte des deutschen Zusammenbruchs* (Berlin, 1920).

Djemal Pasha, *Memoirs of a Turkish statesman 1913–1919* (London, [1922]).

Dockrill, Michael, and David French (eds.), *Strategy and intelligence: British policy and intelligence during the First World War* (London, 1996).

Doerries, Reinhard R., *Washington–Berlin 1908/1917: die Tätigkeit des Botschafters Johann Heinrich Graf von Bernstorff in Washington vor dem Eintritt der Vereingten Staaten von Amerika in den Ersten Weltkrieg* (Dusseldorf, 1975); English edition, *Imperial challenge: Ambassador Count Bernstorff and German–American relations, 1908–1917* (Chapel Hill, 1989).

Doise, Jean, and Maurice Vaïsse, *Diplomatie et outil militaire 1871–1969* (Paris, 1987).

Dschawid-Bei [ie Djavid], *Türkische Kriegsfinanzwirtschaft. Budgetrede, gehalten in der türkischen Kammer am 3. März 1917* (Stuttgart and Berlin, 1917).

Dua, R. P., *Anglo-Japanese relations during the First World War* (New Delhi, 1972).

Ducasse, André, Jacques Meyer, and Gabriel Perreux, *Vie et mort des français 1914–1918* (Paris, 1959).

Duroselle, Jean-Baptiste, *La France et les français 1914–1920* (Paris, 1972).

—— *La Grande Guerre des français: l'incomprehensible* (Paris, 1994).

Egger, Rainer, 'Heeresverwaltung und Rüstungsindustrie in Niederösterreich während des I. Weltkrieges', in Wilhelm Brauneder and Franz Baltzarek (eds.), *Modell einer neuen Wirtschaftsordnung. Wirtschaftsverwaltung in Österreich 1914–1918* (Frankfurt, 1991).

Ehlert, Hans Gotthard, *Die wirtschaftliche Zentralbehörde des deutschen Reiches 1914 bis 1919. Das Problem der 'Gemeinwirtschaft' in Krieg und Frieden* (Wiesbaden, 1982).

Eichengreen, Barry, *Golden fetters: the gold standard and the great depression, 1919–1939* (New York, 1992).

Eley, Geoff, 'The view from the throne: the personal rule of Kaiser Wilhelm II', *Historical Journal*, XXVIII (1985), 469–85.

Ellinwood, DeWitt C., and S. D. Pradhan, *India and World War I* (New Delhi, 1978).

Emin, Ahmed, *Turkey in the World War* (New Haven, 1930).

Epkenhans, Michael, *Die wilhelminische Flottenrüstung 1908–1914. Weltmachtstreben, industrieller Fortschritt, soziale Integration* (Munich, 1991).

—— 'Military–industrial relations in Imperial Germany', *War in History* X (2003), 1–26.

Epstein, Klaus, *Matthias Erzberger and the dilemma of German democracy* (New York, 1971).

Erzberger, Matthias, *Die Rüstungsausgaben des Deutschen Reiches* (Stuttgart, 1914).

—— *Erlebnisse im Weltkrieg* (Stuttgart, 1920).

Evans, R. J. W., and Hartmut Pogge von Strandmann (eds.), *The coming of the First World War* (Oxford, 1988).

Farr, Martin, 'A compelling case for voluntarism: Britain', alternative strategy, 1915–1916', *War in History*, IX (2002), 279–306.

—— 'Reginald McKenna as chancellor of the exchequer 1915–1916', Glasgow University Ph.D. thesis, 1998.

Farrar, L. L., jr, *The short-war illusion: German policy, strategy and domestic affairs, August–December 1914* (Santa Barbara, 1973).

—— *Divide and conquer: German efforts to conclude a separate peace, 1914–1918* (Boulder, Col. 1978).

Farrar, Marjorie Millbank, 'Politics versus patriotism: Alexandre Millerand as French minister of war', *French Historical Studies*, XI (1980), 577–609.

—— *Principled pragmatist: the political career of Alexandre Millerand* (New York, 1991).

Fayolle, Marie-Émile, *Cahiers secrets de la guerre*, ed. Henri Contamine (Paris, 1963).

Feldman, Gerald D., *Army, industry and labor in Germany 1914–1918* (Princeton, 1966).

—— 'The political and social foundations of Germany's economic mobilization, 1914–1916', *Armed Forces and Society*, III (1976), 121–45.

—— *The great disorder: politics, economics and society in the German inflation 1914–1924* (New York, 1993).

—— *Hugo Stinnes. Biographie eines Industriellen 1870–1924* (Munich, 1998).

Ferguson, Niall, 'Germany and the origins of the First World War: new perspectives', *Historical Journal*, XXXV (1992), 725–52.

—— 'Public finance and national security: the domestic origins of the First World War revisited', *Past and Present*, 142 (1994), 141–68.

—— *Paper and iron: Hamburg business and German politics in the era of inflation, 1897–1927* (Cambridge, 1995).

—— *The pity of war* (London, 1998).

Ferro, Marc, *The Great War 1914–1918* (London, 1973).

Ferry, Abel (ed.), *Les Carnets secrets (1914–1918)* (Paris, 1957).

Fiebig-von Hase, Ragnild, and Maria Sturm, 'Die transatlantischen Wirtschaftbeziehungen in der Nachkriegsplanung Deutschlands, der alliierten Westmächte und der USA, 1914–17', *Militärgeschichtliche Mitteilungen*, 52 (1993), 1–34.

Fischer, Fritz, *Germany's aims in the First World War* (London, 1967; first published 1961).

—— *World power or decline: the controversy over Germany's aims in the First World War* (London, 1974; first published 1965).

—— *War of illusions: German policies from 1911 to 1914* (London, 1975; first published 1969).

Fisk, Harvey E., *French public finance in the Great War and today* (New York, 1922).

Flood, P. J., *France 1914–1918: public opinion and the war effort* (Basingstoke, 1990).

Florinsky, Michael T., *The end of the Russian empire* (New Haven, 1931).

Fontaine, Arthur, *French industry during the war* (New Haven, 1926).

Förster, Stig, *Der doppelte Militarismus. Die deutsche Heeresrüstungspolitik zwischen Status-quo-Sicherung und Aggression, 1890–1913* (Stuttgart, 1985).

—— 'Der deutsche Generalstab und die Illusion des kurzen Krieges, 1871–1914. Metakritik eines Mythos', *Militärgeschichtliche Mitteilungen*, 54 (1995), 61–95.

Forsyth, Douglas J., *The crisis of Liberal Italy: monetary and financial policy, 1914–1922* (Cambridge, 1993).

Frantz, Gunther (ed.), *Russland auf dem Wege zur Katastrophe. Tagebücher des Grossfürsten Andrej und des Kriegsministers Poliwanow. Briefe der Grossfürsten an den Zaren* (Berlin, 1926).

Fraser, Peter, 'The British "shells scandal" of 1915', *Canadian Journal of History*, XVIII (1983), 69–86.

French, David, 'The military background to the "shells crisis" of May 1915', *Journal of Strategic Studies*, II (1979), 192–205.

—— *British economic and strategic planning 1905–1915* (London, 1982).

—— *British strategy and war aims 1914–1916* (London, 1986).

—— 'The meaning of attrition, 1914–1916', *English Historical Review*, CIII (1988), 385–405.

Frey, Marc, 'Deutsche Finanzinteressen an der Vereinigten Staaten und den Niederlanden im Ersten Weltkrieg', *Militärgeschichtliche Mitteilungen*, 53 (1994), 327–53.

—— 'Trade, ships, and the neutrality of the Netherlands in the First World War', *International History Review*, XIX (1997), 541–62.

Fridenson, Patrick, *Histoire des usines Renault 1. Naissance de la grande enterprise 1898–1939* (Paris, 1972).

—— (ed.), *1914–1918: l'autre front* (Paris, 1977); English edition, *The French home front 1914–1918* (Providence, RI, 1992).

Galbraith, John S., 'British war aims in World War I: a commentary on statesmanship', *Journal of Commonwealth and Imperial History*, XIII (1984), 25–45.

Gall, Lothar (ed.), *Krupp in 20. Jahrhundent* (Berlin, 2002).

Gall, Lothar, Gerald Feldman, Harold James, Carl-Ludwig Holtfrerich, and Hans E. Büschger, *The Deutsche Bank 1870–1995* (London, 1995).

Gatrell, Peter, 'After Tsushima: economic and administrative aspects of Russian naval rearmament, 1905–1913', *Economic History Review*, 2nd series, XLIII (1990), 255–70.

—— *Government, industry and rearmament in Russia, 1900–1914: the last argument of tsarism* (Cambridge, 1994).

—— and Mark Harrison, 'The Russian and Soviet economies in two world wars: a comparative view', *Economic History Review*, 2nd series, XLVI (1993), 425–52.

Gatzke, Hans W., *Germany's drive to the west (Drang nach Westen): a study of Germany's western war aims during the First World War* (Baltimore, 1950).

Geinitz, Christian, *Kriegsfurcht und Kampfbereitschaft. Das Augusterlebnis in Freiburg. Eine Studie zum Kriegsbeginn 1914* (Essen, 1998).

Geiss, Imanuel, 'The outbreak of the First World War and German war aims', *Journal of Contemporary History*, I (1966), 75–91.

—— *July 1914: the outbreak of the First World War: selected documents* (London, 1967).

George, Mark, 'Liberal opposition in wartime Russia: a case study of the Town and Zemstvo Unions, 1914–1917', *Slavonic and East European Review*, LXV (1987), 371–90.

Geyer, Dietrich, *Russian imperialism: the interaction of domestic and foreign policy 1860–1914* (Leamington Spa, 1987).

Geyer, Michael, *Deutsche Rüstungspolitik 1860–1980* (Frankfurt am Main, 1984).

Gilbert, Bentley Brinkerhoff, 'Pacifist to interventionist: David Lloyd George in 1911 and 1914. Was Belgium an issue?, *Historical Journal*, XXVIII (1985), 863–85.

—— *David Lloyd George: a political life. The organizer of victory 1912–1916* (London, 1992).

Gilbert, Charles, *American financing of World War I* (Westport, Conn., 1970).

Gilbert, Martin, *Winston S. Churchill*, vol. III, *1914–1916*, and companion volume (London 1971–2).

—— *First World War* (London, 1994).

Gleason, William, 'The all-Russian Union of Zemstvos and World War I', in Terence Emmons and Wayne S. Vucinich (eds.), *The Zemstvo in Russia: an experiment in local self-government* (Cambridge, 1982).

Godfrey, John, *Capitalism at war: industrial policy and bureaucracy in France 1914–1918* (Leamington Spa, 1987).

Goebel, Otto, *Deutsche Rohstoffwirtschaft im Weltkrieg einschliesslich des Hindenburg-Programms* (Stuttgart, 1930).

Gordon, Michael, 'Domestic conflict and the origins of the First World War: the British and German cases', *Journal of Modern History*, XLIV (1974), 191–226.

Görlitz, Walter (ed.), *The Kaiser and his court: the diaries, note books and letters of Admiral Georg von Müller, Chief of the Naval Cabinet, 1914–1918* (London, 1961; first published 1959).

Gottlieb, W. W., *Studies in secret diplomacy during the First World War* (London, 1957).

Gourko, Basil, *Memories and impressions of war and revolution in Russia 1914–1917* (London, 1918).

Grady, Henry F., *British war finance 1914–1919* (New York, 1927).

Graf, Daniel W., 'Military rule behind the Russian front 1914–1917: the political ramifications', *Jahrbücher für Geschichte Osteuropas*, XXII (1974), 390–411.

Granier, Gerhard, 'Deutsche Rüstungspolitik vor dem Ersten Weltkrieg. General Franz Wandels Tagebuchaufzeichnungen aus dem preussischen Kriegsministerium', *Militärgeschichtliche Mitteilungen*, 38 (1985), 123–62

Gratz, Gustav, and Richard Schüller, *Der wirtschaftliche Zusammenbruch Österreich-Ungarns* (Vienna, 1930).

Gray, Colin, *The leverage of sea power: the strategic advantages of navies in war* (New York, 1992).

Grebler, Leo, and Wilhelm Winkler, *The cost of the world war to Germany and Austria-Hungary* (New Haven, 1940).

Grieves, Keith, *The politics of manpower, 1914–1918* (Manchester, 1988).

—— *Sir Eric Geddes: business and government in war and peace* (Manchester, 1989).

Grieves, Keith, 'Improvising the British war effort: Eric Geddes and Lloyd George, 1915–18', *War & Society*, VII (1989), 40–55.

Grigg, John, *Lloyd George: from peace to war 1912–1916* (London, 1985).

Guillen, P. (ed.), *La France et l'Italie pendant la première guerre mondiale* (Grenoble, 1976).

Guinn, Paul, *British strategy and politics 1914 to 1918* (Oxford, 1965).

Gutsche, Willibald, 'Die Entstehung des Kriegausschusses der deutschen Industrie und seine Rolle zu Beginn des ersten Weltkrieges', *Zeitschrift für Geschichtwissenschaft*, XVIII (1970), 877–98.

Hadley, Michael L., and Roger Sarty, *Tin-pots and pirate ships: Canadian naval forces and German sea raiders 1880–1918* (Montreal, 1991).

Hagen, Gottfried, *Die Türkei im Ersten Weltkrieg. Flugblätter und Flugschriften in arabischer, persischer und osmanisch-türkischer Sprache aus eines Sammlung der Universitätbibliothek Heidelberg eingeleitet, übersetzt und kommentiert* (Frankfurt am Main, 1990).

Halévy, Daniel, *L'Europe brisée; journal et lettres 1914–1918*, ed. Sébastien Laurent (Paris, 1998).

Haley, Charles D., 'The desperate Ottoman: Enver Pasha and the German empire', *Middle Eastern Studies*, XXX (1994), 1–51, 224–51.

Hamilton-Grace, R. S., *Finance and war* (London, 1910).

Hamm, Michael F., 'Liberal politics in wartime Russia: an analysis of the progressive bloc', *Slavic Review*, XXXIII (1974), 453–68.

Hankey, Maurice, Lord, *Government control in war* (Cambridge, 1945).

—— *The supreme command 1914–1918*, 2 vols. (London, 1961).

Hanssen, Hans Peter, *Diary of a dying empire*, ed. R. H. Lutz, M. Schofield, and O. O. Winther (Port Washington, NY, 1973; first published 1955).

Hardach, Gerd, *The First World War 1914–1918* (London, 1977; first published 1970).

Harvey, A. D., *Collision of empires: Britain in three world wars, 1793–1945* (London, 1992).

Haste, Cate, *Keep the home fires burning: propaganda in the First World War* (London, 1977).

Hatry, Gilbert, *Renault: usine de guerre 1914–1918* (Paris, 1978).

Haupt, Georges, *Socialism and the Great War: the collapse of the Second International* (Oxford, 1972).

Hazlehurst, Cameron, 'Asquith as prime minister, 1908–1916', *English Historical Review*, LXXXV (1970), 502–31.

—— *Politicians at war, July 1914 to May 1915: a prologue to the triumph of Lloyd George* (London, 1971).

Hecker, Gerhard, *Walther Rathenau und sein Verhältnis zu Militär und Krieg* (Boppard am Rhein, 1983).

Helfferich, Karl, *Der Weltkrieg* (Karlsruhe, 1925; first published 1919).

—— *Money* (New York, 1969; from the German edn. of 1923).

Heller, Joseph, *British policy towards the Ottoman empire 1908–1914* (London, 1983).

Hendrick, Burton J., *The life and letters of Walter A. Page* (London, 1930).

Herrmann, David, *The arming of Europe and the making of the First World War* (Princeton, 1996).

Herwig, Holger, *The First World War: Germany and Austria-Hungary 1914–1918* (London, 1997).

Herzfeld, Hans, *Der Erste Weltkrieg*, 7th edn. (Munich, 1985; first published 1968).

Hewins, W. A. S., *Apolgia of an imperialist: forty years of empire policy*, 2 vols. (London, 1929).

Hindenburg, Paul von, *Out of my life* (London, 1920).

Hinsley, F. H., (ed.), *British foreign policy under Sir Edward Grey* (Cambridge, 1977).

Hirschfeld, Gerhard, '1986 regional conference: war and society in modern German history', *German History*, IV (1987), 64–91.

—— Gerd Krumeich, Dieter Langewiesche, and Hans-Peter Ullmann, *Kriegserfahrungen. Studien zur Sozial- und Mentalitatsgeschichte des Ersten Weltkriegs* (Essen, 1997).

Hirst, F. W., and J. E. Allen, *British war budgets* (London, 1926).

L'Histoire, 14–18: mourir pour la patrie (Paris, 1992).

Hobson, J. M., 'The military-extraction gap and the wary Titan: the fiscal sociology of British defence policy 1870–1913', *Journal of European Economic History*, XXII (1993), 461–506.

Holtfrerich, Carl-Ludwig, *The German inflation 1914–1923: causes and effects in international perspective* (Berlin, 1986).

Hope, Nicholas, *German and Scandinavian protestantism 1700 to 1918* (Oxford, 1995).

Horn, Martin, 'Alexandre Ribot et la coopération financière anglo-française 1914–1917', *Guerres mondiales et conflits contemporains*, 180 (October 1995), 7–28.

—— *Britain, France and the financing of the First World War* (Montreal, 2002).

—— 'External finance in Anglo-French relations in the First World War, 1914–1917', *International History Review*, XVII (1995), 51–77.

Horne, John, 'Immigrant workers in France during World War I', *French Historical Studies*, XIV (1985), 57–88.

—— (ed.), *State, society and mobilization in Europe during the First World War* (Cambridge, 1997).

Howard, Harry N., *The partition of Turkey: a diplomatic history 1913–1923* (New York, 1966; first published 1931).

Hull, Isobel V., *The entourage of Kaiser Wilhelm II 1888–1918* (Cambridge, 1982).

Jahn, Hubertus F., *Patriotic culture in Russia during World War I* (Ithaca, 1995).

Janssen, Karl-Heinz, *Der Kanzler und der General. Die Führungkrise um Bethmann Hollweg und Falkenhayn (1914–1916)* (Göttingen, 1967).

Jarausch, Konrad H., 'The illusion of limited war: Chancellor Bethmann Hollweg's calculated risk, July 1914', *Central European History*, II (1969), 48–76.

—— *The enigmatic chancellor: Bethmann Hollweg and the hubris of imperial Germany* (New Haven, 1973).

Jenkins, Roy, *Asquith* (London, 1964).

Jèze, Gaston, and Henri Truchy, *The war expenditure of France* (New Haven, 1927).

Jindra, Zdenek, 'Die Rolle des Krupp-Konzerns bei der wirtschaftlichen Vorbereitung des Ersten Weltkrieges', *Jahrbuch für Wirtschaftsgeschichte* (1976), Teil 1, pp. 133–62.

Joffre, J., *Mémoires du Maréchal Joffre (1910–1917)*, 2 vols. (Paris, 1932).

Johnson, Elizabeth (ed.), *The collected writings of John Maynard Keynes*, vol. XVI, *Activities 1914–1919: the Treasury and Versailles* (London, 1971).

Johnson, Franklyn Arthur, *Defence by committee: the British Committee of Imperial Defence 1885–1959* (London, 1960).

Johnson, Jeffrey Allan, *The Kaiser's chemists: science and modernization in imperial Germany* (Chapel Hill, 1990).

Joll, James, *The Second International 1889–1914* (London, 1975).

—— *The origins of the First World War* (London, 1984).

Jones, G. Gareth, 'The British government and the oil companies, 1912–1924: the search for an oil policy', *Historical Journal*, XX (1977), 647–72.

Jost, Walter, and Friedrich Folger (eds.), *Was wir vom Weltkrieg nicht wissen* (Leipzig, 1936).

Kaiser, David, 'Germany and the origins of the First World War', *Journal of Modern History*, LV (1983), 442–74.

Kann, Robert, Bela K. Kiraly, and Paula S. Fichtner (eds.), *The Habsburg empire in World War I: essays on the intellectual, military, political and economic aspects of the Habsburg war effort* (New York, 1977).

Kaspi, André, *Le Temps des Américains: le concours américain à la France en 1917–1918* (Paris, 1976).

Kautsky, Karl (ed.), *Die deutschen Dokumente zum Kriegsausbruch 1914*, 4 vols. (Berlin, 1922).

Keiger, John F. V., *France and the origins of the First World War* (London, 1983).

—— 'Jules Cambon and Franco-German détente, 1907–1914', *Historical Journal*, XXVI (1983), 641–59.

Kennedy, Greg, and Keith Neilson (eds.), *Far-flung lines: essays on imperial defence in honour of Donald Mackenzie Schurman* (London, 1997).

Kennedy, Paul, *The rise of the Anglo-German antagonism 1860–1914* (London, 1980).

—— *The rise and fall of the great powers: economic change and military conflict from 1500 to 2000* (London, 1988).

Kent, Marian (ed.), *The great powers and the end of the Ottoman empire* (London, 1984).

Kielmansegg, Peter Graf, *Deutschland und der Erste Weltkrieg*, 2nd edn. (Stuttgart, 1980).

King, Jere Clemens, *Generals and politicians: conflict between France's high command, parliament and government, 1914–1918* (Berkeley, 1951).

Kiraly, Bela, Nandor F. Dreisziger, and Albert A. Nofi (eds.), *East Central European society in World War I* (Boulder, Col., 1985).

Kirby, David, *War, peace and revolution: international socialism at the crossroads 1914–1918* (Aldershot, 1986).

Kirkaldy, A. W. (ed.), *British finance during and after the war 1914–21* (London, 1921).

Kitchen, Martin, *The silent dictatorship: the politics of the German high command under Hindenburg and Ludendorff, 1916–1918* (London, 1976).

Klein, Fritz, *Deutschland im ersten Weltkrieg*, 3 vols. (Berlin, 1968).

Klotz, L.-L., *De la guerre à la paix* (Paris, 1924).

Knauss, Robert, *Die deutsche, englische und französische Kriegsfinanzierung* (Berlin, 1923).

Koch, H. W., (ed.), *The origins of the First World War: great power rivalry and German war aims* (London, 1972); 2nd edn. (1984).

Kocka, Jürgen, *Facing total war: German society 1914–1918* (Leamington Spa, 1984; first published 1973).

Koistinen, Paul A.C., *Mobilizing for modern war: The political economy of American warfare 1865–1919* (Lawrence, Kansas, 1997).

Koss, Stephen, *Asquith* (London, 1976).

Koss, Stephen E., 'The destruction of Britain's last Liberal government', *Journal of Modern History*, XL (1968), 257–77.

Kraft, Heinz, *Staatsräson und Kriegführung im kaiserlichen Deutschland 1914–1916. Der Gegensatz zwischen dem Generalstabschef von Falkenhayn und dem Oberbefehlshaber Ost im Rahmen des Bundniskreises der Mittelmächte* (Göttingen, 1980).

Kriegel, Annie, *Le Pain et les roses: jalons pour une histoire des socialismes* (Paris, 1968).

—— and Jean-Jacques Becker, *1914: la patrie et le mouvement ouvrier français* (Paris, 1964).

Krieger, Leonard, and Fritz Stern (eds.), *The responsibility of power: historical essays in honor of Hajo Holborn* (London, 1968).

Kroboth, Rudolf, *Die Finanzpolitik des deutschen Reiches während der Reichskanzlerschaft Bethmann Hollwegs und die Geld und Kapitalmarktverhältnisse (1909–1913/14)* (Frankfurt am Main, 1986).

Krohn, Claus-Dieter, 'Geldtheorien in Deutschland während der Inflation 1914 bis 1924', in Gerald D. Feldman, Carl-Ludwig Holtfrerich, Gerhard A. Ritter, and Peter-Christian Witt (eds.), *Die Anpassung an die Inflation* (Berlin, 1986).

Kronenbitter, Gunther, 'Die Macht der Illusionen. Julikrise und Kriegsausbruch 1914 aus der Sicht des deutschen Militärattachés in Wien', *Militärgeschichtliche Mitteilungen*, 57 (1998), 519–50.

Krumeich, Gerd, *Armaments and politics in France on the eve of the First World War: the introduction of three-year conscription 1913–1914* (Leamington Spa, 1984; first published 1980).

Kruse, Wolfgang, 'Die Kriegsbegeisterung im deutschen Reich zu Beginn des Ersten Weltkrieges', in Marcel van der Linden and Gottfried Mergner (eds.), *Kriegsbegeisterung und mentale Kriegsvorbereitung* (Berlin, 1991).

—— *Krieg und nationale Integration: eine Neuinterpretation des sozialdemokratischen Burgfriedensschlusses 1914/15* (Essen, 1993).

—— (ed.), *Eine Welt von Feinden. Der Grosse Krieg 1914–1918* (Frankfurt am Main, 1997).

Kühlmann, Richard von, *Erinnerungen* (Heidelberg, 1948).

La Gorce, Paul-Marie de (ed.), *La Première Guerre Mondiale*, 2 vols. (Paris, 1991).

Lambi, Ivo Nikolai, *The navy and German power politics, 1862–1914* (Boston, 1984).

Lampe, John R., *The Bulgarian economy in the twentieth century* (London, 1986).

Landau, Jacob M., *Pan-Turkism in Turkey: a study of irridentism* (London, 1981).

—— *The politics of pan-Islam: ideology and organization* (Oxford, 1990).

Langdon, John W., *July 1914: the long debate, 1918–1990* (New York, 1991).

Larcher, M., *La Guerre turque dans la guerre mondiale* (Paris, 1926).

—— 'Données statistiques concernant la guerre 1914–1918', *Revue militaire française*, 140 (février 1933), 190–204; 141 (mars 1933), 291–303; 142 (avril 1933), 44–52.

—— 'Données statistiques sur les forces françaises', *Revue militaire française*, 155 (mai 1934), 198–223; 156 (juin 1934), 351–63.

Le Bon, Gustave, *The psychology of the Great War* (London, 1916).

Le Révérend, André, *Lyautey* (Paris, 1983).

Lewis, Bernard, *The emergence of modern Turkey* (London, 1961).

Lieven, D. C. B., *Russia and the origins of the First World War* (London, 1983).

—— *Nicholas II: emperor of all the Russias* (London, 1993).

Liman von Sanders, Otto, *Five years in Turkey* (Annapolis, 1927; first published 1920).

Lincoln, W. Bruce, *Passage through Armageddon: the Russians in war and revolution 1914–1918* (New York, 1986).

Linke, Horst Günther, 'Russlands Weg in den Ersten Weltkrieg und seine Kriegs-ziele 1914–1917', *Militärgeschichtliche Mitteilungen*, 32 (1982), 9–34.

Lobanov-Rostovsky, A., *The grinding mill: reminiscences of war and revolution in Russia, 1913–1920* (New York, 1935).

Lotz, Walther, *Die deutsche Staatsfinanzwirtschaft im Kriege* (Stuttgart, 1927).

Lowe, Peter, *Britain and Japan 1911–1915: a study of British far eastern policy* (London, 1969).

Lucas, Charles (ed.), *The empire at war*, 5 vols. (Oxford, 1921–6).

Ludendorff, Erich, *My war memories 1914–1918*, 2 vols. (London, 1919).

—— *Urkunden der obersten Heeresleitung über ihre Tätigkeit 1916–18* (Berlin, 1920).

Lutz, Ralph Haswell (ed.), *Documents of the German revolution: fall of the German empire 1914–1918*, 2 vols. (Stanford, 1932).

Lyautey, Pierre, *Lyautey l'Africain: textes et lettres du maréchal Lyautey*, 4 vols. (Paris, 1953–7).

Lyth, Peter J., *Inflation and the merchant economy: the Hamburg Mittelstand 1914–1924* (New York, 1990).

McCallum, Iain, 'Achilles heel? Propellants and high explosives, 1880–1916', *War Studies Journal*, IV (1999), 65–83.

Macdonald, Catriona M. M., and E. W. McFarland (eds.), *Scotland and the Great War* (East Linton, 1999).

McDonald, David MacLaren, *United government and foreign policy in Russia 1900–1914* (Cambridge Mass., 1992).

Macfie, A. L., *The end of the Ottoman empire 1908–1923* (London, 1998).

McKean, Robert B., *St Petersburg between the revolutions: workers and revolution-aries, June 1907–February 1917* (New Haven, 1990).

McKercher, B. J. C., and Keith E. Neilson, '"The triumph of unarmed forces": Sweden and the allied blockade of Germany, 1914–1917', *Journal of Strategic Studies*, VII (1984), 178–99.

McKibbin, Ross, *The evolution of the Labour party 1910–1924* (Oxford, 1974).

—— 'Why was there no Marxism in Great Britain?', *English Historical Review*, XCIX (1984), 297–331.

MacMunn, George, *Turmoil and tragedy in India: 1914 and after* (London, 1934).

McNeill, William H., *The pursuit of power: technology, armed force, and society since A.D. 1000* (Oxford, 1983).

Mai, Gunther, *Das Ende des Kaiserreichs. Politik und Kriegführung im Ersten Weltkrieg* (Munich, 1987).

Maier, Charles S., 'Wargames: 1914–1919', *Journal of Interdisciplinary History*, XVIII (1988), 819–49.

Manchester, William, *The arms of Krupp 1587–1968* (London, 1969).

Marder, Arthur J., (ed.), *Fear God and dread nought: the correspondence of Admiral of the Fleet Lord Fisher of Kilverstone*, 3 vols. (London, 1952–9).

Marder, Arthur J., *From the Dreadnought to Scapa Flow: the Royal Navy in the Fisher era, 1904–1919*, 5 vols. (London, 1961–70).

Marquand, David, *Ramsay MacDonald* (London, 1977).

Martin, Germain, *La Situation financière de la France 1914–1924* (Paris, 1924).

—— *Les Finances publiques de la France et la fortune privée (1914–1925)* (Paris, 1925).

Marwick, Arthur, *The deluge: British society and the First World War* (London, 1965).

März, Eduard, *Austrian banking and financial policy: Creditanstalt at a turning point 1913–1923* (London, 1984; first published 1981).

Materna, Ingo, and Hans-Joachim Schreckenbach, with Bärbel Holtz, *Dokumente aus geheimen Archiven*. Band 4 *1914–1918. Berichte des Berliner Polizeipräsidenten zur Stimmung und Lage der Bevölkerung in Berlin 1914–18* (Weimar, 1987).

Maurin, Jules, *Armée-Guerre-Société: soldats languedociens (1889–1919)* (Paris, 1982).

May, Arthur J., *The passing of the Hapsburg monarchy 1914– 1918*, 2 vols. (Philadelphia, 1966).

Meaney, Neville, *The search for security in the Pacific, 1901–14* (Sydney, 1976).

Meinecke, Friedrich, *Strassburg/Freiburg/Berlin 1901–1919: Erinnerungen* (Stuttgart, 1949).

Menu, Ch., 'Les Fabrications de guerre', *Revue militaire française*, 149 (novembre 1933), 180–210.

Messimy, Adolphe, *Mes souvenirs* (Paris, 1937).

Meynier, Gilbert, *L'Algérie révelée: la guerre de 1914–1918 et le premier quart du XX4 siècle* (Genève, 1981).

Michalka, Wolfgang, (ed.), *Der Erste Weltkrieg. Wirkung, Warnehmung, Analyse* (Munich, 1994).

Michel, Bernard, 'L'Autriche et l'entrée dans la guerre en 1914', *Guerres mondiales et conflits contemporains*, 179 (juillet 1995), 5–11.

Michelson, Alexander M., Paul N. Apostol, and Michael W. Bernatzky, *Russian public finance during the war* (New Haven, 1928).

Miller, Steven E. (ed.), *Military strategy and the origins of the First World War* (Princeton, 1985).

Miller, Susanne, *Burgfrieden und Klassenkampf: die deutsche Sozialdemokratie im Ersten Weltkrieg* (Dusseldorf, 1974).

Millett, Allan R., and Williamson Murray (eds.), *Military effectiveness*, vol. I, *The First World War* (Boston, 1988).

Milner, Susan, *The dilemmas of internationalism: French syndicalism and the international labour movement, 1900–1914* (New York, 1990).

Ministry of Munitions, *History of the Ministry of Munitions*, 12 vols. (London, 1922).

Miquel, Pierre, *La Grande Guerre* (Paris, 1983).

Mollin, Volker, *Auf dem Wege zur 'Materialschlacht'. Vorgeschichte und Funktionen des Artillerie-Industrie-Komplexes im deutschen Kaiserreich* (Pfaffenweiler, 1986).

Mombauer, Annika, 'Helmuth von Moltke and the German general staff— military and political decision-making in imperial Germany, 1906–1916', Sussex University D. Phil thesis, 1997.

—— 'A reluctant military leader? Helmuth von Moltke and the July crisis of 1914', *War in History*, VI (1999), 417–46.

Mommsen, Wolfgang, 'Domestic factors in German foreign policy before 1914', *Central European History*, VI (1973), 3–43.

—— 'Society and war: two new analyses of the First World War', *Journal of Modern History*, XLVII (1975), 530–8.

—— *Max Weber and German politics 1890–1920* (Chicago, 1984; first published 1959).

—— *Imperial Germany 1867–1918: politics, culture, and society in an authoritarian state* (London, 1995).

Le Monde, La Trés Grande Guerre (Paris, 1994).

Morgan, E. Victor, *Studies in British financial policy 1914– 25* (London, 1952).

Morgan, Kenneth O., *Lloyd George* (London, 1974).

Morgenthau, Henry, *Ambassador Morgenthau's story*, (New York, 1919).

Morris, A. J. A., *The scaremongers: the advocacy of war and rearmament 1896–1914* (London, 1984).

Moukbil bey, M., *Le Campagne de l'Irak 1914–1918: le siège de Kut-el-Amara* (Paris, 1933).

Moulton, H. Fletcher, *The life of Lord Moulton* (London, 1922).

Moyer, Laurence V., *Victory must be ours: Germany in the Great War 1914–1918* (New York, 1995).

Mühlmann, Carl, *Deutschland und die Türkei 1913–1914. Die Berufung der deutschen Militärmission nach der Türkei 1913, das deutsch–türkische Bündnis 1914 und der Eintritt der Türkei in den Weltkrieg* (Berlin-Grunewald, 1929).

—— *Das deutsch–türkische Waffenbündnis im Weltkriege* (Leipzig, 1940).

—— *Oberste Heeresleitung und Balkan im Weltkrieg 1914–1918* (Berlin, 1942).

Müller, Herbert Landolin, *Islam, Gihad ('Heiliger Krieg') und deutsches Reich. Ein Nachspiel zur wilhelminischen Weltpolitik im Maghreb 1914–1918* (Frankfurt am Main, 1991).

Müller, Stefan von, *Die finanzielle Mobilmachung Österreichs und ihr Ausbau bis 1918* (Berlin, 1918).

Neilson, Keith, 'Russian foreign purchasing in the Great War: a test case', *Slavonic and East European Review*, LX (1982), 572–90.

Neilson, Keith, *Strategy and supply: the Anglo-Russian alliance, 1914–17* (London, 1984).

—— ' "My beloved Russians": Sir Arthur Nicolson and Russia, 1906–1916', *International History Review*, IX (1987), 521–54.

—— *Britain and the last Tsar: British policy and Russia 1894–1917* (Oxford, 1995).

Nettl, J. P., 'The German Social Democratic Party 1890–1914 as a political model', *Past and Present*, 30 (1965), 65–95.

—— *Rosa Luxemburg*, 2 vols. (London, 1966).

Newbury, Colin, 'Spoils of war: sub-imperial collaboration in South West Africa and New Guinea', *Journal of Imperial and Commonwealth History*, XVI (1988), 86–106.

Nogales, Rafael de, *Four years beneath the crescent* (London, 1926).

Nouailhat, Yves-Henri, 'Un emprunt français au États-unis en juillet 1916: l'emprunt de l'American Foreign Securities Company', *Revue d'histoire moderne et contemporaine*, XIV (1967), 356–74).

—— *France et États-unis août 1914–avril 1917* (Paris, 1979).

Noyes, Alexander D., *The war period of American finance 1908–1925* (New York, 1926).

O'Brien, Phillips Payson, *British and American naval power: politics and policy, 1900–1936* (Westport, Conn., 1998).

Offer, Avner, 'The working classes, British naval plans and the coming of the Great War', *Past and Present*, CVII (1985), 204–26.

—— 'Morality and Admiralty: "Jacky" Fisher, economic warfare and the laws of war', *Journal of Contemporary History*, XXIII (1988), 99–119.

—— *The First World War: an agrarian interpretation* (Oxford, 1989).

Olphe-Galliard, G., *Histoire économique et financière de la guerre (1914–1918)* (Paris, 1923).

Ott, Hugo, 'Kriegswirtschaft und Wirtschaftskrieg 1914–1918: verdeutlicht an Beispielen aus dem badisch-elsässischen Raum', in Erich Hassinger, J. Heinz Müller, and Hugo Ott (eds.), *Geschichte. Wirtschaft. Gesellschaft* (Berlin, 1974).

Owen, Gail L., 'Dollar diplomacy in default: the economics of Russian–American relations, 1910–1917', *Historical Journal*, XIII (1970), 251–72.

Panayi, Panikos, *The enemy in our midst: Germans in Britain during the First World War* (New York, 1991).

Panichas, George A. (ed.), *Promise of greatness: the war of 1914–1918* (London, 1968).

Pares, Bernard, *The fall of the Russian monarchy: a study of the evidence* (London, 1939).

Paret, Peter (ed.), with Gordon Craig and Felix Gilbert, *Makers of modern strategy from Machiavelli to the nuclear age* (Oxford, 1986).

Parrini, Carl, *Heir to empire: United States economic diplomacy 1916–1923* (Pittsburgh, 1969).

Parry, Cyril, 'Gwynedd and the Great War', *Welsh History Review*, XIV (1988), 78–117.

Pearson, Raymond, *The Russian moderates and the crisis of Tsarism 1914–1917* (London, 1977).

Pearton, Maurice, *The knowledgeable state: diplomacy, war and technology since 1830* (London, 1982).

Perrins, Michael, 'The council for state defence 1905–1909: a study in Russian bureaucratic politics', *Slavonic and East European Review*, LVIII (1980), 370–98.

Peters, John, 'The British government and the City–industry divide: the case of the 1914 financial crisis', *Twentieth Century British History*, IV (1993), 126–48.

Petit, Lucien, *Histoire des finances extérieures de la France pendant la guerre (1914–1919)* (Paris, 1929).

Petrovich, Michael Boris, *A history of modern Serbia 1804–1918*, 2 vols. (New York, 1976).

Philpott, William J., *Anglo-French relations and strategy on the western front, 1914–1918* (Basingstoke, 1996).

Pick, Daniel, *War machine: the rationalization of slaughter in the modern age* (New Haven, 1993).

Pigou, A. C., *The political economy of war* (London, 1921).

Pogge von Strandmann, Hartmut (ed.), *Walther Rathenau: industrialist, banker, intellectual, and politician. Notes and diaries 1907–1922* (Oxford, 1985; first published 1967).

Pokrowski, M. N. (ed.), *Die internationalen Beziehungen im Zeitalter des Imperialismus*, ed. Otto Hoetsch, series 1, ii (Berlin, 1933).

Pomiankowski, Joseph, *Der Zusammenbruch des Ottomanischen Reiches. Erinnerungen an die Türkei aus der Zeit des Weltkrieges* (Vienna, 1928).

Popovics, Alexander, *Das Geldwesen im Kriege* (Vienna, 1925).

Pourcher, Yves, *Les Jours de guerre: la vie des français au jour le jour 1914–1918* (Paris, 1994).

Prior, Robin, *Churchill's 'World Crisis' as history* (London, 1983).

Pugh, Martin, *The making of modern British politics 1867–1939* (Oxford, 1982).

Raithel, Thomas, *Das 'Wunder' der inneren Einheit. Studien zur deutschen und französischen Öffentlichkeit bei Beginn des Ersten Weltkrieges* (Bonn, 1996).

Rauchensteiner, Manfred, *Der Tod des Doppeladlers. Österreich-Ungarn und der Erste Weltkrieg* (Graz, 1993).

Reader, W. J., *Imperial Chemical Industries: a history*, 2 vols. (London, 1970).

Reboul, C., *Mobilisation industrielle. Tome 1, Des fabrications de guerre en France de 1914 à 1918* (Paris, 1925).

Redlich, Joseph, *Austrian war government* (New Haven, 1929).

Reichsarchiv, *Der Weltkrieg. Kriegsrüstung und Kriegswirtschaft*, 2 vols. (Berlin, 1930).

Renouvin, Pierre, *The forms of war government in France* (New Haven, 1927).

—— 'La politique des emprunts étrangers aux Etats–Unis de 1914 à 1917', *Annales: économies—societés—civilisations*, VI (1951), 289–305.

—— *La Crise européenne et la première guerre mondiale (1904–1918)*, 6th edn. (Paris, 1969).

Ribot, Alexandre, *Letters to a friend: recollections of my political life* (London, [c. 1925]).

—— *Journal d'Alexandre Ribot et correspondances inédites 1914–1922* (Paris, 1936), edited by A. Ribot.

Riedl, Richard, *Die Industrie Österreichs während des Krieges* (Vienna, 1932).

Riezler, Kurt, *Kurt Riezler. Tagebücher, Aufsätze, Dokumente*, ed. Karl Dietrich Erdmann (Göttingen, 1972).

Ringer, Fritz K., *The decline of the German mandarins: the German academic community, 1890–1933* (Hanover, NH, 1990; first published 1969).

Ritter, Gerhard, *The sword and the sceptre: the problem of militarism in Germany*, 4 vols. (London, 1970–3).

Rivet, Daniel, *Lyautey et l'institution du protectorat français au Maroc 1912–1925*, 3 vols. (Paris, 1988).

Robbins, Keith, *The First World War* (Oxford, 1984).

Robert, Jean-Louis, *Les Ouvriers, la patrie et la révolution: Paris 1914–1919* (Paris, 1995).

Roberts, Richard, *Schröders: merchants and bankers* (Basingstoke, 1992).

Roesler, Konrad, *Die Finanzpolitik des deutschen Reiches im Ersten Weltkrieg* (Berlin, 1967).

Rogger, Hans, 'Russia in 1914', *Journal of Contemporary History*, I (1966), 95–119.

Rohkrämer, Thomas, *Der Militarismus der 'kleinen Leute'. Die Kriegsvereine im Deutschen Kaiserreich* (Munich, 1990).

Röhl, John C. G., 'Admiral von Müller and the approach of war, 1911–1914', *Historical Journal*, XII (1969), 651–73.

—— *The Kaiser and his court: Wilhelm II and the government of Germany* (Cambridge, 1994).

—— (ed.), *1914: delusion or design? The testimony of two German diplomats* (London, 1973).

—— (ed.), with Elisabeth Müller-Luckner, *Der Ort Kaiser Wilhelms II in der deutsche Geschichte* (Munich, 1991).

—— and Nicolaus Sombart (eds.), *Kaiser Wilhelm II: new interpretations* (Cambridge, 1982).

Rohwer, Jürgen (ed.), *Neue Forschungen zum Ersten Weltkrieg* (Koblenz, 1985).

Roosa, Ruth Amenda, 'Russian industrialists during World War I: the interaction of economics and politics', in Gregory Guroff and Fred V. Carstensen (eds.), *Entrepreneurship in imperial Russia and the Soviet Union* (Princeton, 1983).

Rosenberg, Arthur, *The birth of the German republic 1871–1918* (New York, 1962; first published 1931).

Roskill, Stephen, *Hankey: man of secrets, 3 vols.* (London, 1970).

Rothwell, V. H., *British war aims and peace diplomacy 1914–1918* (Oxford, 1971).

Rumbold, Algernon, *Watershed in India 1914–1922* (London, 1979).

Ryder, A. J., *The German revolution of 1918: a study of German socialism in war and revolt* (Cambridge, 1967).

Saatmann, Inge, *Parlament, Rüstung und Armee in Frankreich, 1914/18* (Dusseldorf, 1978).

Sanborn, Josh, 'The mobilization of 1914 and the question of the Russian nation: a reexamination', *Slavic Review,* LIX (2000), 267–89.

Sanders, Michael, and Philip M. Taylor, *British propaganda during the First World War 1914–18* (London, 1982).

Sareen, Tilan Raj, *Indian revolutionary movements abroad (1905–1921)* (New Delhi, 1979).

Sayers, R. S., *The Bank of England 1891–1944,* 2 vols. (Cambridge, 1966).

Scham, Alan, *Lyautey in Morocco: protectorate administration, 1912–1925* (Berkeley, 1970).

Schmidt, Martin E., *Alexandre Ribot: odyssey of a liberal in the Third Republic* (The Hague, 1974).

Schoen, Erich, *Geschichte des deutschen Feuerwerkswesens der Armee und Marine mit Einschluss des Zeugwesens* (Berlin, 1936).

Schöllgen, Gregor, *Escape into war? The foreign policy of imperial Germany* (Oxford, 1990).

Schorske, Carl E., *German social democracy 1905–1917: the development of the great schism* (New York, 1955).

Schulte, Bernd F., *Die deutsche Armee 1900–1914: zwischen beharren und verändern* (Dusseldorf, 1977).

—— *Vor dem Kriegsausbruch 1914. Deutschland, die Türkei und der Balkan* (Dusseldorf, 1980).

—— *Europäische Krise und Erster Weltkrieg. Beitrage zur Militärpolitik des Kaiserreichs, 1871–1914* (Frankfurt am Main, 1983).

Schwabe, Klaus, *Wissenschaft und Kriegsmoral. Die deutschen Hochschullehrer und die politischen Grundfragen des Ersten Weltkrieges* (Göttingen, 1969).

Schwarte, Max, (ed.), *Der Weltkrieg in seiner Einwirkung auf das deutsche Volk* (Leipzig, 1918).

—— (ed.), *Der Weltkampf um Ehre und Recht,* 10 vols. (Leipzig, 1921–33); first published as *Der grosse Krieg 1914/18* (Leipzig, 1921).

Schwarzmüller, Theo, *Zwischen Kaiser und 'Führer'. Generalfeldmarschall August von Mackensen: eine politische Biographie* (Paderborn, 1995).

Scott, Ernest, *Australia during the war* (Sydney, 1940; first published 1936).

Scott, J. D., *Vickers: a history* (London, 1962).

Seabourne, Teresa, 'The summer of 1914', in Forrest Capie and Geoffrey E. Wood (eds.), *Financial crises and the world banking system* (Basingstoke, 1986).

Self, Robert C. (ed.), *The Austen Chamberlain diary letters: the correspondence of Sir Austen Chamberlain with his sisters Hilda and Ida, 1916–1937* (Cambridge, 1995).

Semmel, Bernard, *Liberalism and naval strategy: ideology, interest, and sea power during the Pax Britannica* (Boston, 1986).

Seton-Watson, R. W., J. Dover-Wilson, Alfred E. Zimmern, and Arthur Greenwood, *The war and democracy* (London, 1915; first published 1914).

Shanafelt, Gary W., *The secret enemy: Austria-Hungary and the German alliance, 1914–1918* (Boulder, Col., 1985).

Shaw, Stanford J., and Ezel Kural Shaw, *History of the Ottoman empire and modern Turkey*, 2 vols. (Cambridge, 1976–7).

Sheehan, James J., *German liberalism in the nineteenth century* (Chicago, 1978).

Siegelbaum, Lewis H., *The politics of industrial mobilization in Russia, 1914–17: a study of the war-industries committees* (London, 1983).

Silberstein, Gerard E., *The troubled alliance: German–Austrian relations 1914 to 1917* (Lexington, 1970).

Siney, Marion C., *The allied blockade of Germany 1914–1916* (Ann Arbor, 1957).

Skidelsky, Robert, *John Maynard Keynes*, vol. I, *Hopes betrayed 1883–1920* (London, 1983).

Smith, C. Jay, jr, 'Great Britain and the 1914–1915 straits agreement with Russia: the British promise of November 1914', *American Historical Review*, LXX (1965), 1015–34.

—— *The Russian struggle for power, 1914–1917: a study of Russian foreign policy during the First World War* (New York, 1969; first published 1956).

Smith, Paul, (ed.), *Government and the armed forces in Britain 1856–1990* (London, 1996).

Snell, John L., 'Socialist unions and socialist patriotism in Germany, 1914–1918', *American Historical Review*, LIX (1993), 66–76.

Soames, Mary (ed.), *Speaking for themselves: the personal letters of Winston and Clementine Churchill* (London, 1998).

Sombart, Werner, *Händler und Helden: politische Besinnungen* (Munich, 1915).

Soutou, Georges-Henri, *L'Or et le sang: les buts de guerre économiques de la première guerre mondiale* (Paris, 1989).

Spies, S. B., 'The outbreak of the First World War and the Botha government', *South African Historical Journal*, I (1969), 47–57.

Spitzmüller, Alexander, *Memoirs of Alexander Spitzmüller, Freiherr von Hammerstein (1862–1953)*, ed. Carvel de Bussy (New York, 1987).

Spring, D. W., 'Russia and the Franco-Russian alliance, 1905–1914: dependence or interdependence?', *Slavonic and East European Review*, LXVI (1988), 564–92.

Stamp, Josiah, *Taxation during the war* (London, 1932).

Stanley, William R., 'Review of Turkish Asiatic railways to 1918: some political-military considerations', *Journal of Transport History*, VII (1966), 189–204.

Stargardt, Nicholas, *The German idea of militarism: radical and socialist critics* (Cambridge, 1994).

Stegemann, Hermann, *Geschichte des Krieges*, 4 vols. (Stuttgart, 1918–21).

Steinberg, Jonathan, *Yesterday's deterrent: Tirpitz and the birth of the German battle fleet* (London, 1965).

Steiner, Zara, *Britain and the origins of the First World War* (London, 1977).

Stevenson, David, *French war aims against Germany 1914–1919* (Oxford, 1982).

—— *The First World War and international politics* (Oxford, 1988).

—— *Armaments and the coming of war: Europe, 1904–1914* (Oxford, 1996).

Stoecker, Helmuth (ed.), *German imperialism: from the beginnings until the Second World War* (London, 1986; first published 1977).

Stone, Norman, *The eastern front 1914–1917* (London, 1975).

—— *Europe transformed 1878–1919* (London, 1983).

Strachan, Hew, 'The battle of the Somme and British strategy', *Journal of Strategic Studies*, XXI (1998), 79–95.

—— *The First World War: a new illustrated history* (London, 2003)

—— (ed.), *Oxford Illustrated History of the First World War* (Oxford, 1998).

Stuermer, H., *Two war years in Constantinople* (London, 1917).

Stumpf, R., *The private war of Seaman Stumpf: the unique diaries of a young German in the Great War*, ed. Daniel Horn (London, 1969).

Suchomlinow [i.e. Sukhomlinov], W. A., *Erinnerungen* (Berlin, 1924).

Sumida, Jon Tetsuro, *In defence of naval supremacy: finance, technology and British naval policy, 1899–1914* (Boston, 1989).

—— 'British naval administration and policy in the age of Fisher', *Journal of Military History*, LIV (1990), 1–20.

—— 'British naval operational logistics 1914–1918', *Journal of Military History*, LVII (1993), 447–80.

Tan, Tai-Yong, 'An imperial home-front: Punjab and the First World War', *Journal of Military History*, LXIV (2000), 371–410.

Taylor, A. J. P., *Politics in wartime* (London, 1964).

—— (ed.), *Lloyd George: twelve essays* (London, 1971).

Teillard, Jean, *Les Emprunts de guerre* (Montpellier, 1921).

Teixeira, Nuno Severiano, *L'Entrée du Portugal dans la Grande Guerre: objectifs nationaux et stratgégies politiques* (Paris, 1998).

Thompson, Wayne C., *In the eye of the storm: Kurt Riezler and the crises of modern Germany* (Iowa City, 1980).

Ticktin, David, 'The war issue and the collapse of the South African Labour party 1914–15', *South African Historical Journal*, 1 (1969), 59–80.

Trachtenberg, Marc, '"A new economic order": Étienne Clémentel and French economic diplomacy during the First World War', *French Historical Studies*, X (1977), 315–41.

Trebilcock, Clive, 'The British armaments industry 1890–1914: false legend and true utility', in Geoffrey Best and Andrew Wheatcroft (eds.), *War, economy and the military mind* (London, 1976).

—— *The Vickers brothers: armaments and enterprise 1854–1914* (London, 1977).

—— *The industrialization of the continental powers 1780–1914* (London, 1981).

Trumpener, Ulrich, 'German military aid to Turkey in 1914: an historical re-evaluation', *Journal of Modern History*, XXXII (1960), 145–9.

—— 'Turkey's entry into World War I: an assessment of responsibilities', *Journal of Modern History*, XXXIV (1962), 369–80.

—— 'Liman von Sanders and the German–Ottoman alliance', *Journal of Contemporary History*, I (1966), 179–92.

—— *Germany and the Ottoman empire 1914–1918* (Princeton, 1968).

Turner, John, *British politics and the Great War: coalition and conflict 1915–1918* (New Haven, 1992).

—— (ed.), *Britain and the First World War* (London, 1988).

Turner, L. C. F., *Origins of the First World War* (London, 1970).

Ullrich, Volker, *Kriegsalltag: Hamburg im ersten Weltkrieg* (Cologne, 1982).

Valiani, Leo, *The end of Austria-Hungary* (London, 1973; first published 1966).

Vandenrath, Johannes, *et al.*, *1914: les psychoses de guerre?* (Rouen, 1985).

Verhey, Jeffrey Todd, 'The "spirit of 1914": the myth of enthusiasm and the rhetoric of unity in World War I Germany', University of California, Berkeley, Ph.D. dissertation, 1991; published as *The spirit of 1914: militarism, myth and mobilization in Germany* (Cambridge, 2000).

Vincent, C. Paul, *The politics of hunger: the allied blockade of Germany, 1915–1919* (Athens, Oh., 1985).

Vincent-Smith, John, 'Britain, Portugal, and the First World War, 1914–1916', *European Studies Review*, IV (1974), 207–38.

Vogt, Adolf, *Oberst Max Bauer: Generalstabsoffizier im Zwielicht* (Osnabrück, 1974).

Walker, Eric A., *A history of southern Africa* (London, 1957).

Wallace, Stuart, *War and the image of Germany: British academics 1914–1918* (Edinburgh, 1988).

Wallach, Jehuda L., *Anatomie einer Militärhilfe. Die preussisch–deutschen Militärmissionen in der Türkei 1835–1919* (Dusseldorf, 1976).

Walvé de Bordes, J. van, *The Austrian crown: its depreciation and stabilization* (London, 1924).

Wandruszka, Adam, and Peter Urbanitsch, *Die Habsburgermonarchie 1848–1918*, vol. I, *Die wirtschaftliche Entwicklung*, ed. Alois Brusatti (Vienna, 1973); vol. V, *Die bewaffnete Macht* (Vienna, 1987).

War Office, *Statistics of the military effort of the British empire during the Great War* (London, 1922).

Warhurst, P. R., 'Smuts and Africa: a study in sub-imperialism', *South African Historical Journal*, XVI (1984), 82–100.

Watson, David Robin, *Georges Clemenceau: a political biography* (London, 1974).

Weber, Frank G., *Eagles on the crescent: Germany, Austria, and the diplomacy of the Turkish alliance 1914–1918* (Ithaca, NY, 1970).

Wegener, Wolfgang, *Die Seestrategie des Weltkrieges* (Berlin, 1929); English edn., *The naval strategy of the world war*, ed. Holger Herwig (Annapolis, 1989).

Wegs, James Robert, 'Austrian economic mobilization during World War I: with particular emphasis on heavy industry', Illinois University Ph.D. dissertation, 1970; published as *Die österreichische Kriegswirtschaft 1914–1918* (Vienna, 1979).

Wehler, Hans-Ulrich, *The German empire 1871–1918* (Leamington Spa, 1985; first published 1973).

Wells, H. G., *Mr Britling sees it through* (London, 1916).

Westwood, John, *Railways at war* (London, 1980).

Wette, Wolfram, 'Reichstag und "Kriegswinnlerei" (1916–1918): die Anfänge parlamentarischer Rüstungskontrolle in Deutschland', *Militärgeschichtliche Mitteilungen*, 36 (1984), 31–56.

Wheeler-Bennett, John W., *Wooden titan: Hindenburg in twenty years of German history 1914–1934* (London, 1967; first published 1934).

Whiting, R. C., 'Taxation and the working class', *Historical Journal*, XXXIII (1990), 895–916.

Wiedenfeld, Kurt, *Die Organisation der Kriegsrohstoff-Bewirtschaftung im Weltkriege* (Hamburg, 1936).

Wild von Hohenborn, Adolf, *Briefe und Tagebuchaufzeichnungen des preussischen Generals als Kriegsminister und Truppenführer im Ersten Weltkrieg* (Boppard am Rhein, 1986).

Williamson, D. G., 'Walter Rathenau and the K.R.A. August 1914–March 1915', *Zeitschrift für Unternehmensgeschichte*, XXIII (1978), 118–36.

Williamson, John G., *Karl Helfferich 1872–1924: economist, financier, politician* (Princeton, 1971).

Wilson, Keith, *The policy of the Entente: essays on the determinants of British foreign policy 1904–1914* (Cambridge, 1985).

Wilson, Keith, (ed.), *The rasp of war: the letters of H. A. Gwynne to the Countess Bathurst 1914–1918* (London, 1988).

—— (ed.), *Decisions for war, 1914* (London, 1995).

Wilson, Trevor, *The downfall of the Liberal party 1914–1935* (London, 1966).

—— *The myriad faces of war: Britain and the Great War 1914–1918* (Cambridge, 1986).

—— (ed.), *The political diaries of C. P. Scott* (London, 1970).

Winkler, Wilhelm, *Die Einkommenverschiebungen in Österreich während des Weltkrieges* (Vienna, 1930).

Winter, J. M., *Socialism and the challenge of war: ideas and politics in Britain 1912–1918* (London, 1974).

—— *The Great War and the British people* (London, 1986).

—— *The experience of World War I* (Edinburgh, 1988).

—— (ed.), *War and economic development: essays in memory of David Joslin* (Cambridge, 1975).

Winter, Jay, and Blaine Baggett, *1914–18: the Great War and the shaping of the 20th century* (London, 1996).

Witt, Peter-Christian, *Die Finanzpolitik des Deutschen Reiches von 1903 bis 1913: eine Studie zur Innenpolitik des wihelminischen Deutschland* (Lübeck, 1970).

—— (ed.), *Wealth and taxation in Central Europe: the history and sociology of public finance* (Leamington Spa, 1987).

Wolff, Theodor, *Vollendete Tatsachen 1914–1917* (Berlin, 1918).

—— *Tagebücher 1914–1919*, ed. Bernd Sösemann, 2 vols. (Boppard am Rhein, 1984).

Woodward, Llewellyn, *Great Britain and the war of 1914–1918* (London, 1967).

Wrisberg, Ernst von, *Heer und Heimat 1914–1918* (Leipzig, 1921).

—— *Wehr und Waffen 1914–1918* (Leipzig, 1922).

Zagorsky, S. O., *State control of industry in Russia during the war* (New Haven, 1928).

Zeman, Z. A. B., *The break-up of the Habsburg empire 1914–1918: a study in national and social revolution* (London, 1961).

Ziemann, Benjamin, *Front und Heimat: ländliche Kreigserfahrungen im südlichen Bayern 1914–1923* (Essen, 1997).

Zilch, Reinhard, *Die Reichsbank und die finanzielle Kriegsvorbereitung 1907 bis 1914* (Berlin, 1987).

Zürcher, Erik Jan, *The Unionist factor: the role of the Committee of Union and Progress in the Turkish national movement 1905–1926* (Leiden, 1984).

INDEX